Praise for *The Thieves' Opera*

"A remarkably vivid and convincing portrait of London in the age of Hogarth . . . Immensely entertaining, in the best sense of that word, and informative in the bargain . . . With considerable gusto, Moore devotes herself to a depiction of this criminal world in all its squalid glory. Excellent." —*The Washington Post*

"This nifty popular history spotlights the interrelated careers of the Georgian era's two most notorious good-for-nothings: Jonathan Wild and Jack Sheppard. . . . An extended overview of London's wild and woolly street culture. The result is edifying, richly colorful, and, at times, enthralling." —*Kirkus Reviews*

"A treasure-house of intriguing information on the social history of early Georgian London, the hidden life that has escaped the history books." —*The Daily Mail*

"Enthralling . . . Lucy Moore handles her material with aplomb." —*The Spectator*

"A fascinating history that wades deep into the criminal mire of Georgian London." —*Scotland on Sunday*

"An elegantly composed book by an author with an interesting mind and a deep commitment to her subject . . . An auspicious debut by a talented writer." —*The Independent* (London)

"In these days of sleaze and corruption, the eighteenth-century world of crime and crime-busting assumes a new relevance. Lucy Moore leads the reader through the thieves' den of Georgian London, portraying that underworld with panache and bringing its hero-villains once more back to life." —Roy Porter, author of *London: A Social History*

The Thieves' Opera

Lucy Moore

The Thieves' Opera

A Harvest Book • Harcourt, Inc.

San Diego   New York   London

Requests for permission to make copies of any part of the work should
be mailed to: Permissions Department, Harcourt, Inc.,
6277 Sea Harbor Drive, Orlando, Florida, 32887-6777.

First published in Great Britain in 1997 by Viking.

Library of Congress Cataloging-in-Publication Data
Moore, Lucy, 1970–
The thieves' opera: the mesmerizing story of two notorious criminals in
eighteenth-century London/Lucy Moore.—1st U.S. ed.
p.   cm.
Originally published: London: Viking, 1997.
Includes bibliographical references.
ISBN 0-15-100364-5
ISBN 0-15-600640-5 (pbk.)
1. Wild, Jonathan, 1682?–1725. 2. Sheppard, Jack, 1702–1724.
3. Criminals—England—London—Biography. 4. Crime—England—
London—History—18th century.
HV6245.M56 1998
364.16'2'0942'09033—dc21 97-36740

Text set in Monotype Garamond
Printed in the United States of America
First Harvest edition 2000
A C E F D B

Contents

CONTENTS

List of Illustrations

Grateful acknowledgement is made to Fotomas Index, who provided photographs for all the illustrations except No. 1.

Endpapers
The City Guide or A Pocket Map of London, Westminster and Southwark, 1753, Thomas and John Bowles (Guildhall Library, Corporation of London)

A Note on the Text

A brief note on money. I am not an economic historian, so this is a very rough estimate based on my own understanding of what things were worth in the eighteenth century as compared to the present day. Although goods had different comparative values in the eighteenth century, roughly one can assume that a shilling was worth about ten pounds in today's money, and a pound, or twenty shillings, was worth about 200 pounds. I think some historians would say that this is over-generous, but considering how much lower the standard of living would have been then, the actual value of money and goods would have been far higher because they were accessible to so small a proportion of the population.

A shilling was made up of twelve pence (each penny worth just under a pound in today's money). A groat was 4d.; a crown was 5s.; and half a crown was 2s. 6d.; a mark was 13s. 4d., a guinea 21s., a moidore, 27s.

A skilled labourer, for example a tailor or carpenter, would earn about 20s. a week; an unskilled labourer about half that. When prices were high, more than half of his salary would be spent on bread to feed his family. A pound of bread cost between 1(1/2)d. and 2d. (£1.50–£2). The gulf between rich and poor was vast: some peers spent more on wine each year than their humblest tenants would earn in a lifetime.

Stealing anything worth more than a shilling carried the death penalty. Lace and silk were luxury items, handmade and often imported at great expense; they were frequently stolen because they were hard to trace and easy to dispose of, as well as being much in demand. A lace neckcloth would have cost about 5s., or £50. Similarly, wigs were favourites with thieves; they might be worth anything up to 40 guineas – well over £8,000 in modern money. London was rich, even if the wealth was concentrated in a small proportion of the population; and crime paid, even if the penalty for being caught was high. It was worth the risk.

Generally, when quoting eighteenth-century writers, I have modernized grammar and spelling and taken out random italics and capitals, to the extent that it makes the text easier to read.

Introduction

I see Jonathan Wild and Jack Sheppard on several levels. In the first place, and perhaps most important for the purposes of this book, their lives were full of excitement and adventure – a great story to tell. As much as possible, I have quoted from original sources to allow the story and the characters to speak for themselves.

Secondly, they were a means through which I could explore and discuss aspects of the society in which they lived – its rituals and mores as well as the day-to-day details of living and surviving. Structurally, I have tried to insert my digressions, for example on hanging or prison life, where they seemed most relevant to the story; they do interrupt the narrative, but I hope the information they provide overrides the inconvenience.

The fictionalized accounts of Wild's and Sheppard's lives, most notably *The Beggars' Opera* and *Jonathan Wild the Great*, gave their lives an additional resonance: they became literary figures as well as mere historical ones. Dickens based aspects of Fagin on Wild, and the Artful Dodger is not wholly unlike Jack Sheppard. Later in the nineteenth century, Sherlock Holmes compared his arch-enemy, Moriarty, to Wild.

Wild's story is particularly relevant to criminal history. Fielding's Bow Street Runners used techniques employed by Wild in his self-created role as Thief-taker General. The techniques of interrogation that Wild perfected – dividing suspects to elicit confessions, promising pardons in return for information – are still used by policemen today. On the other hand, his criminal empire can be seen as the prototype of modern criminal organizations, including the American Mafia and East End gangs like those of the Kray brothers.

In a sense, they are archetypal figures, too: Wild, the criminal bureaucrat who appears to conform in order to achieve his ambitions; and Sheppard, the individualist for whom freedom is the only aim, the original, uncontainable rebellious youth.

I would like to thank Georgina Capel; Robin Birley and Andrew Roberts for introducing me to her; Peter Carson, Andrew Kidd, Keith Taylor, Richard Duguid and Jessica Brooks at Penguin; Bela Cunha; and Clare Paterson and Jonathan Burnham for their initial encouragement.

This book is dedicated to my grandparents.

TOM CLINCH

As clever Tom Clinch, while the rabble was bawling,
Rode stately through Holborn to die in his calling,
He stopt at the George for a bottle of sack,
And promised to pay for it when he came back.
His waistcoat, and stockings, and breeches, were white;
His cap had a new cherry ribbon to tie't.
The maids to the doors and the balconies ran,
And said, 'Lack-a-day, he's a proper young man!'
But, as from the windows the ladies he spied,
Like a beau in his box, he bow'd low on each side!
And when his last speech the loud hawkers did cry
He swore from his cart, 'It was all a damn'd lie!'
The hangman for pardon fell down on his knee;
Tom gave him a kick in the guts for his fee:
Then said, 'I must speak to the people a little,
But I'll see you all damn'd before I will whittle!
My honest friend Wild (may he long hold his place)
He lengthen'd my life with a whole year of grace.
Take courage, dear comrades, and be not afraid,
Nor slip this occasion to follow your trade;
My conscience is clear, and my spirits are calm,
And thus I go off without prayer-book or psalm;
Then follow the practice of clever Tom Clinch,
Who hung like a hero and never would flinch.

JONATHAN SWIFT, 1726/7

PART ONE

London is their scene of action; and to live in any other
place is living like fishes out of water.

G. E.,
*Authentic Memoirs of the
Life and Surprising Adventures of John Sheppard by Way of
Familiar Letters from a Gentleman in Town,*
1724

London

In 1708, when Jonathan Wild arrived in London from the Midlands town of Wolverhampton, it was 'undoubtedly the largest and most populous city in the whole of Europe'.[1] The city boasted a population of over 600,000, more than a hundred times that of Wolverhampton and twenty times larger than that of Norwich, the second-largest city in Britain. London's circumference, encompassing its many fast-growing suburbs like Chelsea, Hampstead and Camberwell, as well as the city proper from the Tower of London to Westminster, was estimated in 1725 to be thirty-six miles.

Much of the centre of the city had been destroyed in the Great Fire in 1666, and the old timber buildings had been replaced hurriedly and cheaply in the rush to rehouse London's new homeless. The cobbled streets were full of mud and dust because of the building work that was constantly under way, which combined with the clouds of sooty smoke that hung over the city to coat its buildings and inhabitants with a layer of dusty grime. The new houses were made of brick or stone, rather than wood, for obvious reasons, and on the whole were more hygienic, healthier places in which to live; but the haste with which they had been constructed made them unstable. It was not uncommon to hear the loud crash of masonry tumbling or even to see a whole building collapsing, as the house in the background of Hogarth's *Gin Lane* is doing (illustration 14, page 94). Dr Johnson described the London of his youth as a place where 'falling houses thunder on your head'.

Although efforts were made in some areas to rebuild London on modern lines, with wide pavements and stately houses, these kinds

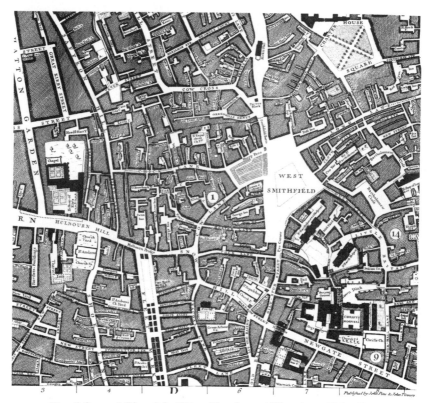

1. Detail from *A Plan of the Cities of London and Westminster* (John Rocque)

of improvements were expensive and time-consuming, and were largely restricted to the new residential area of Mayfair, which was patronized almost exclusively by the gentry and aristocracy. Most streets in central London, stretching from Cheapside down along the Thames past Blackfriars and along the Strand, were still narrow and ramshackle, laid out largely as they had been before the fire. Gutters ran down the centre of them, filled with refuse that would be washed away by the rain. At intervals, 'causeways' allowed people to cross the road on broader stones. The streets were overhung with painted signs marking shops, taverns and businesses. 'Our streets are filled with blue boars, and black swans, and red lions; not to mention flying pigs, and hogs in armour, and many other creatures more extraordinary than any in the deserts of Africa.'[2] These signs might be so 'large, and jut out so far, that in some narrow streets they touch one another; nay, and run across almost quite to the other side', wrote Cesar de Saussure, a Swiss visitor to London whose letters home were circulated throughout Europe but not published in England until 1902. Every shop had 'a sign of copper, pewter, or wood painted and gilt'[3] suspended over the street on iron or gilt branches and could cost up to £100 to make.

Houses were not numbered, and directions were commonly given by descriptions of prominent shop signs and landmarks – making London's maze of streets almost indecipherable to a new-comer like Jonathan Wild. A toy shop advertising in the *Female Tatler* was 'at the sign of the Griffin, at the corner of Bucklersbury in the Poultry' – impossible to find if one did not know the city well. To make matters even more complicated, many businesses operated under signs that had been erected for previous proprietors and did not relate to their work at all. 'What can be more inconsistent,' complained Joseph Addison in the *Spectator* in 1711, 'than to see a bawd at the sign of the Angel?'

London's street names, like its signs, were exuberantly colourful: in Southwark alone there were streets with names like Melancholy Walk, Dead Man's Place, Love Lane, Bear Garden and Maid Lane. Others elsewhere included Dog and Bitch Yard, Labour in Vain Hill, Flying Horse Yard, Soldier and Trumpet Alley, Pelican Stairs and Dancing Bridge. Street names often indicated the character of a place, like the physiognomy of a face, or recalled a local landmark: thus one would look for a prostitute in Maiden Lane, or find New-gate Gaol (actually housed in an old, but once new, gatehouse) in Newgate Street. Hogarth's Idle Apprentice (illustration 20, page 111) is arrested in Plate IX of the series at Blood Bowl House, in Hanging Sword Alley, off Fleet Street – an area notorious as a hid-ing-place for violent criminals and used deliberately by Hogarth to indicate the depths to which Tom Idle has sunk.

The streets were filled with as much bustling activity as their names often indicated. The provincial Jonathan Wild, his eyes ac-customed to the slow pace of life in a small Midlands town, would have been amazed by the city's energy and excitement. This description of Fleet Street was written in the 1770s by a German visitor to London, but still conjures up what must have been the atmosphere of the city streets the incredulous Jonathan first gazed on at the start of the century:

In the road itself chaise after chaise, coach after coach, cart after cart. Through all of this din and clamour, and the noise of thousands of tongues and feet, you hear the bells from the church-steeples, postmen's bells, the street-organs, fiddles and tambourines of itinerant musicians, and the cries of the vendors of hot and cold food at the street corners. A rocket blazes up storeys high amidst a yelling crowd of beggars, sailors and urchins. Someone shouts 'Stop, thief,' his handkerchief is gone. Everyone runs and presses forward, some less concerned to catch the thief than to steal a watch or a purse for themselves. Before you are aware of it a young, well-dressed girl has seized your hand. 'Come, my lord, come along, let us drink a glass together,' or 'I'll go with you if you please.' An accident happens not forty paces away. 'God bless me,' calls one. 'Poor fellow,' cries another. A stoppage ensues and you look to your pockets. Everyone is intent on helping the victim. There is laughter again: someone has fallen into the gutter. 'Look there, damn me,' cries a third, and the crowd passes on. Next comes a yell from a hundred throats as if a fire had broken out, or a house were falling, or a patriot had looked out of a window. In Gottingen you can go anywhere and get within forty paces to see what is happening. Here, that is at night and in the City, you are lucky to escape with a whole skin down a side alley until the tumult is over. Even in the wilder streets all the world rushes headlong, as if summoned to the bedside of the dying. That is Cheapside and Fleet Street on a December evening.[4]

'Crowds heaped on crowds,' was how John Gay described London in his ode to the city, *Trivia*. Fashionable women glittered in dazzling colours – pinks and greens and yellows of all shades – creamy bosoms rising out of fitted bodices, slender waists accentuating wide, flowing skirts, frothy lace or ribbon at the neck and cuffs, holding delicate squares of perfumed muslin to their noses. Men were no less gorgeous, wearing knee-length jackets over pale breeches and silk stockings or spit-shiny boots, their wide sleeves open to reveal a cascade of lacy cuff beneath, flashes of embroidered waistcoats just visible, swords slung by their sides, perhaps holding a silver-topped cane. Fops minced past in red high-heeled shoes, clouds of powder like flour billowing out behind them. Both men and women of the upper classes wore powdered wigs, but people of lesser means could not afford them. The best were made out of female hair – the lighter the shade the more desirable – and could cost up to forty shillings. Women allowed their own hair to grow underneath their wigs, or wore hairpieces, but men shaved their heads and glued the wigs to their bald pates; Hogarth's Rake's wig has slipped off his head in the frenzy of the gambling house (illustration 13, page 92). When they were not wearing their wigs, men wore night-caps or turbans to cover their bald heads.

Chimney-sweeps marked passers-by with tiny sooty paws; round-cheeked, white-capped girls with grubby petticoats sold musk-melons or oysters, lace or ribbons. Trade in London, as in the rest of England, was seasonal and transitory for much of society. A woman living poorly in the city might follow 'sometimes the business of picking up rags and cinders, and at other times that of selling fruit and oysters, crying hot-pudding and grey-peas in the streets, and the like'.[5] Their cries filled the busy streets, each item with its own individual, recognizable song. Jonathan Swift wrote several verses 'made for women who cry apples, &c.' including asparagus- and oyster-sellers' cries:

> Ripe 'Sparagrass,
> Fit for lad or lass,
> To make their water pass:
>   O, tis a pretty picking
>   With a tender chicken.

> Charming oysters I cry,
> My master come buy,
> So plump and so fresh,
> So sweet is their flesh,
> No Colchester oyster,
> Is sweeter and moister,

7

Your stomach they settle,
And rouse up your mettle,
They'll make you a Dad
Of a lass or a lad;
And, Madam your wife
They'll please to the life;
Be she barren, be she old,
Be she slut or be she scold,
Eat my oysters, and lie near her,
She'll be fruitful, never fear her.

Street-sellers mingled with lords and pickpockets rubbed shoulders with merchants. Steele, writing for the *Spectator*, describes being accosted in Warwick Street:

As I was listening to a new ballad, a ragged rascal, a beggar who knew me, came up to me, and began to turn the eyes of the good company upon me, by telling me he was extreme [*sic*] poor, and should die in the street for want of a drink, except I immediately would have the charity to give him sixpence to go to the next alehouse and save his life. He urged, with a melancholy face, that all his family had died of thirst.

Although it was one of the largest cities in Europe at the time, by modern standards London's population was so small – there were probably only 70,000 inhabitants within the city walls – that it was common for a gentleman to be familiar with a beggar. In such a closed environment, it was easy to stand out or to become notorious. Jonathan Wild would have quickly been able to recognize the faces of London's more prominent figures. The nobility, for instance, who were identifiable by their liveried servants and crested carriages, were celebrities whose comings and goings and doings were related regularly in the daily newspapers: 'The Duke of Marlborough, who is in good health, went lately on horseback as far as Fulham, and designs to reside next summer at Blenheim House,' reported the *Weekly Journal* on 24 January 1719. An advertisement like this one, in *Parker's London News* on 8 April 1724 – 'A liver-coloured and white small spaniel bitch, with a mottled face and turn up nose, she is very fat; taken from an alehouse in Mark Lane, on

2. *A Harlot's Progress II* (William Hogarth)

The Harlot is tipping over a table to distract the attention of the man who keeps her from her lover, a fencing master, who is being ushered out of the door behind him. Her protector, a Jewish merchant, has clearly just arrived; he is holding his hat under one arm. The merchant's expression is mirrored by the monkey (a symbol of lust) at his feet.

Wednesday last: whoever shall bring her to Mr Martin's at the lower end of Mark Lane shall have 5s. reward' – which today would only be effective in a local newspaper, presumably produced results. Individual, random occurrences were noted with interest. The *Weekly Journal* of 8 August 1724 reported that 'Last Monday morning, a working man fell down dead suddenly in the Temple.'

In eighteenth-century Europe, London was the apogee of sophistication and fashionable life. But it was seen by contemporaries as a city of sin, of corruption and dissolution, populated by tawdry whores, thuggish porters, insolent footmen, desperate gamblers, painted courtesans and argumentative hackney-coach drivers. Its 'chaotic uncontrollability'[6] obsessed its literary inhabitants, including Alexander Pope, Jonathan Swift, Henry Fielding and Dr Johnson.

The capital was a magnet for men and women from the country, like Jonathan Wild, seeking their fortune. As late as the 1770s, two out of three Londoners had been born elsewhere. The Irish populated St Giles and the East End; about 20,000 Jews lived in London, mostly in Whitechapel or around Petticoat Lane; many of the silk-weavers in Spitalfields were Huguenots; Welsh immigrants monopolized the meat, dairy and livestock trades. The rest of England was undoubtedly blinkered and provincial in its attitude to the outside world, but London, though riddled by social divisions and prejudices, was a cosmopolitan city. Exotic nationalities from far-flung corners of the earth were represented there: Indian sailors and traders, and perhaps 10,000 Africans, seamen or escaped slaves. It had been considered the height of chic for a lady to have a black dwarf as a slave since Henrietta Maria, Charles I's queen, had been painted by Van Dyck with her favourite, so the sight of an African or Indian face would not have been as unusual or shocking as one might imagine. Hogarth's Moll Hackabout is served by a black house-boy in Plate II of *A Harlot's Progress* (illustration 2, page 9) as an illustration of her social pretensions. The black beggars who populated St Giles, one of the poorest areas of London, with a high immigrant population, were disparagingly known as 'St Giles's Blackbirds'.

St Giles was the area for which the word 'slum' was coined in Regency times.[7] Rickety tenement buildings had sprung up since the Great Fire, with as many boarders taken in as possible. Apprentices usually slept in the attics of their masters' homes, on straw mattresses placed on boards between the joists. The owners of the house, the master, his wife and children, generally lived on the top floor; the rooms below were rented out (illustration 3, page 11; *The Distressed Poet*, showing hired attic accommodation). The cheapest place in a house was always the basement, with the poorest tenants packed tight like sardines, with their pigs and chickens, into damp cellars with little ventilation or light.

3. *The Distressed Poet* (William Hogarth)

The poet, his wife and their child use this one room for eating, sleeping and working. The poet's pretensions to gentility, despite his penury, are shown by the wig he wears. His selfishness towards his wife and child, making them live in this state of poverty while he tries to make a success of his art, is apparent. Lying on the floor is a copy of Alexander Pope's *Grub Street Journal*, while above the poet's head is a contemporary satirical print of Alexander Pope.

A typical middle-class family's house, such as Dr Johnson's behind Fleet Street, would have had stairs, bedrooms, brick chimneys that did not smoke, doors with locks, looking-glasses, pottery and ironware that was cheaper and more easily available than ever before. People sat in chairs rather than on benches, and slept in real beds rather than on mattresses on the floor. Glass windows were increasingly common, but still expensive, due to a high window tax that forced the poor to block up existing windows if they could not afford the tariff. Water-closets were not in widespread use, even among the aristocracy, until the late eighteenth century. Every household, however luxurious or modern, would have been plagued by lice and vermin; even the king had a Flea Catcher Royal and a Rat Catcher Royal.

It would have cost from £100 a year to rent a large house with stables in a fashionable area in the 1710s. Jonathan Swift paid 8s. a week for a dining room and bedchamber in Bury Street, which he considered 'plaguey deep'. A night in a cheap lodging-house would have cost about tuppence, and a respectable, clean, but basic lodging-house would have been about a groat, or 4d., a night. A good salary for a London labourer was about 13s. a week; Defoe estimated in 1730 that a poor man in steady work would earn only between 4 and 5s. a week. It was hard to make ends meet at the bottom end of the social and economic scale, but generally conditions were still better than on the continent. Cesar de Saussure reported that even the poorest workers wore shoes, unlike in France. A bad harvest would cause hunger and want, but not widespread starvation. Some people, though, were worse off than others: Henry Fielding, the author and magistrate who founded the Bow Street Runners in the 1750s, once emptied a derelict house in St Giles of its thirty Irish inhabitants; when they turned out their pockets, they had less than a shilling among them.

The parish of St Giles was where Hogarth placed his fictional *Gin Lane* (illustration 14, page 94). The gin-making process had been imported from Holland at the time of Wilham III's accession in 1689. By the start of the eighteenth century gin-drinking was endemic. Every fourth house in St Giles was a gin shop; some estimates go so far as to say that by 1736 every sixth house in London was a gin shop. It was cheap (the inscription over the shop in Hogarth's *Gin Lane*, 'Drunk for a penny/Dead drunk for two pence/ Clean straw for nothing,' was supposedly taken from a real sign), plentiful in supply, and, taken with sweet fruit cordial, palatable. It was the perfect vehicle for dulling the pain of lost hopes and failed dreams. Everyone drank it – men, women and children, old and young, infirm and able. The effects of gin could be heartbreaking. One young mother, Judith Dufour, fetched her two-year-old child from the workhouse where, unable to support it herself, she had left it. The little child had been dressed in a new set of clothes, and desperate for money to buy more gin, Judith strangled it and left the small stripped body in a ditch. She sold the clothes it was wearing for 1s. 4d., which she spent on gin. 'Should the drinking of this poison be continued in its present height during the next twenty years, there will, by that time, be very few of the common people left to drink it,' lamented Fielding.

If the effects of failure in London were achingly apparent in the city's slums, equally apparent were the signs of success. 'New squares, and new streets rising up every day to such a prodigy of buildings, that nothing in the world does or ever did equal it,' wrote Defoe. This building was particularly prevalent in the West End. Fashionable London had been moving west since the last century, first creating Covent Garden, then building up the area around Leicester Fields and moving slightly north to Soho Square and south to St James's.

Enormous social gulfs existed between the upper, middle and lower classes, heightened in London by the close proximity to each other in which different members of society lived. The rapidity of London's growth after the Great Fire, and the increasing segregation between social groups, had created a population of enormous variety, with each group knowing – and caring – almost nothing of the others. 'The inhabitants of St James's notwithstanding they live under the same laws, and speak the same language, are a distinct people from those of Cheapside, who are likewise removed from those of the Temple on one side and those of Smithfield on the other,' wrote Addison, in the *Spectator*. This combination of 'close physical proximity, and vast social distance'[8] led to social alienation, exacerbated in London by the localization of government in the separate neighbourhoods, the danger of some areas, and the slow speed of travelling around the city. Rigid lines were drawn between classes, occupations and trades, making each section of the population feel completely separate from the others.

The aristocracy of the eighteenth century felt it had the right to dominate the rest of society by virtue of its birth, breeding and, above all, its wealth. 'Dominion follows property,' wrote Bernard de Mandeville. The English upper classes were considered unique in Europe for their involvement with their tenants; one continental visitor to England, Madame du Boccage, commented, 'In France we cringe to the great, in England the great cringe to the people.'[9] The traditional view that authority rested on consent was prevalent; conscientious paternalism was considered the duty of every land-owner. La Rochefoucauld was horrified to find that local gentry and rich farmers were included in social events at the country houses of his grand English hosts, who insisted on involving themselves in the lives of their tenants. However, many landlords believed that this very involvement lessened their obligation to respect the rights of their tenants, riding roughshod over local interests when it suited them. Game laws were exploited, common lands enclosed, poach-ers violently prosecuted. Thomas Coke transported an entire village to expand his parkland, designed by Capability Brown, at Holkham in Norfolk.

The upper classes lived within a cordon sanitaire of political dogma and self-appeasing paternalism. They were separated from their inferiors literally as well as ideologically, their houses and parks surrounded by high fences preventing any contact with such undesirable sights as hungry, ragged vagabonds, gin-soaked moth-erless children, or cowed, frightened under-servants. No sense of a common humanity existed for the most rigidly aristocratic: 'It is monstrous,' commented the Duchess of Bedford on the egalitari-anism of Methodism, 'to be told that you have a heart as sinful as the common wretches that crawl the earth.' The greater the gulf be-tween the two sides of society became, the more urgently the upper ranks felt they had to defend that which set them apart. Even John Wesley, the evangelical Methodist preacher whose ideas so shocked the Duchess of Bedford, believed that a government could not af-ford to share authority with its people, at the risk of jeopardizing social stability and the greater good. 'The greater the share the peo-ple have in government, the less liberty, civil or religious, does a nation enjoy.' John Wild, Jonathan's brother, was defying the very foundations on which the state was believed to rest by supporting the Pretender in 1715, as much for the sake of voicing his opinion as for challenging the king's authority.

'Mankind are happier in a state of inequality and subordination,' wrote Dr Johnson. This philosophy eased the consciences of the rich, justifying their view that the lower classes existed only to supply their needs and desires. The harder the poor worked, the better the wheels and cogs of daily life would turn, and the more assured the sense of social stability would be. Henry Fielding summed up this school of thought in 1751:

To be born for no other purpose than to consume the fruits of the earth is the privilege (if it may really be called a privilege) of very few. The greater part of mankind must sweat hard to produce them, or society will no longer answer the purpose for which it was ordained. Pleasure always hath been, and always will be, the principal business of persons of fashion and fortune, and more especially of the ladies . . .

In order to ensure that the privilege of pleasure was unattainable to the rest of society, political and economic thinkers stressed the undesirability of allowing the poor to better themselves. 'Reading, writing and arithmetic, are . . . very pernicious to the poor,' wrote de Mandeville, in a 1723 essay on charity schools. 'Men who are to remain and end their days in a laborious, tiresome and painful station of life, the sooner they are put upon it at first, the more patiently they'll submit to it for ever after.' Charity schools and workhouses, first instituted under Queen Anne, were the manifestations of this belief, their proponents arguing that hard work from an early age would instil not only discipline, but also a proper sense of subordination: 'children fed by charity ought in a more special manner to be clothed in humility'.[10] In short, the poor ought to feel towards their masters not resentment, as the youthful Jonathan Wild did, but gratitude. William Temple, writing in 1758, reiterated this idea. 'The only way to make them [workers] temperate and industrious is to lay them under a necessity of labouring all the time they can spare from meals and sleep, in order to procure the common necessities of life.'

An income of £40 a year was enough for a family of five to survive independently, without getting into debt or being forced to accept charity or poor relief. The annual salary of a London labourer was just under £30; providing he worked all year, and his wife took in work or they let out a room, his family would just get by. But work was seasonal, and transitory; he probably wouldn't have owned a house to let out a room; and an emergency – if prices rose unexpectedly, or a child fell ill, when a single visit from a doctor cost a guinea – would cripple them. Perhaps a fifth of the population received poor relief. Gregory King, the late seventeenth-century census-taker, thought the figure was more like 50 per cent. Poor relief was a form of wage subsidy, supplementing incomes to a level that allowed poor families to scrape by year after year, while keeping the costs of manufacturing down. 'Were it not for what they receive out of the tax . . . they would not knit or spin for so small wages as they receive for that work, because they would starve by it,' wrote Lord Townsend in 1730. In the countryside, the poorest sections of society were more cushioned by the community than in London. A Wolverhampton family like Wild's, brought suddenly to hard times, would have been helped by their neighbours, acutely conscious of the fact that it might just as easily have been them.

Markets, fairs and holidays celebrated the cycle of rural life and its strength of community feeling. The annual parish wake was a week-long holiday, honouring the patron saint of the local church, but centred on secular festivities – football games, wrestling and boxing matches, dancing, feasts, contests in hot hasty-pudding eating or chasing greased pigs, stalls selling delicacies such as gingerbread. Lord of Misrule holidays turned the accepted order of society upside down, with villagers dressing up as local dignitaries, and local dignitaries the focus of teasing and pranks, temporarily relieving the pressure of life in a rigidly ordered society. Courting traditionally took place at May Day festivities, but fairs and markets also provided an opportunity for young people to meet each other. 'The women are especially impudent for that day,' observed Defoe of market-days, 'as if it were a day that justified them giving themselves a loose [licence] to all manner of indecency and immodesty, without any reproach, or without suffering the censure which such behaviour would deserve at another time.' These centuries-old customs provided country folk with a sense of pride in their culture, inspired a feeling of class solidarity, and helped them make light of the hardship under which their daily lives laboured. They were encouraged in this by the local gentry and landowners, whose almost deliberate 'rural paganism', a glorification of fresh air and country pursuits, was a reaction against the Puritanism of the seventeenth century.[11]

In London, though, there were no such escape valves. The impersonal nature of living in a large city, combined with the transience of much of the population, prevented the creation of a sense of communal feeling. The only recourse for many of London's poor was a gin shop or tavern, which instead of providing solace only sent men and women into a vicious cycle of despair, drunkenness and deeper despair.

Initiation

Although the exact date of Jonathan Wild's birth is unknown, records show that he was baptized in the ancient church of St Peter's, Wolverhampton on 6 May 1683. 'He was the first fruit of his father and mother's nocturnal labours,'[1] the eldest of five children born to John Wild, a carpenter, and his wife, who sold herbs and fruit in the local market. Although they were poor, they were known as an honest, industrious couple.

Seventeenth-century Wolverhampton was the second-largest town in Staffordshire, with a population of about 6,000, most of whom earned their living in the iron-working and locksmithing trades. Wolverhampton had been rewarded handsomely by Charles II on his restoration in 1660 for its loyalty to the royalist cause during the Civil War, and by 1683 it was a thriving, prosperous town situated on a hill.

Wolverhampton was well known for its Catholicism. Cromwellian ministers, visiting the town in the 1640s, declared that it was swarming with papists, 'styled by many a little Rome'.[2] The reactionism of the Glorious Revolution in 1688 checked these tendencies, and a flourishing Jesuit mission that ran a school in Wolverhampton was summarily dissolved. Still, an underlying sympathy to the Jacobite cause and the Catholic religion remained beneath a convenient loyalty to the new regime, exacerbated by strong anti-dissenter feelings and a latent resentment of the enclosures instituted by the Protestant gentry in the late seventeenth century. During the risings of 1715, the whole of Staffordshire displayed its loyalty to the Pretender, celebrating his birthday with much bell-ringing and rejoicing, publicly (and treasonously) drinking his health. Jonathan's younger brother, John Wild, who had acquired some local status as a bailiff and then as Town Crier, led the Jacobite riots that erupted in Wolverhampton in July 1715 when the Pretender's arrival was expected at any day. He raised toasts to 'James III' and headed a mob that tried to pull down the Presbyterian meeting houses in Wolverhampton and nearby West Bromwich.

Jonathan was sent to the Free School in St John's Lane, where he was taught to read and write. At fifteen he was apprenticed to a local buckle-maker. By 1700 he had served out his apprenticeship and set up in business. Two years later he married a local girl on whom he quickly sired a son. John Wild must have looked on his son with pride, anticipating a future for him of industry rewarded, if not with luxury, then at least with contentment. But Jonathan had ideas above his station: as Defoe put it, 'his soul was too great to be confined to such servile work'.

Daniel Defoe, whose biography of Wild was based on interviews he conducted with him, relates that the young Jonathan's 'thoughts, as he said, [were] above his trade'. Clearly Wolverhampton, and the opportunities it held, were too restricted for a man like Jonathan who was possessed, from a very early age, of 'a genius that would bend and stoop to anything'.[3] Defoe believed that Jonathan's slow descent into crime was the result of his idleness.

Jonathan wanted application, which is generally observed to be the fault of many men of brisk parts; work and he were too much at variance for him to thrive by his trade; he seemed to follow it only at a distance, often playing the loose, wandering from one alehouse to another, with the very worst, though the merriest, company in the place; and he was very fond of the strolling actors that now and then frequented the country.

It may have been mere laziness; but perhaps that is too simple an explanation. Wild might also have had some vague sense that his destiny lay beyond the limits of Wolverhampton, a feeling that he had talents that could be fully exploited only in a larger arena.

Certainly he was desperate to get to London. He first left Wolverhampton, and his wife and infant son, in 1704, as a manservant to a local gentleman who was soon dissatisfied with his service and sent him back home. An anonymous biographer says that the man Wild accompanied to London was a lawyer; and that after his dismissal, Wild used the experience he had gained in legal affairs to get a job as a 'setter', who hunted down and brought in debtors to appear before the Marshalsea Court – a job that would have required to the full the ruthlessness and brutality that were later to serve him so well.

Another story related by Defoe tells how, on his return to Wolverhampton, Wild borrowed a horse from a neighbour and, in need of money, sold it without asking the owner's permission. The man found out what Wild had done, and agreed that, instead of prosecuting Wild, he would accept a weekly payment from him until the cost of the horse had been repaid. The first two instalments were paid in full and on time, but when the third payment was several weeks overdue the man confronted Wild and demanded his money. Wild replied that he had no intention of paying him a penny more.

'That contract is obsolete, and of no effect.'

'How so?' asked the man, perplexed.

'Why,' replied Wild, 'you'll allow that articles of agreement, or contracts, not fulfilled, are broken; and articles, once broken, cannot subsist afterwards. Now our articles are broken for I have made but two payments, when there are three due long ago, therefore I owe you nothing, and nothing I will pay you.'

About four years later, Wild left Wolverhampton for a second time, determined never to return.

Nothing is known of his early years in London, but in March 1710 five people accused Jonathan Wild of debt and brought a joint action against him. He was committed to Wood Street Compter, one of London's two ancient debtors' prisons (the word Compter derives from 'Counter'), just off Cheapside. The length of his stay in the Compter is unclear; by his own admission he was in Wood Street for four years and he left the gaol in September 1712. What is certain is that on arriving in London Wild's tastes must quickly have outstretched his means. 'By the misfortunes of the world, he was subject to the discipline of the Compter, for above the space of four years, during which time it was impossible but he must be in some measure let into the secrets of the criminals there under confinement. . .'[4]

Wild looked back on his years in Wood Street Compter as his introduction to the world of crime. Eighteenth-century prisons were well known as schools of vice. Because manpower was limited, and in any case the authorities were utterly corrupt, no attempts were made to separate prisoners from each other according to their crimes. Thus a twelve-year-old boy who had stolen a handkerchief – a type of thief known to his peers as a 'Wiper Puller' – awaited his first trial beside a convicted house-breaker or highwayman waiting to be hanged. The innocence of the prisoners awaiting trial was not assumed; they were just thrown in with the rabble regardless. While some had more privileges than others, these distinctions were largely theoretical because all of them, whatever their crimes or status, were jumbled up together.

This confusion and lack of discipline was particularly in evidence at Wood Street, with a large semi-permanent population of debtors who could not leave until their debts, including those incurred while in gaol, were paid off. As well as these indigenous residents, almost everyone arrested in London was taken first to Wood Street for a night or two before being assigned to another prison in London, where they would await trial. Thus every member of London's criminal underworld would probably pass through Wood Street at some point in their career. It was the perfect place for a man like Jonathan Wild to develop contacts and start to carve out a reputation for himself.

Working in a prison could be a lucrative career if one was prepared to cast aside all moral scruples, as most prison officials seemed to be able to do. Each office-holder bought his office from the government, usually at a very high price – the office of Under-Marshal, the second-highest in the prison hierarchy, cost £700 in 1712 – and felt entitled, after spending so much to achieve his position, to recoup his costs by milking prisoners for as much as he could get. Because gaols were independent of state control, there were no limits on the powers of the keepers and turnkeys, known in criminal slang as 'Quod-Culls'.

They charged an entrance fee, or 'garnish', to each new arrival, as well as a discharge fee when someone left. Their biggest source of profit was the tap-room, which sold tobacco, beer and spirits, principally gin, often brewed at the prison. Newgate gin was known by several slang names: 'Kill-Grief', 'Cock-my-Cap' or 'Washing and Lodging'. In 1787 a keeper suggested that the proliferation of drink available in prisons improved discipline because 'when the prisoners are drunk they tend to be docile and quite free from rioting'. Liquor was also a comfort to those preparing themselves to meet Jack Ketch (the slang name for the hangman): 'great fear is overcome by great drinking'.[5]

Keepers also made money charging inmates for extras: a bed, and on top of that sheets and blankets; edible, and sufficient, food; cleanliness – often mere necessities of life, as well as luxuries such as newspapers and books. Law books were popular reading, as many prisoners could not afford legal representation and had to defend themselves on the stand. Although many could not read, they asked or paid literate prisoners to read to them. Dogs were not forbidden to inmates until 1792 and 'pigs, pigeons and poultry' were kept by them until 1814. Visitors were charged 3s. a head, but they were allowed in and out as often as they were willing to pay.

Some prisoners (rather unkindly) brought their wives to gaol to live with them; in 1717 the keeper regretfully informed several inmates that although he would like to house their wives in gaol there simply wasn't room for them all. In such a situation, perhaps he would have been as lenient as Diderot's gaoler at Vincennes, who in return for a small fee allowed the philosopher to scale the prison walls each night to visit his mistress in Paris.[6] Clearly, in some cases keepers did allow their charges to leave the confines of the prison, because Swift parodies their corruption and avarice in a poem of 1709:

The turnkey now his flock returning sees,
Duly let out o'nights to steal for fees.

Any request was considered, provided it was backed up with 'rhino', or ready cash. William Pitt, the keeper of Newgate in 1716, was estimated to have made three to four thousand pounds in 'garnish', the slang word for the bribe demanded by the keepers, over a period of three or four months when Newgate was full of rich, noble Jacobite prisoners awaiting trial for their part in the risings of 1715. 'They [the prisoners] are debarred from nothing but going out,'[7] wrote an eighteenth-century observer. Perhaps the only reason prisoners were not allowed to buy their liberty was that it would remove from the turnkeys their lucrative source of income.

As with all institutions, some inmates adapted more readily than others to the situation in which they found themselves. Defoe's Moll Flanders describes her gradual acclimatization to Newgate: 'I degenerated into stone; I turned first stupid and senseless, then brutish and thoughtless, and at last raving mad as any of them were; and in short, I became as naturally pleased and easy with the place as if indeed I had been born there.'[8]

There were few rules, incomprehensible to the outsider, and until they were mastered life for the initiate was unbearable. Garnish had to be paid not only to the keepers, but also to certain prisoners who demanded tribute from new arrivals and would not hesitate to use force to extract it. If a prisoner, like Wild when he first arrived, did not have ready cash, he or she was treated harshly. Until he found his feet, Wild probably lived with about seventy others in a room roughly thirty-foot long by fifteen-foot wide by twelve-foot high. There was almost no light and no circulation of the heavy, fetid air; it was cold and damp all year round, sometimes with up to a foot of water on the ground; cockroaches and rats were everywhere, and every prisoner was plagued by lice. They relied for food on scraps that keepers might give them out of rare kindness, or on what they could beg for out of the 'begging grate' that opened into Newgate Street. Wild's most recent biographer, Gerald Howson, estimates

4. *A Rake's Progress VII: In the Debtors' Prison* (William Hogarth)
The turnkey on the right behind the Rake is demanding 'garnish' and the little boy
is waiting to be paid for the beer he has brought the Rake. The room is lit by a tiny
window. At the rear, a man is stoking an alchemists' forge, showing the desire of
the prison's inhabitants to transform their fortunes. A pair of wings like those made
by Icarus lie on the canopy in the top left-hand corner of the print.

that there were four to eight deaths a week in Wood Street Compter at this time because of the dreadful conditions the prisoners
were forced to suffer (illustration 4, above; Fleet Prison, another of
London's debtors' prisons, shown in Plate VII of *A Rake's Progress*).

If, like Wild, one had no money, total subservience to the keepers was the only option. Debtors had to find a way of making
money while in gaol because although they were kept there at their
creditors' expense, they could not leave for good until they had
paid their entrance and departure fees, and their upkeep while in
prison, as well as cleared their original debts. Some, in desperation,
sold themselves into slavery in the colonies for a limited period, a

sort of voluntary transportation; others just gave up and stayed in gaol until they died.

Wild was gradually able to gain a foothold in the prison hierarchy because he was willing to do any chore, no matter how degrading or disgusting, to earn a little money. Bit by bit he gained the trust of the turnkeys, who allowed him more and more authority within the prison, which was run internally by a select group of inmates, known as 'Partners', chosen by the turnkeys to assist them. By working for the keepers, Wild was able to pay back his debts and even to lend money to other prisoners. By the time he left the Compter in 1712 he had been given the office of 'Liberty of the Gate', which required him to check the 'Rats', or newly arrested prisoners, into Wood Street before taking them to a magistrate to be charged. This meant that he had a good deal of freedom both within the prison and beyond its walls.

He acquired a name for himself among the prisoners as well.

There seemed to be a kind of sympathy betwixt their natures and that of Jonathan, so that they soon crept into one another's secrets; he became acquainted with all their tricks and stratagems; and when the iron hand of justice had laid hold of them, and they were entangled in difficulties, he often put such quirks and evasions in their heads, and gave them such advice, as sometimes proved of great advantage to them; so that he became a kind of oracle among the thieves.[9]

The tortuous deviousness of mind that had lain dormant, unfulfilled, in Wolverhampton came to his aid in Wood Street. His fellow prisoners not only borrowed money from him and, apparently, lent it to him, they also sought his advice on their cases. This preoccupation with trials made mock trials a popular prison pursuit. In 1725 Bernard de Mandeville wrote that the inmates of Newgate spent 'their most serious hours . . . in mock trials, and instructing one another in cross questions to confound witnesses'. These exercises were sometimes a form of internal prison discipline, sometimes practice for real trials – in which Wild, one imagines, would have excelled. They often contained elements of rural Lord of Misrule festivals, savage parodies of the institution which had condemned them to prison in the first place. The 'judges' tied white towels around their heads to imitate wigs, and spoke in language that made a mockery of the courts and the ideals of justice on which they were based. 'The most trifling bribe of the judge will secure an acquittal,' recorded one observer of this phenomenon in 1817.

A year later Wild was able to re-ingratiate himself with William Smith, one of the five who had originally brought the action against him, so much so that Smith lent him another £3. Wild evidently did not like being beholden to Smith: in 1720, when Wild was near the pinnacle of his power, he had Smith arrested and transported to America and sent back again when Smith escaped in 1721 before he had served his full seven years sentence. However, he did not bear a grudge against everyone he associated with in Wood Street. Another man he lent money to during his stay behind bars was Obidiah Lemon, a 'Rattling Lay', or thief specializing in robbing coaches. The two men built up a relationship that endured long beyond their stay in Wood Street; Lemon worked for Wild for many years, both stealing and acting as an informer

During his imprisonment, Wild also learned about the violence, drunkenness and depravity that characterized the daily lives of his fellow criminals. Bernard de Mandeville, writing to advocate harsher measures in prisons, was shocked by his visits to Newgate: 'the licentiousness of the place is abominable, and there are no jests so filthy, no maxims so destructive to good manners, or expressions so vile and profane, but what are uttered there with applause, and treated with impunity'.

The motley group of pickpockets, whores, highwaymen, forgers and confidence tricksters who periodically inhabited Wood Street Compter and London's other gaols were known to each other by aliases like Cocky-my-Chance, Black-Waistcoat Dick, Irish Ned and Jemmy the Shuffler. The criminal underworld had its own language, or cant, by which its members defined and recognized each other. The 'slang patter' they used marked criminals off from other people, emphasizing their sense of alienation from normal society, and perhaps also the pride they took in this separation. French cant illustrates the criminals' attitude to their way of life. To introduce someone to a life of crime was to set them free; the slang name for a thief was *l'ami*; to steal was the verb *servir*; French criminals had eighty words for drunkenness and none for sobriety. Some cant terms have slipped out of common usage – for instance, a ladder was known as a 'jacob' and the dark was called the 'mung'. But many cant words and phrases are still used in modern English: a 'baggage' is a slut; to 'twig' is to notice; and to 'nail' is to catch or seize. And cockney rhyming slang retains elements of eighteenth-century cant in its spirit and humour.

The villains with whom Wild associated would all have been able to justify their actions.

> We care not a straw
> For reason and law
> For conscience is all in all.[10]

proclaimed one seventeenth-century thieves' ballad. Joseph 'Blue-skin' Blake, who later worked for Wild, held that 'All the world's a cheat, and he was a fool that had no hand in it.' John Gay, author of *The Beggars' Opera*, romanticized this view. His hero, Macheath, saw himself as a Robin Hood figure, taking from the rich to give to the poor, even if the poor only included himself and his associates. 'We are for a just partition of the world, for every man hath a right to enjoy life . . . Money was made for the free-hearted and generous, and where is the injury of taking from another what he hath not the heart to make use of?' Jemmy Twitcher, a member of Macheath's gang, agreed with his master: 'What we win, gentlemen, is our own by the law of arms, and the right of conquest.' Men like Macheath and Twitcher looked down on the people on whom they preyed as stupid, for not appreciating what they had; and weak, for not being able to defend it from rogues like themselves. The cant word for a man was 'Cull', which also meant a robbed man. Thus, according to the criminals' own definition, every man was a potential victim, a sitting target for thieves.

In 1710, of greater London's population of just over 600,000, perhaps 10,000 were criminals of one sort or another.

. . . Vast numbers of our people are compelled to seek their livelihood by begging, robbing, stealing, cheating, pimping, forswearing, flattering, suborning, forging, gaming, lying, fawning, hectoring, voting, scribbling, stargazing, poisoning, whoring, canting, libelling, free-thinking and the like occupations,

Gulliver told his Houyhnhnm master in Swift's 1726 satire, *Gulliver's Travels*.

An act of 1744 categorized vagabonds into three groups: drunks and beggars, 'idle and disorderly people' who refused to enter a workhouse, and thus were refused poor relief; 'rogues', including fortune-tellers, mountebanks, charlatans, strolling players and peddlers, all of whom made a living, but still had no roots or ties; and 'incorrigible rogues', escaped criminals, returned transportees and second or multiple offenders.[11] Almost all criminals fitted one of the vagabond categories at some point, but most fell unintentionally into crime and its associated lifestyle, rather than being born into it. Older men and women who turned to crime usually did so as a last resort, after a life of constant struggle which finally broke their spirit. Many young people were attracted to crime by the aura of glamour and danger that surrounded those involved in it. Some, bankrupted by gambling debts or high living, turned to robbery to clear their debts; others went to gaol because of their debts, and fell in with villains there. The average miscreant was opportunistic in his approach to crime, and modest in ambition. Petty crime was a normal part of life for most poor people, especially in London, where the contrast between rich and poor was so clear, and the opportunities for theft or other forms of wrong-doing were so obvious. Most criminals were 'unremarkable people, distinguished from their fellows by little else except the fact that by bad luck or worse judgement they got caught up in the toils of the law'.[12]

There also existed a criminal élite, whose lives and careers were intimately bound up with one another's. These men and women had often been trained in the arts of crime from an early age; their friends and families were usually connected with law-breaking in some way. A sub-culture of crime existed in Hanoverian London, allowing people to achieve power and material satisfaction via alternative avenues, since the accepted routes to the top – land, wealth, education and social connections – were out of their grasp. They sought access to the goals which society held to be worthwhile, but which, to them, were unavailable.

The criminal philosophy was marked by brave defiance and a devil-may-care attitude. 'The greater rogue the greater luck,' went the saying. Cocky pickpockets plied their trade at hangings, refusing to be cowed by the example the government hoped to set for them through the public display of capital punishment. The fixed concentration of the crowd at the moment when the cart moved away from the gallows and the condemned man's convulsing form swung out made it the ideal place to pick pockets: observers would not notice anything was missing until the thief was well hidden among the crowd. Hanging days, because of the opportunities they presented as well as their festive atmosphere, were known as 'Sheriff's Balls' or 'Hanging Fairs'. Hanging itself was not seen as a deterrent, principally because no criminal really believed he or she would be caught in the first place. Charles Dickens, in his research for *Oliver Twist*, found this was true in the nineteenth century; and indeed this attitude is still prevalent in the twentieth. And even if one were caught, thought many, what did it matter? Isaac Atkinson, an Oxford-educated murderer, who stabbed the chaplain accompanying him to the gallows, cried out to the audience before he was hanged, 'There's nothing like a merry life and a short one!'[13] His attitude was representative of that of many of his peers.

Carnival is not a spectacle seen by the people; they live it, and everyone participates because its very idea embraces all the people. While carnival lasts, there is no other life outside it. During carnival time life is subject only to its laws, that is the laws of their own freedom.[14]

Criminals seemed to live in a perpetual state of carnival, avoiding the strictures of normal life, labour, order and sobriety, enforced on them in the form of workhouses and charity schools, in favour of libertine carnival values – pleasure-seeking, recklessness and abandonment. Their daily lives were governed by misrule, defiance and disorder, blurring the distinctions between criminal activity and an ideological or political stand against conventionality. The criminal underworld was a mirror image of normal society, a complement as well as a threat to it. Unwritten codes of honour, obligation and respect reflected acceptable modes of behaviour; the formality of eighteenth-century life had as its counterpart and balance the lawlessness, bravado and cruelty of the life of crime.

Wild spent four years becoming initiated into this world, learning its peculiarities and hierarchies, its taboos and allowances. When he managed to con his way out of Wood Street Compter at the end of 1712, he was part of London's criminal establishment, with his future in that world ahead of him.

Struggle

Whereas Jonathan Wild was an immigrant, aspiring towards the wealth and respectability of London's new middle classes, Jack Sheppard was born into the irascible, Nonconformist, Huguenot traditions of the East End of London. The streets he played in as a child were steeped in sectarianism, determined independence of mind and conscience, resistance to oppression – as well as poverty, want and crime.

Sheppard was born on 4 March 1702 (while Jonathan Wild still languished in Wolverhampton) in White's Row, Spitalfields. Presumably because he was a weak or sickly baby, he was baptized the next day at St Dunstan's, Stepney. He was named for a brother, John, who had died aged three a year before Jack was born. Jack's father, a carpenter, died while Jack, his brother Thomas and their younger sister Mary were still small; his mother, although she doted on her children, was unable to support them without her husband's income. Mary, the youngest, died two years after her father. At about the same time, Mrs Sheppard sent the young Jack, aged six, to Mr Garrett's School near Great St Helen's in Bishopsgate. The school, or workhouse, had been founded in 1700 in the spirit of reforming zeal that marked Anne's reign; it was more a house of correction (or 'house of corruption', as they were popularly known) than an institution of education and growth.

Workhouses were a new method of social control, devised at the turn of the eighteenth century; in 1711 there were about 4,000 children at over a hundred workhouses or charity schools throughout London. The conditions at the London Workhouse, also in Bishopsgate, were described in 1708: thirty or forty children to a ward, sleeping two to a bunk on tiers circling the walls. Two was the recommended number of children per bunk, but in reality six or eight of them were crammed in with each other on a single bunk. They woke at half past six, had half an hour for prayers and an inadequate breakfast of gruel, and started work at seven. They cobbled, spun, knitted and sewed until six in the evening, with an hour's break for lunch, and then slept, exhausted, until the routine began again. They were sent off for an hour's lessons a day, but the teaching was at best perfunctory. The strict discipline enforced by this regime was a deliberate attempt to instil fear of disobedience and idleness into the hearts of the pupils.

This harsh attitude towards the poor was due to the prevailing belief that even the slightest taste of extra money or free time would corrupt them so much that they would no longer be willing to work to support the extravagances of their masters. A pamphlet called *The Servant's Calling: With Some Advice to the Apprentice*, published in 1725, advised masters that 'a frequent taste of any kind of diversion is apt to grow upon the palate, and to give too strong a relish for them; and when the inclination is turned strongly towards them, the shop or work-room is like the confinement of a prison, and labour like a weight that goes up hill'.

Fielding laid the blame for the increase in violence and crime in London squarely on the moral dissolution of the poor, which led to social and material aspirations:

Now what greater temptation can there be to voluptuousness, than a place where every sense and appetite of which it is compounded, are fed and delighted; where the eyes are feasted with show, and the ears with music, and where gluttony and drunkenness are allured by every kind of dainty; nay where the finest women are exposed to view, and where the meanest person who can dress himself clean, may in some degree mix with his betters, and thus perhaps satisfy his vanity as well as his love of pleasure?

The fear of moral and social deterioration that inspired Fielding's vitriolic outburst was widespread throughout the eighteenth century.

The luxurious lifestyle of the rich was considered beneficial to society as a whole, because their demands created jobs, while any hint
of the poor doing any more than getting by was frowned on, because it was assumed that if they had any money to spare on drinking or finery, they were being paid too much. People wrote
scathingly of lamplighters wearing silk stockings, common labour-
ers' families being able to afford tea and sugar, and shopkeepers'
wives priding themselves on having hot chocolate and white bread
for breakfast. This expenditure, regardless of whether it had been
honestly earned, was regarded as a subtle form of insubordination.

The gin-drinking and gambling of the poor were seen not as the
results of abject poverty, but as an innate corruption that drove men
to crime. Fielding called gin an 'intoxicating draught [which] itself
disqualifies them [the poor] from using any honest means to acquire
it, at the same time that it removes all sense of fear and shame, and
emboldens them to commit every wicked and desperate enterprise'.
The poor were not credited with having self-control or an independent work ethic – 'Good drunken company is their delight;/
And what they get by day, they spend by night,' wrote Defoe – so
the educated élite believed discipline should be forcibly instilled in
them. The views of reformers like this contributor to the pamphlet
The Craftsman, were unusual, and rarely stated: 'As for the corruptions
of servants, I can look upon them in no other light than as the
natural consequences of the corruptions of those in a higher sphere.'

Workhouses like Mr Garrett's were intended to be the first stage
in a lifetime of submission. 'The advantage of the workhouse to the
parish does not arise from what the poor people can do towards
their subsistence, but from the apprehension the poor have of it,'
wrote one social commentator in 1725. They were guided by two
basic principles: that poverty was evil; and that labour was the religious and moral duty of the poor, the only thing that would free
them from the sin inherent in their lowly position.

Ironically, workhouses, like prisons, were also considered to be
schools of crime, where potential miscreants met and made contact
with one another. 'These workhouses though in appearance bene-

ficial yet have in some respects an evil tendency for they mix the good and the bad; and too often make reprobates of all alike,' wrote Defoe. So just as Wild served his criminal apprenticeship in Wood Street Compter, Jack Sheppard from an early age was tutored by the youthful members of London's underworld in another of the city's academies of vice.

When he was ten years old, Jack's mother found him a place as a shop-boy. After her husband died, she had gone to work for William Kneebone, a woollen draper whose house and office was in the Strand; and Mr Kneebone agreed to provide Jack with a home and work. He was a kindly, generous man who took trouble with the lad, teaching him to read and write. Five years later, he arranged for Jack to be apprenticed to his friend Owen Wood, a carpenter who lived in Wych Street, off Drury Lane. Wood agreed to take the boy in because Kneebone promised to use his influence to secure a large building contract on a house in Hampstead for Wood. On 2 April 1717 Jack was bound apprentice to Wood for seven years, the usual period of service, in the presence of Sir William Fazakerley, a Chamberlain of the City of London.

In the seventeenth century apprenticeship had been seen as a positive force for betterment in society. Richard Burton, in *The Apprentice's Companion*, written in 1681, described it as 'that genteel servitude which by a few years' service faithfully and diligently performed towards their masters, lays a certain foundation for attaining riches and honour in this world, and by God's grace everlasting happiness in the life to come'. Defoe noted that in the mid seventeenth century, apprentices were less rebellious, less scornful, easier to control, and more pious than they had become by 1726.

By the time Jack Sheppard was apprenticed to Owen Wood, apprentices were increasingly seen as no more than servants or skivvies. Henri Misson, writing in 1719, called an apprentice 'a sort of slave', tied to his master by his indenture, but bound by no loyalty or gratitude. A century earlier, the master had given his apprentice a home, looking after him both materially and emotionally, providing not only lodging and food but also clothes, laundry and doctors

5. *Industry and Idleness I: The Fellow 'Prentices at their Looms* (William Hogarth)
Tom Idle has a copy of the ballad of Moll Flanders pinned to his loom while
Francis Goodchild has a pristine copy of the *'Prentices' Guide* at his feet and Dick
Whittington's advice pinned to the wall behind him. Goodchild works, smiling to
himself, while Idle is asleep on his feet, a mug from a tavern in Spitalfields (Jack
Sheppard's birthplace) on the loom in front of him.

if necessary. The hard work demanded of an apprentice had been
seen as an investment in his future; but more and more, apprentices
were asked to do work that bore little relation to the trade they
were supposed to learn. In many cases, apprentices had learned
their trade after two or three years of service but were legally
banned from practising it, and remained beholden to a master who
continued to set them menial tasks. Sheppard's extraordinary skill
as a carpenter and engineer was evident throughout his criminal career; after a few years working for Wood, he must have felt that his
contract was a restraint on his abilities.

Increasingly, apprentices were paid wages instead of merely living as part of their master's family, a practice unheard of in Eliza-

bethan times. This heightened the feeling that they were little more than domestic servants, whose unruliness and unreliability were well known in the early eighteenth century. It also meant that they had pocket money to spend on drinking, whoring and gambling. The eighteenth-century stereotype of the 'Idle Apprentice' immortalized by Hogarth (illustration 5, page 35) was made possible by this new allowance of money. However, most social commentators believed idleness was inherent in the makeup of all apprentices. 'An apprentice is likely to be idle, and almost always is so, because he has no immediate interest to be otherwise,' declared Adam Smith.

The taste for luxury and licentiousness that spending money encouraged also drew apprentices and domestic servants towards crime. Because they did not save their wages – what was the point, when they were forbidden to work for themselves? – money only relieved them from boredom, drudgery and frustration in the short term, and they often turned to petty crime to supplement their incomes. Maidservants might prostitute themselves, or apprentices rob the houses where they worked. Many did not actually steal themselves, but sold information about their master's possessions, or when the house would be empty, to thieves. Footmen were well known for turning to highway robbery when their extravagant tastes and expenditure had exceeded their incomes. The material gains of crime were probably enhanced by a *frisson* of satisfaction at defying their master's authority. Although manifestations of resentment by the poor would have been squashed where possible – and so do not often survive in written form today – Bernard de Mandeville reported that 'they [the poor] murmur at Providence, and loudly complain, that the good things of the world are chiefly enjoyed by those who do not deserve them'.

Despite the new freedom that having money conferred on journeymen, their behaviour was still tightly constrained by their masters. Apprentices were fined for swearing, drunkenness, fighting, gambling and slack work. If they refused to pay a fine, they were given eleven strokes across the buttocks with a board. This type of harsh physical punishment was typical of the age. Authority within the household was maintained by violence. A wife's, child's or servant's resistance to their master's rule was considered petty treason, rebellion on a personal level, and as such could provoke a savage response. Even Samuel Pepys, essentially a kind, warm-hearted man, thought nothing of boxing his clerk's ears, whipping his boy-servant, and beating his fifteen-year-old maid with a broomstick before locking her up for a night in the cellar.[1]

Horror stories of cruel treatment to servants and apprentices abounded. Mrs Brownrigg was a respectable midwife, married to a prosperous painter and plasterer. They owned their home, 'lived in credit', and took in parish apprentice girls to help in the house. These girls were treated with unbelievable cruelty. They were fed on stale bread and water, if at all, and made to sleep on rough straw on the floor of the coal cellar. One desperate girl, Mary Clifford, frozen to the bone by the damp against which her ragged clothes and inadequate diet gave little protection, tried to steal some food. Mrs Brownrigg caught her reaching up to the cupboard, and stripped her naked before beating her savagely with the butt end of a whip. Mary Clifford was sent back to the cellar, bleeding, raw, with a chain around her neck that barely allowed her to breathe. A few days later she complained to one of the Brownriggs' lodgers about the conditions under which she and her companions were forced to live; Mrs Brownrigg overheard, and slashed viciously at Mary's tongue with a pair of scissors, cutting it in two places. Eventually, someone informed the courts of Mrs Brownrigg's brutality to her apprentice girls, and she was tried and hanged in 1767. It was too late for Mary Clifford, though; she was discovered locked in a cupboard, in a condition 'impossible to describe', and she died a few days later.[2]

On the whole, however, as long as it was possible, a blind eye was turned to this kind of behaviour. In 1733 a fisherman from Hammersmith was found guilty only of the manslaughter of his apprentice, whom he had beaten with rope and a tiller before leaving him outside, mortally wounded. The boy had 'died of wounds and want of looking after and hunger and cold together'. Two years later a ribbon-weaver called James Durant was acquitted of the murder of his apprentice, described as 'a very little boy' of thirteen or fourteen, whom he had beaten to death with a mop-stick.[3] It was considered a man's prerogative to maintain control over his household, including his wife, children and servants, by whatever means he saw fit; any resistance to his word was considered a challenge to his authority, and thus deserving of punishment. If a wife was convicted of adultery, her punishment, for petty treason, was to be burned at the stake.

If apprentices were often dealt with callously by their masters, parish apprentices were treated with even less consideration. They were farmed out to anyone willing to take them; once the parish had relieved itself of the responsibility for the child, little attention was paid to its future life, as in the case of Mary Clifford and Mrs Brownrigg. Sally Salisbury, the celebrated prostitute, was put out at the age of nine as a parish apprentice to a seamstress near Aldgate; 'but having the misfortune to lose a piece of lace, of a considerable value, she ran away from her mistress, and never returned'.[4] If Sally had been treated cruelly by her mistress, the fear of punishment would have seemed to the little girl to be a fate far worse than wandering the streets alone. Parish apprentices usually took with them a settlement of 20s.; many masters simply agreed to take a child for the money, and then overworked and abused it until it ran away. The more vulnerable a child was and the more pitiful its condition, the more a cruel master could take advantage of it without fear of reprisal from family or friends.

Jack was more fortunate than most because his interests were looked after by his mother and Mr Kneebone. As a child, he was sent out as a parish apprentice to a cane-chair maker, but his master soon died; another cane-chair maker took him on but he 'used him so ill'[5] that Jack left and went to his mother at Mr Kneebone's. Sheppard stayed with Owen Wood apparently quite happily for several years, working hard and learning his chosen trade. Two years after he started work for Wood, the silk-weavers of Spitalfields rioted after their petitions to Parliament for laws to limit the imports of Indian cotton that threatened their trade had gone unheeded. They molested women wearing Indian cotton and calico, throwing ink over their dresses or tearing them off their bodies. The government was forced to limit the importing of cheap Indian printed cottons to appease the weavers.

The silk-weavers of Spitalfields were among the most independent and politicized sections of England's population at this time. Of Huguenot descent, their traditional religious Nonconformity extended to their political views. They refused to work in the factories that were springing up all over the rest of the country, harbingers of the Industrial Revolution; they would not accept that their masters were their 'betters'; they resented the power that these men wielded over them. The silk they wove was worn by the rich as a mark of wealth and success. A proverb of 1732 expresses the hostility the weavers felt towards the upper classes: 'We are all Adam's children, but silk makes the difference.'

Although Jack was not directly involved in these riots, he shared a common ancestry with the silk-weavers and their families. He had been brought up alongside the rebels, and must have understood the resentment they felt towards the state and the powerful minority that controlled government policy. In smaller ways, too, he and his fellow workers suffered under a burden of oppression. Traditionally, men were paid their wages in taverns on Saturday nights – workers on Westminster Abbey, historically, were always paid at the Cock tavern, in Tothill Street – and publicans arranged for employers to plan to meet their workers in the evening, but they deliberately arrived at eleven or twelve at night. By this time, the waiting men would have drunk all their wages, so the employer would simply give their money directly to the publican, and the worker would be left with nothing to take home to his family. Thus a man earnestly intending to save his small pay packet would have his good intentions thwarted by the duplicity of those above him.

While on one side London's workers had to contend with a long tradition of oppression, on the other they had always had popular heroes on whom they focused to relieve the dissatisfaction and frustration of their lives. Wat Tyler, leader of the Peasant Revolt in

1381, was still revered in the eighteenth century. John Gay used the names Wat and Robin for two members of Macheath's gang of highwaymen in *The Beggars' Opera*. A 1730 play entitled *Wat Tyler and Jack Strawe: Or, the Mob Reformers* initially applauds Wat's courage in confronting the king to demand reform. He is hailed as 'Wat the First' and the 'Prince of Popular Princes'; but soon he is corrupted by his success, and threatens treason, and with Jack Straw is killed – 'Pull from that saucy, lousy head, the crown, and put it where it should be – upon mine.' The mob, appalled that they have supported one who desired to overthrow the king, are welcomed back into the royal fold. The ambivalence of the mob's response to Tyler is typical of the popular view of rebellion, which was as a form of protest, of seeking change and reaction, but not as a movement for social reform. The king's position was sacrosanct, and every member of society still knew and accepted his place within it.

It was those people who lived outside society, rather than merely rebelled against it, who were the true heroes of their contemporaries. The historian Peter Linebaugh calls 'the growing propensity, skill and success of London working people in escaping from the newly created institutions that were designed to discipline people by closing them in', for instance in workhouses, or houses of correction, 'Excarceration'. Criminals, in particular, refused to fulfil the roles society had mapped out for them; and common people adored them because they defied the law, throwing off the restrictions of poverty and submission under which they had been born.

PART TWO

It is the general complaint of the taverns, the coffee-houses,
the shopkeepers and others, that their customers are afraid when
it is dark to come to their houses and shops for fear that their
hats and wigs should be snitched from their heads or their swords taken
from their sides, or that they may be blinded,
knocked down, cut or stabbed.

CHARLES HITCHIN,
*The Regulator: Or, a Discovery of
the Conduct of Thieves and Thief-Takers*, 1718

Underworld

In 1712 an Act was passed for 'the relief of insolvent debtors' (10 Anne c.29). Jonathan Wild, using the legal skills he had honed during his four years' residence at Wood Street, submitted a successful application and was released from prison. He and his lover, a woman named Mary Milliner, set up a small brothel together in Lewkenor's Lane, now Macklin Street, in Covent Garden. Mary Milliner, a 'jade of some fame',[1] was a familiar figure at Wood Street Compter, although she seems not to have been imprisoned there. Whores of the cheaper sort found a good many of their clients were prisoners. For a small bribe the keeper or turnkey would let them in to solicit business.

Prostitutes, like thieves, were known by many names: trumpery, buttered buns, squirrels, bunters. The women, displaying their solidarity, called each other Sister or Cousin. The cheapest prostitute available was a three-penny-upright, but one could pay up to £250 for a night with a girl at the most exclusive whorehouses, situated in rooms above a piazza at Covent Garden. Many women living on the streets prostituted themselves when it suited them, or when the opportunity arose, like Defoe's Moll Flanders, admittedly of loose moral makeup to start with, who was propositioned by a rich-looking gentleman and thought she might be able to make a bit of money by picking his pocket as well as charging for her services. Some girls would brazenly pull open their dresses to display their wares as a well-dressed man walked past them in the street.

Men of all classes and occupations thought little of going to a prostitute; it was completely acceptable. Men were expected to be sexually active, while their wives were not supposed to be interested – in fact it was thought unwise, generally, to try to interest one's wife too much in sex lest she develop a voracious appetite for it. The health and sanity of prostitutes, unlike wives', was not considered. Medically, the practice was approved, because retention of semen was considered injurious to a man's health. Thus whores and whorehouses proliferated, profiting from a steady stream of customers, with Covent Garden recognized as the centre of this industry. A guidebook, Harris's *New Atlantic: The Whoremonger's Guide to London*, was produced annually, detailing the addresses of brothels, and describing the physical characteristics and specialities of the girls. Eight thousand copies were distributed each year to subscribers.

The German philosopher Georg Lichtenberg describes, in amazement, how women were available:

got up in any way you like, dressed, bound up, hitched up, tight-laced, loose, painted, done up or raw, scented, in silk or wool, with or without sugar, in short, what a man cannot obtain here, if he have not money; upon my word, let him not look for it anywhere else in this world of ours.[2]

Another German visitor to London, in the 1710s, was likewise impressed by the array of whores available but found they cost a 'prodigious deal'.

The easiest way of finding a whore was on the street. The young James Boswell describes picking up a prostitute in 1763:

At the bottom of the Haymarket I picked up a strong, jolly young damsel, and taking her under the arm I conducted her to Westminster Bridge, and then in armour complete [wearing a condom] I did engage her upon this noble edifice. The whim of doing it there with the Thames rolling beneath us amused me greatly.[3]

By the late seventeenth century condoms were in popular use, less for contraceptive purposes than to avoid venereal disease. Casanova called them 'English overcoats'. The best condoms were made of sheep's intestines, and cheaper, more uncomfortable ones were available made of linen soaked in brine, which needed washing after use. Both types were re-usable. They came in three sizes, and were sold in silk-bound packets of eight, tied up with silk ribbons.

Brothels were the expensive alternative to streetwalkers. They were known as vaulting academies, or nurseries, or seminaries, or nunneries. In his satirical novel *Mr Jonathan Wild the Great*, Henry Fielding describes 'those eating houses in Covent Garden, where female flesh is deliciously dressed, and served up to the greedy appetites of young gentlemen'. Different whorehouses catered not only for different price ranges, but also for different tastes. Some offered floor shows, others naked dancing. A particular fashion was for girls striking 'postures', either naked or scantily dressed, something Emma Hamilton, Nelson's mistress, was later famous for. The servant in the background of Scene III of *A Rake's Progress* is carrying a large plate on which a posturer is about to perform (illustration 16, page 97). Mrs Theresa Berkely ran a flagellants' brothel in Charlotte Street, specializing in what was known as the 'English perversion'. Jonathan Wild described going to a house of 'He-Whores' near the Old Bailey with his future associate, Charles Hitchin, Under-Marshal of London:

which they no sooner enter'd, but the M-l [Hitchin] was complemented by the company with the titles of Madam and Ladyship . . . The men calling one another 'My Dear', hugging and kissing, tickling and feeling each other, as if they were a mixture of wanton males and females; and assuming effeminate voices, female airs etc., some telling others that they ought to be whipp'd for not coming to school more frequently.

Another house like this existed in Holborn, run by the aptly named Mother Clap, where men could 'dress themselves in women's apparel for the entertainment of others of the same inclinations, in dancing etc. in imitation of the Fair Sex'. This house was raided in the 1710s, and the transvestites were taken to court and tried,

completely rigged in gowns, petticoats, head cloths, fine lac'd shoes, fur-below scarves, and masks; some had riding hoods; some were dressed like shepherdesses; others like milkmaids with fine green hats, waistcoats and petticoats, and others had their faces patched and painted, and wore very expensive hoop-petticoats, which were then very lately introduced.

The guilty were condemned to be 'publicly conveyed through the streets in their various female habits'. According to Wild, the utter humiliation of this ordeal was 'so mortifying to one of the young gentlemen that he died within a few days' of the punishment. At trials held in the late 1720s, it came out in the evidence against these houses of 'He-Whores' that mock marriages were performed between men, complete with veils, rings and bridal chambers.

Sally Salisbury, born Sarah Pridden in 1692, was one of the most famous prostitutes of her day. She grew up living on the streets of St Giles. 'At different seasons of the year, she shelled beans and peas, cried nose-gays and newspapers, peeled walnuts, made matches, turned bunter &c., well knowing that a wagging hand always gets a penny.'[4] By the time she was fourteen, she had been abandoned by her first rich lover, the notorious rake Colonel Charteris. From then on, she worked principally for Mother Wisebourne, whose Covent Garden establishment was the best-known and most expensive whorehouse in London at the time. Mother Wisebourne's girls came to her from various sources – she regularly visited prisons and had made arrangements with the keepers to 'sell' her the freedom of female prisoners with potential; she also frequented the church of St Martin-in-the-Fields, where she looked over the children, whose parents rented them out to beggars for the day, 'as a butcher might choose a mare at Smithfield [meat market]' – but, paradoxically, she had a house chaplain who read prayers to her girls twice a day and a Bible lay open in her house at all times.

Sally's beauty, wit and high spirits made her a favourite with clients such as Viscount Bolingbroke, the Secretary of State, who paid 'the highest price for the greatest pleasure'. On one occasion, she was given a ticket to a grand society ball. Her hostess commented cattily on the splendour of Sally's jewels.

'They had need be finer than yours, my Lady,' said Sally. 'You have but one Lord to keep you and to buy you jewels, but I have at least half a score, of which number, Madam, your Ladyship's husband is not the most inconsiderable.'

'Nay, my Lady—' cried another guest. 'You had much better let Mrs Salisbury alone, for she'll lay claim to all our husbands else, by and by.'

'Not much to yours, indeed, Madam,' replied Sally tartly. 'I tried him once and am resolved I'll never try him again; for I was forced to kick him out of bed, because his —— is good for nothing at all.'[5]

Her biographer, writing for a large popular audience to whom characters like Sally Salisbury were the eighteenth-century equivalent of movie stars, in his preface addressed to her a justification of prostitution:

For the usefulness of it, it will be readily granted. The ladies of your universal character are of wondrous service to those who cannot comply with the indolence, clamour, insatiableness, laziness, extravagance or virtuous nastiness of a wife . . . It must be allowed, that by such gay volunteers as your ladyship, give a young fellow an handsome prospect of the town, lead him through all the enchanting mazes, and even surfeit him with delight; so that by the time he is come out of your hands, he is grown very tame, and prepared for the dull solemnity of marriage.[6]

Cesar de Saussure described her death:

Some time ago a courtesan, of the name of Sally Salisbury, famed for her rare and wonderful beauty, her wit and fun, became the fashion in London, and was favoured by distinguished personages. One night, at a wine supper, one of her admirers having displeased her by some uncomplimentary speech, she seized a knife and plunged it into his body. Next morning she was conveyed a prisoner to Newgate. You will suppose her lovers abandoned her in her distress. They did no such thing, but crowded into the prison, presenting her with every comfort and luxury possible. As soon as the wounded man – who, by the way, belongs to one of the best known English families [John Finch, the son of the Countess of Winchelsea] – was sufficiently recovered, he asked for her discharge, but Sally Salisbury died of brain fever, brought on by debauch, before she was able to leave the prison.

She was twenty-two at the time; the 'brain fever' was probably syphilis. Her life provided a model both for Hogarth's *A Harlot's Progress* and for John Cleland's *Fanny Hill*.

Hogarth's *A Harlot's Progress* is perhaps the best depiction of prostitution in London in the early eighteenth century, following

6. *A Harlot's Progress I* (William Hogarth)

The Harlot's country innocence, her simple dress and the bloom at her bodice, are contrasted with the ruffles and furbelows of Mother Needham's clothes. The procuress wears several beauty spots, a French fashion as well as a common method of disguising the ravages of disease. At the bottom right of the picture is a goose that Moll has brought to give to her cousin in London; 'Winchester goose' was a slang term for a prostitute.

the progression of a simple country girl to utter dissolution. In the first scene (illustration 6, above), an innocent girl, recently arrived from the country, is approached by a procuress. The country maiden seduced by her new master, or made her mistress's confidante in her sordid intrigues, or taken in by a friendly Madam, was such a familiar stereotype that some fallen women went so far as to leave London for a few days in order to return to town on a wagon, rosy-cheeked and with their innocence mysteriously restored, able once more to pass as fresh flesh. Some returned after 'being made free of the wagon [-driver] (which is the phrase amongst these sort of gentry for the last favour) the honest fellow gives them a character [reference], knows abundance of aunts and cousins, all extremely honest etc.'. Mother Wisebourne's partner, Mrs Bennett, could 'restore' a girl's virginity, as many times as was needed.

The depravity of the first scene is underlined by the arrangement of the figures, which echoes that of the biblical Visitation, when the Virgin Mary visits Elizabeth, the expectant mother of John the Baptist, after she has been impregnated by the Holy Spirit, to ask her advice. This visual parallel is reinforced by the names of the characters: Mother Needham, the real-life model for the procuress, was called Elizabeth, and Moll, the name Hogarth gave his Harlot, was a derivative of Mary. This interpretation of the scene casts an ambiguous light on the subject matter: in the Visitation, Mary has sought out Elizabeth to ask her advice. Does Hogarth mean to imply that Moll, fresh and innocent though she may seem, has sought out Mother Needham; that she is not an innocent victim, but an accomplice to her own eventual guilt?[7]

Mother Needham was a famous brothel-keeper of the 1720s, who died in May 1731, three days after being viciously pelted by onlookers as she stood in the stocks. The crowd was so excited that 'a boy, getting upon a lamppost [to see the action better] . . . fell from the same upon iron spikes' and 'expired after a few hours, in great agony'.[8] The *Grub Street Journal* commented caustically after her death that those who had caused her fatal injuries 'acted very ungratefully, considering how much she had done to oblige them' throughout her career.

Her employer was Colonel Charteris, Sally Salisbury's first seducer, who is seen hovering in the doorway behind Needham and Moll Hackabout, ogling the girl. In 1729 Charteris was convicted of raping a servant girl at gunpoint, but was pardoned by the king and released in 1730. It was highly unusual for a gentleman to be convicted – or even accused, or tried – of rape; but his pardon demonstrates how this type of behaviour, by a well-connected man, was considered by his peers to be no more than a silly mistake, if that.

Blood! Must a Colonel, with a lord's estate
Be thus obnoxious to a scoundrel's fate?
Brought to the bar, and sentenced from the bench
For only ravishing a country wench?
Shall gentlemen receive no more respect?
Shall their diversion thus by laws be checked?[9]

He died, most probably of a venereal disease, in 1731; his funeral provoked a public demonstration, with an indignant mob throwing 'dead dogs &c. into the grave' with him. Arbuthnot's damning epitaph of him reads: 'Francis Charteris, who with an inflexible constancy, and inimitable uniformity of life, persisted in spite of age and infirmities, in the practice of every human vice. . .'[10]

Hogarth comments further on the Harlot's trade and her opinions in the third scene (illustration 7, page 51), in which a magistrate bursts into her chamber. Hanging on a hook above her bed is a handy bundle of birch twigs, either a part of a masquerade costume or for flogging clients; condoms litter the table; an anodyne necklace, used for treating venereal disease and relieving children's teething pains, is also shown, a reference not only to the Harlot's health but also to her illegitimate child (not shown until the final scenes). Next to her bed are two engravings, one of a fictional highwayman, Macheath, the hero of Gay's *The Beggars' Opera*, and the other of the popular preacher Dr Sacheverell, who was impeached for his High Church views interpreted by the Puritanical monarchs William and Mary as seditious: both images of renegades, flouting law and order. The romanticism of his Harlot is plain, her yearning for escapist idealism exemplified by these two images.

But the magistrate condemns her to Bridewell, a 'house of correction' where she stands in Plate IV (illustration 8, page 52) beating hemp in an expensive gown – perhaps a gift from a lover in better days, but now apparently the only dress she owns. Like the Harlot, Sally Salisbury was in and out of prisons and houses of correction throughout her life; she died in Newgate on a charge of manslaughter but on other occasions she had been held in Mar-

7. *A Harlot's Progress III* (William Hogarth)

The 'bunter' who attends Moll has no nose, a common sign of syphilis. Her presence brings clearly to mind Moll's eventual fate, showing what she is doomed to become. Moll holds up a watch that she has stolen from a lover the night before. When this print was published, the employees of Sir James Gonson, the magistrate William Hogarth used as his model for the magistrate at the rear of the engraving, closed down his office in their haste to rush out and buy copies of the print.

shalsea Debtors' Prison and in Bridewell. It was not unusual for whores to be found beating hemp in inappropriate clothing. The *Grub Street Journal* of 1730 describes Mary Moffat, a well-known prostitute, as beating hemp 'in a gown very richly dressed with silver'.

The prostitutes who worked for Jonathan Wild and Mary Milliner would never have been able to afford to buy dresses embroidered with silver. They would have been more like 'Corinna, pride of Drury Lane' (an area notoriously populated by whores), to whom Swift addressed his satirical poem, 'A Beautiful Young Nymph Going to Bed'.

8. *A Harlot's Progress IV* (William Hogarth)

The woman on the far right of the print is delousing herself while her neighbour jeers at Moll's weak efforts to beat the hemp. On Moll's right is a well-dressed gambler, identified by the torn playing card on the ground in front of him. The warder chastising Moll was used by Fielding as a model for Thwackum on his novel *Tom Jones*.

> Corinna, pride of Drury Lane,
> For whom no shepherd sighs in vain;
> Never did Covent Garden boast
> So bright a battered, strolling Toast;
> No drunken rake to pick her up,
> No cellar where on tick to sup;
> Returning at the midnight hour;
> Four storeys climbing to her bower;
> Then, seated on a three-legged chair,
> Takes off her artificial hair:
> Now, plucking out a crystal eye,
> She wipes it clean, and lays it by . . .

Now dextrously her plumpers draws,
That serve to fill her hollow jaws.
Untwists a wire; and from her gums
A set of teeth completely comes.
Pulls out the rags, contrived to prop
Her flabby dugs, and down they drop . . .
Up goes her hand, and off she slips
The bolsters that supply her hips.
With gentlest touch, she next explores
Her shankers, issues, running sores;
Effects of many a sad disaster,
And then to each applies a plaster.
But must, before she goes to bed,
Rub off the dawbs of white and red; . . .
She takes a Bolus e'er she sleeps;
And then between two blankets creeps.
With pains of love tormented lies;
Or, if she chance to close her eyes,
Of Bridewell and the Compter dreams,
And feels the lash, and faintly screams; . . .
Or, to Jamaica seems transported,
Alone, and by no planter courted.
Or, near Fleet-Ditch's oozy brinks,
Surrounded with a hundred stinks: . . .
Or, struck with fear, her fancy runs
On watchmen, constables, and duns,
From whom she meets with frequent rubs;
But never from religious clubs;
Whose favour she is sure to find,
Because she pays them all in kind.

Corinna wakes. A dreadful sight!
Behold the ruins of the night!
A wicked rat her plaster stole,
Half ate, and dragged it to his hole.
The crystal eye, alas, was missed;
And Puss had on her plumbers p—st.
A pigeon picked her issue-peas;
And *Shock* her tresses filled with fleas.

'Corinna' was an example of the cheapest type of streetwalker, known as a Buttock-and-File: 'buttock', for obvious reasons – clearly, a piece of ass meant the same thing then as it does today – and 'file', for the tool that thieves used in house-breaking. Buttock-and-Files could combine their trades, robbing their clients of their purses during a moment of abandonment. Some whores used to take the purse out of their client's pocket as they had sex, and replace it with another one weighted with lead so that when the client left, feeling his pocket to ensure the purse was still there, he would believe he hadn't been robbed. A Buttock-and-File usually worked with a 'Twang', a male companion who watched covertly as his partner found her victim and engaged him in intercourse while she robbed him. At a given signal, he would come up to them and knock the 'Cull', or victim, down so that they could make their escape before he realized he had been robbed.

Wild worked as Twang for Mary Milliner, and for the other girls in their establishment. He was of average height, but strong. As a Twang he was ideal because he was ruthless enough to consider any cruelty fair play; his victims would seldom have been able to pursue him or raise a hue and cry. He also fenced, or sold, the goods the girls stole. This was more to his taste, for although he was physically brave he preferred to remain in the background masterminding situations, rather than being actually involved himself. 'Nor indeed, had he any occasion to run a hazard himself, he finding himself as much a gainer in the part he acted as if he had shared in the adventure,' recorded Defoe. Small-time receiving was the perfect introduction to thief-taking, the profession Jonathan Wild was to dominate and transform during his career.

Britain in the early eighteenth century could be a brutal, frightening place. Violence was an inescapable fact of life at all levels of society. 'Anything that looks like fighting is delicious to an Englishman,' wrote Henri Misson, a French visitor to England, who published his observations of the differences between the French and the English in 1719. Even recreations might involve violence, albeit somewhat randomly. Hogarth and some friends went on a junket to Kent in 1732. Their country ramble degenerated into an extraordinary scene when they started throwing bits of dung at each other, which led to 'a battle royal with sticks, pebbles and hog's dung'.[11] Lionel Copely, a Yorkshire gentleman, was indicted in 1664 for beating a man, putting a bridle into his mouth, and after climbing on to his back, riding him for half an hour.

Disputes were often settled by force. Duelling was still common, and was carried out quite openly in the fields in and around London. Hyde Park, which was five or six miles in circumference, filled with deer and still very wild, was a particular favourite but any open space, such as Lincoln's Inn Fields or Leicester Fields, might be used. In 1712, Lord Mohun and the Duke of Wharton slew each other in Hyde Park. Killing one's opponent in a duel was generally considered manslaughter, not murder, in the eyes of the law, and was punished only as a common law misdemeanour. Seconds sometimes got carried away and joined in the fray: Captain John Hamilton, one of the seconds, was tried for his complicity in the deaths of the principals in the Wharton–Mohun duel. An eyewitness testified that both seconds had their swords in their hands, 'assisting the Lords'. All four probably took off their wigs for ease of movement and vision, and fought bare-headed.

Cesar de Saussure commented on the frequency with which fist-fighting was used to settle an argument. 'Would you believe it, I have actually seen women – belonging, it is true, to the scum of the people – fighting in this same manner.' Sometimes this might have tragic results. William Yates was tried for murder in Surrey in 1726. His defence shows the ease with which spontaneous violence could rage out of control.

I and the Deceased were playing a match at cricket, and the Deceased doing some things which I did not like, together with my being in a fair way to lose, ruffled my temper; whereupon I went up to the Deceased and desired him to be easy, otherwise I would knock him on the head with my bat. The Deceased still persisting to provoke me, I challenged him to box, but he refusing . . . I was easy, and all was quiet.

A few minutes later, his opponent had challenged him to fight, and 'not wishing to be thought a coward', Yates accepted. They 'stripped, and went into a pound, where we fought some time, till he allowed me to be the best man. The pound being locked, we were both obliged to get over the rails, and he, in all appearances got over as well as I', but he died half an hour later, from 'mortal bruising' inflicted by Yates. Yates was found guilty of manslaughter, not a capital offence, burned, or branded, in the hand, and discharged.[12]

The nobility were not exempt from fighting in the street in this manner. In 1719 Henri Misson described seeing 'the late Duke of Grafton at fisticuffs in the open street, with such a fellow [a hackney-coach driver; the Duke was disputing the fare], whom he lamed most horribly'. Misson's footnote reads: 'In the very widest part of the Strand. The Duke of Grafton was big and extremely robust. He had hid his blue riband [the mark of his rank] before he took the coach, so that the coachman did not know him.'

This volatility, a speed and heat of reaction when slighted or crossed, was common. In 1714 Henry Plunkett killed the wig-maker with whom he lodged, when he refused to lower his price for a wig Plunkett had ordered more than a guinea: Plunkett slit Thomas Brown's throat from ear to ear with a razor lying on the counter. A newspaper report of 1719 reveals an incident of similar mindless violence. 'On Saturday night last, a Link-Boy, lighting two gentlemen home to their lodgings in the Strand, and not going fast enough for them, they stabbed him in the back, of which he died the next morning but the murderers escaped.'[13]

Group violence was as prevalent as individual acts of brutality. They might be politically or socially motivated, like the actions of mobs. In 1723 a group of rioters called the Waltham Blacks, in their struggle against the gamekeepers of Waltham Forest who were trying to enforce their masters' orders to tighten poaching restrictions, threatened murder, assaulted people, burned down houses, and staged dramatic rescues of imprisoned offenders. Riots might also be genuine acts of treason, like the risings in support of Jacobite pretenders. Wild rumours circulated constantly in this period of Jacobite invasions from Scotland or France.

It was not just the needy and desperate who created this powder-keg atmosphere. Upper-class disturbances were not unknown. The Mohocks were a band of young rakes who roamed through London causing havoc. Their name was a bastardization of Mohawk, an Indian tribe renowned for its reckless bravery. The only qualification for membership was 'an outrageous ambition of doing all possible hurt to their fellow creatures . . . In order to exert this principle in its full strength and perfection, they take care to drink themselves to a pitch. . .' Members had different areas of specialization: some, called 'Dancing Masters', taught 'their scholars to cut capers by running swords through their legs'; others stuffed their victims in barrels and rolled them down hills; still others assaulted and defaced people they met on the street. Cutting off people's noses was a particular favourite. They went down streets tearing the knockers off the front doors of every house they passed.[14] In March 1712 a group of Mohocks, 'all peers and persons of quality', killed the landlady of a tavern after causing a fight on her premises; all five were acquitted, despite the atmosphere of terror the Mohocks had created.[15] 'Who has not trembled at the Mohocks' name?' asked John Gay. That year, Swift mentioned them in a letter: 'Our Mohocks go on still, and cut people's faces every night; faith they shan't cut mine, I like it better as it is.' He thought the destruction the Mohocks caused was part of a Whig conspiracy to create an atmosphere of chaos on London's streets, under cover of which they could have Lord Oxford, the leader of the Tories, assassinated undetected.

The Bold Bucks, of which the Duke of Wharton was a member, was another aristocratic association like the Mohocks, but with blasphemy rather than violence as its *raison d'être*. To join, its would-be members had formally to deny the existence of God; every Sunday the club ate a dish called 'Holy Ghost Pie'. The Bucks' activities were more specific than the Mohocks'; they concentrated on sexual adventures, in which women were usually unwilling participants. The Hell-Fire Clubs had similar tenets and aims to the Bold Bucks, guided by principles of 'atheism and sexual depravity'. Black Masses were held, read by members dressed as monks, attended by prostitutes in nuns' habits; books of erotica were bound as Books of Common Prayer; group masturbation and orgies were held. Its members included Sir Francis Dashwood, whose mistress, Mrs Stanhope, a brothel-keeper, was known as 'Hell-Fire Stanhope'; and John Montague, the future Earl of Sandwich, who was 'completely depraved, as mischievous as a monkey and as lecherous as a goat'. In April 1721 George I released an order against 'certain scandalous clubs or societies of young persons who meet together . . . [to] insult the most sacred principles of our holy religion . . . and corrupt the minds and morals of one another'. The specific acts in which they indulged were obviously too scandalous to spell out in an official document.[16]

The streets of London were so dangerous that one had to travel fully armed to go out to dinner. Men habitually carried swords, and often pistols as well. No one could be trusted in the dank, unlit streets. Even link-boys, whose job it was to light the street lanterns intended to make London's streets safer at night, didn't hesitate to put out their torches and rob passers-by, or for a penny or two lead them into the clutches of a gang of armed footpads; they were known as 'Moon Cursers'. Servants in a big London house were armed and prepared to defend their master's property as if it were under siege. Footmen were not just used to decorate the back of a carriage; they were also there to defend their master and his family against robbers. Stagecoaches and private coaches took outriders with them to protect their passengers from violent highwaymen. In 1720 ladies going to court carried blunderbusses in their carriages 'to shoot at rogues'. Later in the century, Horace Walpole, who had been shot at in Hyde Park by a highwayman, said, 'One is forced to travel, even at noon, as if one was going to battle.' London was a battlezone. '. . .The streets of this town, and the roads leading to it, will shortly be impassable without the utmost hazard.'[17]

Rates of crime were particularly high after a war, when demobilized soldiers returned home. The army was a hotbed of corruption:

a bribe could arrange anything; in fact, little could be done without bribery. Commissions were sold illegally; officers took advantage of their soldiers for their own profit; drinking, gambling and whoring were glorified; violence was a way of life. The mechanics of life in the army thus predisposed demobilized soldiers to a life of crime. Furthermore, ex-soldiers often had no skills, some having joined up to avoid the strictures of apprenticeship, others tempted by the promise of two guineas and a new suit of clothes 'for every rake that will run away from his wife and family'.[18] Many were thrill-seekers, who joined the army to see the world and make their fortune; frustrated, empty-handed, they returned to grab what they could. With the end of the War of Spanish Succession in 1713, there was the usual rise in criminal prosecutions, and this increase was sustained well into the 1720s. Crime was rife; London was being 'plundered wholesale'.[19]

Most offences were crimes against property. London, as the principal city in the country, was where the country's wealth was concentrated. The gulf between the lives of the lower and upper classes was vast – the ostentatious luxury of the rich was flaunted without modesty, and the poor saw the consumption of their betters and knew that nothing they could ever achieve would bring this type of life within their reach. Crime was their only method of venting their feelings of frustration at this inequality. But crime generally meant theft; although robberies often involved brutality, injury was not the chief aim of the exercise. Rape was common, but it was little reported and still less prosecuted. The age of consent was set at ten in 1576, and there was not much moral support for the victims of sexual abuse. Premeditated murder was rare, but victims of crime were sometimes killed when they were attacked by a gang of footpads or held up by a highwayman.

Practically the only check on this outbreak of violence and lawlessness were thief-takers. Since Elizabethan times, people had sought them out to retrieve their stolen property. Any means might be used, even the supernatural; John Bonner, of Short's Gardens near Covent Garden, advertised his services in 1703, claiming to be able to track down missing items by necromancy. The limitations of the legal system allowed thief-taking to flourish; quite simply it was cheaper and easier for the government to defer responsibility for controlling crime by putting it in the hands of men willing to deal with it. Thief-takers were often receivers of stolen goods, or fences, whose knowledge of the criminal world provided them with unique access to criminals, and by the 1710s thief-taking had become a complex trade involving blackmail, informing, bribery, framing and organization of theft, as well as mere receivership. 'Black Dog' was the cant name for a receiver in sixteenth-century London. Moll Cutpurse was known as the 'High Directress' of crime in Restoration London, with an office on Fleet Street. She was an unusual woman,

troubled by none of those longings which poor maidens are subject to: she had the power and strength to command her own pleasure of any person who had reasonable ability of body; and therefore she needed not whine for it, as she was able to beat a fellow to a compliance, without the unnecessary trouble of entreaties.[20]

An anonymous report in the *British Journal* in 1725 recalled the activities of thief-takers, from the point of view of the people who worked for them, at the start of the century:

The thief-takers are our absolute masters; and they have intelligence from tapsters, ostlers, and porters etc., at inns, and from people, that only for a disguise [enough gin to get drunk on] cry things about the streets; and others, who draw in servants to be accessory in robbing their masters; and they send us into several wards and stations (as a corporal sends soldiers to stand sentinel); and if we refuse to go, they'll immediately have us committed for some former crime; or . . . bring evidence to swear away our lives wrongfully.

The author knew six thief-takers working in London at this time, 'and where they kept their nightly clubs, to which if their gangs did not repair, they were in danger; and from whence they must go wherever he sent them'. He detailed how they would go to prisons daily to look for new offenders, whom they could free in return for their future loyalty, and 'whichever thief-catcher came first to such new offender, he must be his slave for ever after, and rob when he bid him, or be hanged for refusing'.

Thief-takers informed on the thieves who worked for them − 'these people swear my life away for the sake of the reward' protested a defendant on trial in 1738 − but the thieves were forced to rely on thief-takers because, without them, the property they stole was worthless to them. They were hugely unpopular because the nature of their profession kept them from any sentimental attachment or loyalty, and they were always willing to turn someone in if they deemed it necessary. Some thief-takers actually enticed young men into crime specifically to impeach them for the £40 reward the government offered to anyone providing evidence that would convict a criminal. Thief-takers were far and away the best placed to reap these rewards; only they had the necessary sources of information on individual miscreants, and the contacts to secure their arrests. The rewards offered, instead of helping to curb robbery, allowed thief-taking to flourish.

Sir Salathial Lovell, a City Recorder and well-known hanging judge, was the most prominent and productive thief-taker to date when he died in 1713. Tom Brown said the 'shoals' of criminals condemned by Lovell were 'mere sacrifices to his avarice or his malice'. Defoe revealed his activities in his 'Reformation of Manners':

> He trades in justice and the souls of men,
> And prosecutes them equally to gain:
> He has his public Book of Rates to show,
> Where every rogue the price of life may know:
> Fraternities of Villains he maintains,
> Protects their robberies, and shares their gains,
> Who thieve with toleration as a trade,
> And then restores according as they're paid.

A year later, in 1703, Defoe was tried by Lovell for another satirical poem, 'The Shortest Way with Dissenters', which contradicted government policy. He was treated particularly harshly, sentenced to stand in the stocks, a choice of punishment usually reserved for ill-educated ruffians, arguably because he had touched a raw nerve by accusing Lovell of being involved in criminal activities.[21]

After Lovell's death, Charles Hitchin, Under-Marshal of Newgate gaol, took his place as the principal thief-taker in London. A tall, striking man, he paraded through the streets of the city wearing a long powdered wig and a tricorn hat and carrying a sword, with a raggle-taggle gang of pickpockets, whom he called his 'Mathematicians', dancing attendance at his heels. The office of Under-Marshal was responsible to the Court of Aldermen of the City of London, and subordinate to an Upper-Marshal. The two marshals had six men on their staff, and their duties were those of a small, rudimentary, private police force over the area encompassing greater London. Hitchin's official powers of arrest, and the right to issue warrants, reinforced his dominance over the criminals he controlled.

Apprenticeship

Sometime in 1713, soon after Wild was released from Wood Street Compter, Under-Marshal Hitchin asked him if he would like to work for him as an assistant in his thief-taking/receivership business. In both his official and his criminal capacities, Hitchin would certainly have visited Wood Street; if he had not actually met Wild, he would have heard of him. Wild himself said that it was during his time at the Compter that he had become acquainted with the 'secrets of the criminals there under confinement, and particularly Mr Hitchin's management'. It is more than likely that one of Hitchin's 'Mathematicians', William Field, who later worked as an informer for Wild, knew him from his Wood Street days. Perhaps the two men became better acquainted when Wild began fencing the goods Mary Milliner and her girls brought him. Possibly Hitchin saw that Wild had talent, and, worried that he might develop into a serious rival, determined to contain Wild by bringing him closer.

Hitchin had been suspended from his office as Under-Marshal in 1712, ostensibly because thief-taking and government office-holding were incompatible activities, realistically because he was charging such extortionate prices for the stolen goods he recovered. However, because the government did not want to embarrass itself by looking for a replacement so soon after Hitchin had been appointed (only the year before), not to mention the difficulty of finding someone to pay £700 for the office as he had done, they simply hired someone else to perform his duties while Hitchin's fate was decided. He retained his official title, and used the privileges of his office where they were useful to him, but did not have to bother himself with the boring details of day-to-day responsibilities.

Wild's 1718 account of Hitchin's application to him runs as follows:

I am very sensible that you . . . are let into the knowledge of the intrigues of the Compter, particularly with relation to the securing of pocketbooks. But your experience is inferior to mine. I can put you in a far better method than you are acquainted with, and which may be facilitated with safety. For though I am suspended, I still retain the power of acting as a constable; and notwithstanding I can't be heard before my Lord Mayor as formerly, I have interest among the Al[derme]n. But I must first tell you . . . that you'll spoil the trade of thief-taking in advancing greater rewards than are necessary. I give but half-a-crown a [pocket] book; and when the thieves and pickpockets see you and I confederate, they'll submit to our terms and likewise continue their thefts for fear of coming to the gallows by our means. Concluding, you shall take a turn with me as my servant or assistant, and we'll commence our rambles this night.

Wild's job was to assist Hitchin by accompanying him on his daily rounds, visiting recalcitrant thieves who were not stealing enough, or who were taking their goods elsewhere to be fenced; buying friendly magistrates drinks in the taverns they frequented; finding out who owned the goods that were brought in by the thieves so they could offer to sell the items back. It required an inexhaustible memory for faces, names and places, as well as determination and egotism, and the right combination of menace and charm that would ensure absolute loyalty, awe mixed with terror.

Hitchin possessed these qualities to some degree, but he lacked Wild's criminal genius and opportunistic drive. He was protected by his official position, but his timidity prevented him from dealing in anything other than either relatively anonymous goods, such as bankbills, or items with which he could blackmail their owners, such as pocketbooks or diaries containing compromising material of some sort. His technique was also risky, because he approached the owners of the stolen goods himself, usually by letter, in which he anonymously recommended 'Hitchin's' skills as a thief-taker. He would continue, 'But I must also give you this caution, that you are to go to him with your pockets well-lined, or he'll have nothing to say to you.' This practice implied Hitchin's own complicity: he already knew how the goods had been stolen and by whom. Finally, his high-handed, bullying attitude antagonized the criminals he wanted to intimidate, just as his greed alienated his clientele. To judge by Wild's later refinements of receiving and thief taking, watching Hitchin's clumsy methods must have driven him crazy.

By 1714, when Hitchin was reinstated as Under-Marshal, Wild had outgrown his partnership with Hitchin. He continued to use their association to his advantage – calling himself Hitchin's 'Deputy', although the office did not exist; and, like Hitchin, carrying a sword as mark of his authority – but in December 1714 he had an office of his own in a room in Mrs Seagoe's Blue Boar tavern in the Little Old Bailey. From this period onward, he worked alone.

His partnership with Mary Milliner had also come to an end. He had used the silver sword he carried to cut off her ear – 'to mark her for a bitch' – during an argument, and although they continued to work together sometimes, and he still paid her a weekly allowance, their sexual relationship was over. It is hard to fathom what could have persuaded her to remain in contact with Wild after his brutal treatment of her; one has to assume that she either saw a side of him she believed redeemed him, like Nancy in *Oliver Twist*, or that she was simply paralysed by her fear of him.

From this new office Wild was able to develop and hone his skills. Because he had a base, which he called the 'Office for the Recovery of Lost and Stolen Property', he was always available to his clients, and was able to stop seeking out the victims of crime as Hitchin had been forced to do. His fame became the magnet that brought his clientele to him. Everyone in London knew that if something was stolen, Jonathan Wild was the man to recover it (for a small fee).

Wild worked in a far more organized and wide-ranging manner than Hitchin. He played on people's desperation when something valuable or with sentimental value was stolen. To them, the loss was irreparable; they were willing to pay anything to anyone to recover the watch their father had left them or get back the letter from their mistress that was hidden in their pocketbook. Defoe described the procedure when someone went to Wild's office to ask him to recover something. Jonathan would come out from behind his desk, shake hands warmly, and offer his client a seat in the strong Staffordshire accent he never lost. After accepting a guinea finding fee – more than twice the average weekly wage of a labourer; his fee was only 5s. when he first opened his office in the Old Bailey – and writing his client's name and details down in his ledger, he would take extensive notes about the place and time of the theft, what exactly was taken, and then promise to do his best to recover it. Defoe says tartly that this note-taking was 'not for his information, but for your amusement'; it was certainly an effective method of gaining his client's trust and confidence.

Wild would usher the client out, and ask him to return in two or three days to see what he'd been able to produce. When the client came back, Wild would say he'd been able to track down the thief, but that he wanted an extortionate price for the goods, and would he mind waiting a day or two more while he tried to beat the price down for him? The client, thrilled that Wild seemed to have his interests so much at heart, would agree to wait. A few days later, the client would receive a message telling him to be at a certain place at a certain time, with five or ten guineas to exchange for the stolen goods which would be delivered by a messenger. Thus Wild never actually seemed to come into contact with the goods he recovered for people; in his defence, he claimed he only acted as a go-between. The profits he made were 'clean', because they were invisible and untraceable. The money would go straight back to Wild, who had usually already paid for the goods the day they arrived at his office through the back door. When he insisted that he couldn't accept an additional fee for finding something – 'No, no, it is an honour to serve you in this manner; my satisfaction lies in serving the public; I could not possibly accept anything more' – it was a ruse to make his clients think his actions were altruistic. In reality, he was becoming rich at the public's expense. By 1717 Wild was making £200–£300 a year, and had moved across the road to another, larger office at number 68 Little Old Bailey.

Hitchin had warned Wild at the start of their association that he paid the thieves too much for the booty they brought him; certainly, they made more in using Wild as a fence than by using a pawnbroker, who would estimate the worth of their loot without adding in the sentimental value the owner would attach to it. Wild, unlike the pawnbrokers, aimed to return the goods to their rightful owners, and therefore could pay a thief proportionately more because he knew that he would get more for a watch or snuffbox if he returned it to someone who was desperate to get it back. Similarly, Wild found there was a profit to be made in stolen account books, which were worth nothing to anyone except the shopkeeper. However, because he dealt with the thieves and their victims separately, he negotiated his own profit privately; no one could disprove him if he said he had sold a watch back to its owner for two guineas, even if he had taken twenty for it.

Wild frequently used advertising to find the owners of the items he was brought. The following, dating from 1724, was a typical example of the type of advertisement Wild perfected during his career. He placed them in any of the many newspapers published daily and weekly in London:

Lost, the 1st of October, a black shagreen pocketbook, edged with silver, with some notes of hand. The said book was lost in the Strand, near the Fountain Tavern, about 7 or 8 o'clock at night. If any person will bring the aforesaid book to Mr Jonathan Wild, in the Old Bailey, he shall have a guinea reward.

This advertisement could have served two purposes. Either Wild had been approached by the wallet's owner, and didn't have the book or know who had it; but this is unlikely given the knowledge he had of the happenings in London's underworld. More probably, he knew where to get hold of the book – or actually had it in his possession – but advertised to display publicly his detachment from the world of crime and his ignorance of the workings of London's thieves, thus supporting the highly moral stance he took with his clients. He could also have received the book from a thief, but not yet been approached by its rightful owner. If so, this advertisement is a masterpiece of veiled blackmail; the Fountain was a well-known brothel, and anyone who was there in the evening almost certainly had intentions of visiting it. The references to notes of hand show that Wild knew who owned the pocketbook, for notes of hand were always signed. Thus a gentleman not wanting his wife to find out where he had been on 1 October would have had to contact Wild, and pay whatever he asked, to avoid being compromised. Advertisements served the further purpose of bringing Wild's name into the public eye, and promoting his reputation, so that when people lost something Jonathan Wild was the name they associated with its recovery.[1]

Wild also encouraged the thieves who worked for him to learn specialized techniques. In eighteenth-century London there was almost no such thing as a common criminal: each tiny difference in style and technique merited an individual, descriptive name. There were over sixty different types of thieves alone described by contemporary cant phrases or names. A 'Hook Pole Lay' was a thief who used a long pole, with a hook attached to its tip, to pull unsuspecting riders off their horses to rob them; an 'Angler' was a thief who, using a fishing-rod and line from a high window or carriage, fished wallets out of the inside pockets of men walking beneath him, or wigs and hats off their heads. Wigs were a particularly popular target (illustration 9, page 69; Hogarth's *The Five Orders of Periwigs*). Wig-thieves were known as 'Wool-Pullers', and had many techniques. Gay describes some thieves cutting holes in the back of coaches, and putting their hands through to grab the wig of the man sitting unsuspectingly inside.

> Nor is thy flaxen wig with safety worn;
> High on the shoulder, in a basket borne,
> Lurks the sly boy; whose hand to rapine bred,
> Plucks off the curling honours of thy head.

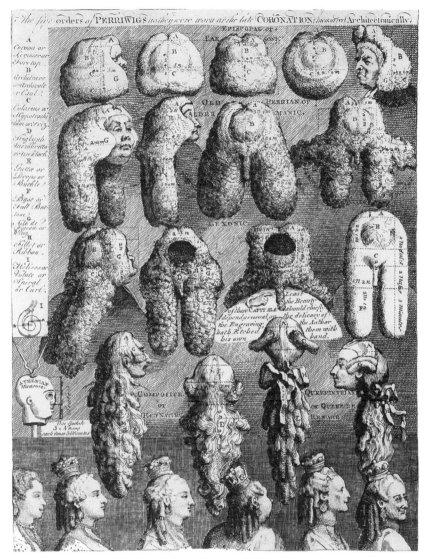

9. *The Five Orders of Periwigs* (William Hogarth)

A 'Milken' was a house-breaker, and a 'Ripping Cove' a house-breaker whose speciality was breaking into houses by tearing open the roof to gain entry. Burglars were sometimes so bold as to knock on a door in broad daylight and force their way inside. They might enlist the help of dissatisfied servants, resentful of their languid mistresses and boorish masters; or one member of a gang might become the lover of a maid, who, after slipping through the door left open for him, could leave it open for his accomplices. The lad who kept a lookout for the watch or an inadvertent witness was called a 'Pushing Tout'. One of Jonathan's men, dressed in servants' livery, entered a house of tenement flats in King Street, near Longacre, and slipped into an apartment, whose owner he had observed leaving a minute before. Seeing nothing else of value to steal, he rolled the bedlinen up into a bundle and went off with it. On the stairs, he bumped into the flat's owner, returning home. She asked him what he was doing there, and he replied that he worked for an upholsterer and was delivering some goods, but that he thought he was in the wrong building. She directed him next door, he went off on his way, and, unsuspecting, she climbed the stairs to discover her loss.

Shoplifters and pickpockets roamed the streets, eyes peeled for the chance opening. 'No cleverer pickpockets exist than in this country,' wrote Cesar de Saussure, slightly ruefully, after his snuffbox had been stolen from him. He had 'placed it into the pocket of my carefully buttoned waistcoat; my coat was buttoned likewise, and I was holding both my hands over the pockets of my coat'. London's street thieves were highly skilled, as Gay attests:

> Here dives the skulking thief, with practised sleight
> And unfelt fingers makes the pocket light.

A 'Stroller' would enter a shop or tavern claiming to be the servant of a rich gentleman, and explaining that his master followed close behind him, would trick the owner out of money or goods. An 'Adam Tiler' was used by a pickpocket to distract his victim while he robbed him. A 'Tail Drawer' slipped the swords away from the sides of unsuspecting gentlemen. New shops were easy prey:

It was always reckoned a safe job when we heard of a new shop, especially when the people were such as were not bred to shops; such may depend on it, that they will be visited [robbed] once or twice at their beginning, and they must be very sharp indeed if they can prevent it.[2]

'Starring the Glaze' was a method of shoplifting by which a glazier's diamond was used to cut a hole in the window of a shop, so that a hand could be thrust in to take whatever lay on display inside. Little boys hidden by the crowd cut the silver buckles off gentlemen's shoes, or snipped silver and gold buttons off jackets. A couple, working together, would jostle passers-by and in the ensuing confusion lift pocketbooks out of breast pockets. The lowest form of thief was a 'Pudding Shammer', just a step above a beggar in the street hierarchy, who stole food to stay alive.

Disguise and acting were key elements in street robbery. Both pickpockets of a sort, the 'Abraham Men' pretended madness, and the 'Confek Cranks' epilepsy, to distract and disarm their prey.

> The lurking thief, who while the day-light shone,
> Made the walls echo with his begging tone:
> That crutch which late compassion moved, shall wound
> Thy bleeding head, and fell thee to the ground.

All eighteenth-century criminals were actors of a sort, because the skills that they needed were so similar to those required on the stage; Jonathan Wild, whose childhood was spent tagging along with the strolling players that passed through Wolverhampton, must have understood this. He employed a dancing master to teach his 'Spruce Prigs' (special thieves) dancing so that they would blend in with the crowds at society balls, the opera or theatres, where rich pickings were to be had. He used ex-footmen for these jobs, whose training in grand households enabled them to mingle with aristocratic guests without being detected. One of these Spruce Prigs removed a gold and diamond watch from a woman on George I's arm at a court ball; another stole a diamond buckle from a guest staying at Windsor Castle. A specialized type of Spruce Prig was the 'Beau Trap', whose expertise lay in fleecing young country gentlemen, newly arrived in the capital, and ignorant of London ways.

One of Wild's Spruce Prigs hired an expensive house in the newly constructed Queen Square on a twenty-one-year lease. Each time the landlord visited the house, he was dismayed to find that his tenant had not yet moved in, but seemed to be ordering the fittings the landlord had just had installed at great expense to be ripped out. The tenant, who was well spoken and immaculately turned-out, assured him that he was only readying the house for the arrival of his wife and family. He spoke vaguely about the fine paintings and furniture that he was having brought up from his country estate; and the landlord, his suspicions allayed by his greed, was reassured. Several weeks later, he returned to the house to find that it had been completely stripped of its panelling, wainscoting, looking-glasses, chimney-pieces – even a staircase. And of the respectable, rich-looking tenant, there was no sign. The landlord had been duped by a master of the art known among the criminal classes as the 'Lodging Lay'.

Other valuable criminal skills included the ability to look inconspicuous, to blend into the crowd. Mental agility was as important as manual or physical dexterity, with a combination of steadiness and shrewdness vital for spotting and grasping opportunities, and for getting out of tricky situations. What was known as 'larceny sense' to twentieth-century American gangsters, the instinctive knowledge about when it was safe to commit a crime, was every bit as important in eighteenth-century London. Thieves took great pride in their specialized skills and individual expertise: 'the craftsman's satisfaction in being master of his mystery'.[3]

Mary Young, alias Jenny Diver, executed in 1740, was one of the most celebrated pickpockets of her day, known for her subtlety, timing and flair. Her most successful disguise was a costume that made her look heavily pregnant. She had artificial arms folded across her belly, allowing her to slip her real arms unnoticed out of the sides of her dress to cut watch-chains and purse-strings. She would go to church dressed as a fine lady, attended by a footman, to rob wealthy worshippers at Mass. 'Diver' was a cant word for a prostitute, and in *The Beggars' Opera* Jenny Diver is one of Macheath's loose women. Gay also warns against female pickpockets in *Trivia*:

But do not, like that bold chief, confide
Thy vent'rous footsteps to a female guide;
She'll lead thee, with delusive smiles along,
Dive in thy fob, and drop thee in the throng.

Defoe's Moll Flanders describes how she avoided arrest after an unsuccessful attempt to rob a lady in the crowd:

I had full hold of her watch, but giving a great jostle, as if someone had thrust me against her, and in the juncture giving her watch a fair pull, I found it would not come, so I let it go at that moment, and cried out as if I had been killed, that somebody had trod upon my foot, and that there were certainly pickpockets there; for somebody or other had given a pull at my watch; for you are to observe, that on these adventures we always went very well dressed, and I had very good clothes on, and a gold watch by my side, as like a lady as other folks.

I had no sooner said so, but the other gentlewoman cried out a pickpocket too, for somebody, she said, had tried to pull her watch away.

When I touched her watch, I was close to her, but when I cried out, I stopped as it were short, and the crowd bearing her forward a little, she made a noise too, but it was at some distance from me, so that she did not in the least suspect me; but when she cried out a pickpocket, somebody cried Ay, and here has been another, this gentlewoman has been attempted too.

At that very instant, a little farther in the crowd, and very luckily too, they cried out a pickpocket again, and really seized a young fellow in the very fact. This, though unhappy for the wretch was very opportunely for my case, though I had carried it off handsomely enough before, but now it was out of all doubt, and the loose part of the crowd run that way, and the poor boy was delivered up to the rage of the street [mob justice], which is a cruelty I need not describe, and which however they are always glad of, rather than be sent to Newgate, where they lie often a long time, till they are almost perished, and sometimes they are hanged, and the best they can look for, if they are convicted, is to be transported.

Although a man reported in 1735 that he had been held up by a 'well-mounted' woman riding side-saddle, most female criminals worked as pickpockets and prostitutes – Buttock-and-Files, like Mary Milliner. The other crime that women commonly committed was infanticide. 'Not a session passes but we see one or more merciless mothers tried for the murder of their bastard children,' wrote a shocked Defoe. Unmarried mothers, terrified of the life of prostitution and destitution that they saw as inevitable after the shame of bearing an illegitimate child, covered up their pregnancies, and when their child was born either left it exposed to the elements to die, or abandoned it by a hospital or workhouse where they hoped it might be given the chance to live – a practice known as 'dropping'. In the first six months of 1743, a dozen babies were dropped in the parish of St George's, Hanover, a prosperous neighbourhood where presumably a child would have more chance of survival than in St Giles or Smithfield.

Three in four of London's children died before they reached the age of six; the Committee on the Care of the Poor in St Martin-in-the-Fields reported that 900 of the 1,200 babies born in the parish in 1715 had died. Even in workhouses the chances of reaching adulthood were slim. A contemporary estimate of the infant death rate in workhouses set up after 1720 was 88 per cent. Swift offered a solution to this problem in his satirical essay 'A Modest Proposal'. He suggested that unwanted children should be used for food, thus eliminating in one stroke both infanticide and hunger. 'A young healthy child well-nursed is at a year old a most delicious, nourishing, and wholesome food.'

Thieves on foot were known as 'footpads', and they usually worked in groups of two or three, though a gang might number up to twenty. They roamed the streets at night, like the Mohocks, taking advantage of the poor lighting and inefficient watches. 'Street robberies are generally committed in the dark,' observed Henry Fielding. 'The persons on whom they are committed are often in chairs and coaches, and if on foot, the attack is usually begun by knocking the party down, and for the time being depriving him of his senses.' Footpads were forced to use more savage methods than highwaymen to disable their victims to allow them enough time to escape on foot. In 1738 a man was attacked in Ludgate Hill by a gang of three footpads, who cut him with a sword, 'so that his teeth and jawbone could be seen', knocked him down, 'to stop him crying out', and ran off with only a shilling.[4]

Stolen goods were usually resold through safe pawnshops for a fraction of their value. Most thieves used their wives or girlfriends as receivers and distributors of stolen goods, or fences like Hitchin and Wild. Some gangs had warehouses and workshops that altered goods so that they could be resold without attracting suspicion, or hid them until they could be sold safely.

Whoever considers the cities of London and Westminster, with the late vast addition of suburbs, the great irregularity of their buildings, the immense number of lanes, alleys, courts and by-places; must think that, had they been invented for the very purpose of concealment, they could scarce have been better contrived. Upon such a view, the whole appears as a vast wood or forest, in which a thief may harbour with as great security, as wild beasts do in the deserts of Africa or Arabia.[5]

London was the perfect setting for crime, with a network of safe taverns, inns, stables and receivers. The Hawkins gang of highwaymen regularly used a livery stable just outside the city, paying the owner a share of their profits, his 'snack', in return for the use of his horses. The stable provided them with a hideaway, as well as a constant supply of fresh horses. The Dog and Duck in St George's Fields, south of the river, was a popular resting place for highwaymen; young boys used to go there to watch them mount up and say goodbye to their 'flashy women' before setting off to earn their living on the highways. Horse thieves could dispose of their spoils easily in London, because individual horses were unlikely to be recognized as easily as they would be in the country. Some gangs of horse thieves – individually known as 'Priggers of Prancers' – simply sold in the north what they had stolen in the south, and vice versa.

Many criminals operated within a loosely organized gang. Edward Burnworth, giving evidence in court of his criminal activities during the 1720s, provided details of forty-one burglaries he had committed with accomplices. He used ten men at different times, but he never worked in a group of more than three for any single robbery. He had also carried out nine street robberies, working in a pair with one of seven different men. Large groups of over five were unwieldy, so a gang of fifteen or twenty would split up into smaller groups to ply their trade. His gang, active in the mid-1720s, was formed after Wild broke up Carrick's Gang, in which Burnworth had cut his teeth as a footpad.

These gangs, by their nature, had a very fluid membership. Members would drift in and out of gaol, go back to their families in other parts of the country, be hanged or transported, sometimes return from the colonies; new members would join. The highwayman Dick Turpin's career was typical of this type of mobility and adaptability. He was able to use the skills he had learned as an apprentice butcher in his first criminal enterprise, stealing cattle. He began holding up stagecoaches soon after, and for a short while managed an inn, the Bull-Beggars'-Hole in Clayhill, Essex, where he used to rob his customers as they slept. He also worked on and off with Gregory's Gang, a notorious band of about twenty outlaw housebreakers who used a clearing in Epping Forest as their base. As a highwayman, he worked with Tom King, whom he met by accident as he tried to rob him. 'What, dog eat dog? Come, come, brother Turpin; if you don't know me, I know you, and shall be glad of your company.'[6] He dealt in stolen horses, and carried on stealing cattle and sheep until his arrest and execution.

The transience of gangs meant that despite the oaths of friendship and allegiance sworn by their members, incentives of pardon or reward often tempted them to inform on their companions. John James and Nathaniel Hawes were highwaymen who had performed eighteen successful hold-ups in their first two weeks together, but soon ruined their working relationship by arguing. They fell out initially because Hawes insisted on returning a ring to a man they held up despite James swearing he'd shoot Hawes through the head if he didn't retrieve it. Soon after, they quarrelled again when James refused to give a whip back to its lady owner at Hawes's request. Their mutual distrust was exacerbated by arguments over division of the spoils. Finally, convinced that James would inform against him, Hawes went to Jonathan Wild and impeached James; his evidence earned him a gaol sentence but hanged his ex-partner. Hawes managed to escape from gaol, but was captured by a gentleman he held up on Finchley Common, who seized the pistol with which Hawes was trying to hold him up, and took the crestfallen highwayman back to Newgate on a passing cart.

This pattern of distrust, fuelled by motives of self-preservation, was common. 'It was not my common method to rob with comrades,' recalled John Wigley, another victim of Wild's system of informers, at his trial in 1721:

For though they swore to be true to each other, and there was sometimes found some faith among them when their interest was not too nearly concerned, yet when their lives were in danger they grew regardless of their oaths and would betray and impeach their most intimate friends.[7]

Some gangs were better organized than others. Smuggling, for instance, required a sophisticated system, under strong, efficient leadership, as did horse-thievery and forgery. Fraudsters and forgers abounded, many of them men like Jonathan Wild, with a training in metal-working. By George III's reign, it was thought that there were more forged shillings in circulation than real ones. Gold coins were clipped, and the clippings sold as bullion. Coins were also 'sweated', put into bags and shaken until particles of gold from them lined the bag. This residue was collected and sold. Gold and silver were melted down, and mixed with base metals before being recast. The debased coins were then recirculated. Guineas were heated, to make the gold soft, and then restamped with a die of a higher value, for example a moidore, which was worth 27s. Banks issued their own notes, a virtual invitation to swindlers and confidence tricksters. Forgeries were made of stamps, of bonds, of deeds of exchange, even of the seal of the Bank of England.

It was vital for these activities to have a distribution system that covered a large area of the country, as well as an efficient network of spies and informers. An estimated 3,000,000 lb. of tea was imported annually by smugglers in the eighteenth century, which would have required a system of almost military precision. Efficiency was one of Jonathan Wild's strongest skills, and it was that, combined with his ability and willingness to manipulate people, which enabled him to gain control over the wide-ranging network of thieves operating in London in the 1710s.

Wild encouraged those who worked for him to do so in specific areas at specific times, thereby creating a system of gangs of highly specialized thieves each with their own patch of London to work. He told them that following his orders would benefit them because it made them more efficient and thus made his job, finding the real owners and returning the goods, simpler. In fact, all it did was make it easier for him to control them. He could check up on their stories to see if they had lied to him about what they had taken, or disposed of their loot through anyone other than him. He asked his clients detailed questions about where and when they were robbed, and of what, and if their answers were corroborated by the thieves' stories, he knew they were serving him well. It also enabled him to find out if there were thieves on London's streets working independently of him.

On one occasion, Wild was approached by a gentlewoman who let lodgings in Hackney. She had been robbed by a female lodger, attended by a footman and a maid, who had stripped her rooms of everything she could carry. Wild looked through his books and saw that Wapping ['Fucking'] Moll, Tawney Bess and Harry Smart – all experts in the Lodging Lay – had last been heard of in Hackney. According to their usual practice, Moll had used the alias Lady Smith, Bess had played her lady's maid, and Harry Smart had completed the illusion of respectable gentility dressed as Moll's footman. To their surprise, Wild tracked them down and forced them to fence their loot through him. Incidents like this demonstrated to his thieves that Wild knew as much about their actions as they did, and they learned not to disobey or deceive him. 'It was no less than death to *sink* upon him, as he termed it, for there was scarce anything stolen which was worth having again but he heard of it, and knew who the person must be that took it, as well as those who lost it.'[8]

In September 1714 Wild had one of his first major successes working alone. A gang of house-breakers broke into the Banqueting Hall at Whitehall and made off with some of the communion plate from the nearby chapel. Using methods similar to modern interrogation techniques, Wild persuaded one member of the gang to 'impeach' two others, and another one to betray the rest of them. Within three months he had had seven people arrested and collected over £700 in reward money. Wild's hands were clean, because he had never touched the goods. This was an approach that he was to use frequently with great success throughout his career, persuading a gang member to inform on his fellows in return for a reduced sentence. As an added bonus, after the trial and sentence had passed, he had another criminal to add to his 'Corporation of Thieves', one who owed his life to Wild – and on whom he had enough information to have him hanged, which ensured his continued loyalty.

Wild did not hesitate to bring to justice those who displeased him. He would send to the gallows people who he knew had passed on their goods through another fence, or who would not accept the price he offered them for a stolen item, or who challenged his authority by inciting dissatisfaction among the other thieves. He was able to do this because he always made sure that he gathered enough evidence against those who worked for him that he could have them hanged at any time. The expression 'double-cross' is derived from Jonathan's ruthless business techniques. He kept immaculate ledger books, detailing criminals working for him and the crimes they had committed. He would mark an 'X' by each name in his ledger once he had the evidence to convict them – for instance, when the information on a certain robbery given to him by both the victim and the thief tallied. When he had given them up to the law, he would mark another 'X' by their name: they had been double-crossed, or betrayed.[9]

Turning thieves in served a dual purpose for Wild. Not only did it set an example to the criminals who worked for him by showing them how much control he had over them, how much he knew and could use against them – it was said of Wild that he slept with his eyes open – but it also made him into a popular hero. He became known as a benefactor, a friend and protector of society. Although thief-taking and receiving had always been seen as allied professions, Wild was the first thief-taker to risk his own skin to capture wanted criminals, as well as finding and returning people's stolen property to them.

The case that made him famous was that of Mrs Knap, the 'murdered gentlewoman', who was killed in the spring of 1716. She was walking home from a concert in Sadler's Wells, a popular destination for city-dwellers taking day-trips to the country (illustration 10, page 81; Hogarth's *Evening*), with her son when they were accosted by thieves in the 'Jockey Fields' near Gray's Inn, and in the ensuing mêlée she was killed. Her son described the accident in court:

In an instant, some fellows coming up, my link [lamp] was blown out, my hat and wig were taken off, and I was knocked down, upon which my mother screamed out, and thereupon one of them fired a pistol close by me, and immediately I heard my mother cry 'Lord help me! Help me!' and then the rogues fled . . . Having lighted my link, I went back and found my mother on the ground.[10]

This story outraged Londoners, who were accustomed to being robbed every day of the week but for whom the senseless murder of an elderly lady was a different and shocking matter. 'I never pardon murder,' Wild declared pompously, and used his network of thieves to track down the men who had committed the crime. They were found within a few days and Wild persuaded one of the gang, Isaac Ragg, against whom he had hanging evidence for a different offence, to impeach the others. Ragg testified that his companion, Will White, had done the deed, 'to frighten the woman, and make her hold her tongue'. They had all been carrying loaded pistols, and after Mrs Knap was shot, they had retired to a tavern where they had checked their guns to see who had fired theirs, and there White had confessed. All of Ragg's accomplices were tried and convicted except one, Timothy Dun, who was in hiding, holed up in a cellar in Southwark.

10. *Evening* (William Hogarth)

The couple at the centre of this piece are an indictment of London's new middle classes. The wife, a corpulent, self-satisfied woman, overshadows her long-suffering husband, whom William Hogarth, by an optical illusion, has crowned with the horns of the cuckold. Their dog walks wearily ahead of the couple.

Wild had bet that he would have Dun before the next sessions, and though he could not find his hiding place he was determined to get him. One day he saw Mrs Dun in the street outside his office – Dun had sent her to find out if Wild was still on his trail – and had her followed back to her husband's hide-out. Collecting a warrant for Dun's arrest, Wild crossed the river with his posse and surrounded the criminal's house in the dim light of dawn. Dun heard the men coming and tried to sneak out of a back window on to the pantry roof, but one of Wild's men, Abraham Mendez, spotted him and shot him in the shoulder. Dun rolled off the ledge into the waiting arms of his captors.

Wild received a huge cash reward for his part in the adventure, as well as dramatically improving his reputation – both among respectable citizens who saw him as a hero, and among criminals, who saw the wisdom in working for rather than against him.

Another incident from this period illustrates Wild's hands-on approach to thief-taking. In 1720 he captured James Wright, a highwayman who had stolen a sapphire ring from the Earl of Burlington and a gold watch from Lord Bruce when he held them up in Richmond, by holding him 'fast by the chin with his teeth, till he dropped his firearms, surrendered, and was brought to Newgate'.[11] Wright was a member of the Hawkins gang, which worked independently of Wild.

Another gang member, Ralph Wilson, was one of several eighteenth-century criminals who agreed, for a large fee, to dictate 'their 'memoirs' to a publishing house such as Applebee's, for which Defoe worked. These ghost-written lives were accessibly written and cheaply produced, ensuring their widespread popularity with London's increasingly literate lower classes. Wilson claimed, 'We never dealt with Wild, and neither did he know any of us.' This was a little naive, since Wild would have made it his business to seek out any criminals working in London outside his sphere of influence – and it explains Wild's savagery in dealing with Wright. Lord Bruce had offered Wild £100 for the return of the ring alone, and Wild, who had no contact within the gang, was humiliated at not being able to get it back for him, and furious about losing such a large reward. Wright's fate was unusual: he was tried and acquitted for lack of evidence; then he reopened his barber-shop on Ludgate Hill and apparently lived happily ever after.

Wild was canny as well as brave. Two 'ancient' women came to his office with a proposal a year or two after he had set himself up in the Old Bailey. They lodged at the house of a wealthy cane-chair maker in Wormwood Street, and they wanted to assist Wild's men in robbing their landlord in return for a share of the profits.

Wild, howsoever he might approve of the proposal, thought it not advisable to be an adventurer in such an enterprise, the application being so odd, and the women strangers, without recommendations or proper credentials from any of the 'Business', he very discreetly made a merit of the matter, by seizing them; they were committed to Newgate, and at the ensuing sessions, convicted of the misdemeanour, and for it fined and imprisoned.[12]

But Wild could be merciful to those who had served him well, even if they did turn against him at the end. Jack Butler had stolen a pair of diamond earrings, a gold watch and a packet of lace and instead of bringing them straight to Wild had hidden them in his lodgings. Wild, who found out that Butler was holding out on him, raised a hue and cry and led a posse to the dyer's shop where the thief lived. They searched the house up and down, and finally found Butler hiding under a large upturned tub. 'So Mr Son-of-a-Bitch!' cried Wild. 'Have I caught you at last!' He swore that he would hang Butler for this betrayal if there were never another rogue in England. But the criminal, terrified, admitted everything. 'If you'll step into my room again, and look behind the bed's head, you may find something that will make you amends for your trouble.' Wild found what he wanted, and was 'well satisfied', but because he had come with a posse he could not prevent Butler's arrest (even if he had wanted to; since Butler had intended to swindle him, Wild would have been unlikely to let him back into his trust). He was, however, able to have his sentence transmuted from hanging to transportation.[13]

At about this time Wild was accused of selling stolen goods that he had in his possession, not just acting as a broker between the thief and his victim. Cornelius Tilburn, a quack doctor, had consulted Wild about recovering some stolen property, but was outraged at the amount he suggested would be necessary to tempt the robbers to part with it. Tilburn accused Wild of having the stuff in his possession, a heated row ensued, and Tilburn stormed out of the Lost Property Office and reported Wild to the police. Wild held firm; he insisted that he was only an agent, and went to court to defend himself; he won the case, and his position was vindicated. After this incident, he appeared invincible. His business had been proved to be beyond the reach of the legal system, and the thieves who worked for him were astounded at the ease with which he had vanquished his enemy, challenged the law, and defeated it on its own ground.

In 1718, when Wild had established himself as the best and most powerful thief-taker in London, an anonymous pamphlet was published, supposedly by a prisoner in Newgate, condemning him and his work. 'The thief-taker is a thief-maker,' it declared. Wild's response was to reveal the true author of the article, his one-time associate Under-Marshal Charles Hitchin, whose business was suffering as a result of Wild's success. Calling it a 'nonsensical treatise', he turned the tables on Hitchin in his own pamphlet, accusing him of sins as great as his own – if not worse. '[My reply] will fully show, by former practice, that the greatest progress this pretended reformer is likely to make in the work of reformation is by plundering the purses, abusing the persons, and the highest impositions, as well upon the guilty as the innocent.'[14]

It was in this pamphlet that Wild first used the title 'Thief-taker General of Great Britain and Ireland', as a mark of his victory over Hitchin. He claimed in his defence that 'no person has been more forward [than Wild] in apprehending and bringing to justice the boldest criminals even to the hazard of life'. Hitchin had accused Wild of having the power to hang whom he liked; Wild countered, 'To say that justice is governed by a thief-taker is such a slur to the reputation of a magistrate, and such an affront to authority, that nothing can equal it.' When Hitchin decried the spread of crime, Wild reminded him of his position as an officer of the City of London, and accused him of not performing his duty: 'The asking by what means these irregularities [i.e., the incidence of crime] are suffered is a plain implied arraignment of justice.' Although Wild dictated the pamphlet to a lawyer, his mastery of tortured logic, his ambition, and his determination to wear a mask of respectability throughout his career are evident.

He went on to expose Hitchin as a homosexual, concluding his reply to Hitchin's attempt to dethrone him thus:

I'll assure you I'll serve your Excellency with the same infidelity and per-fidiousness as you have hitherto done the Magistracy of the City of London in your office of Marshal. Particularly I'll take care that no woman of the town shall walk the streets or bawdy house be kept without your Excellency's licence and trial of the ware; that no sodomitish assembly be held without your Excellency's presence and making choice for your own use, in order to which I'll engage to provide a female dress for your Excellency much further than what your Excellency has been accustomed to wear . . .

This accusation, repeated throughout Wild's testimony and backed up by a good deal of anecdotal detail, destroyed Hitchin's reputation, although he retained his position as Under-Marshal. Nine years later Hitchin was accused of 'sodomitical practices' by a man who seems to have acquiesced fairly willingly to his advances at the time of the alleged incident. He was tried, convicted and fined £20, sentenced to stand in the pillory at the end of St Catherine Street in the Strand, and given six months' imprisonment. Although he had taken the precaution of wearing a suit of armour to the stocks, he was so badly beaten that he had to be removed from the pillory before his allotted hour was up because he was close to death; he died less than six months after this ordeal, from injuries sustained at the stocks.

Contemporary attitudes towards homosexuality were unequivocally intolerant. In 1707 several men were tried and convicted for 'the loathsomeness of their wicked crimes of unnatural lewdness with their own sex, contrary to the order of human nature, and that not having the fear of God before their eyes, did commit very filthy and unseemly actions, not fit to be named in a civilized nation'.

One can almost hear the judge spluttering in horror as he read out the sentence.

Ironically, these views often displayed almost as much misogyny as homophobia. A popular satire on London street society by the journalist Ned Ward in 1709 described a 'Mollies' Club': 'Thus everyone in turn makes scoff of the little effeminacy and weaknesses, which women are subject to, when gossiping o'er their cups on purpose to extinguish that Natural Affection which is due to the Fair Sex & to turn their juvenile desires towards preternatural pollotions.' The attitude of the time was evidenced by slang terminology: 'Mollies' could be either homosexuals or transvestites, and they so assiduously frequented the path dividing the two gardens that made up Moorfields that it was known as 'Sodomites' Walk'.

Moorfields, just outside the city walls on the north-east, was one of the most notorious areas of early eighteenth-century London. It was considered disreputable for more than just its high population of 'sodomites' and prostitutes, both male and female. The bodies of suicides, which could not be afforded a Christian burial, were burned in the ditches there. Some parts were used as refuse tips. Thieves were stripped to the waist and flogged on the edge of the fields as public punishment for their crimes. And New Bethlehem, or Bedlam, which had housed London's lunatics since 1676, stood in Moorfields.

In this period there was no compassion in dealing with the insane. Bedlam's inmates were left to rot in their own filth and depravity, tormented by their nightmares, with no attempts made to calm their delusory visions or provide standards of cleanliness, comfort and nutrition that would ease their terrible distress. To add insult to injury, a popular pursuit of the fashionable classes was visiting Bedlam to laugh at the antics of the mad men and women housed there, just as the two simpering ladies in the background of the madhouse scene of Hogarth's *A Rake's Progress* are doing (illustration 11, page 87). The keepers used to feed the inmates in front of visitors to shock and frighten them, and to give them their money's worth. The highwayman Ralph Wilson, aware that he would shortly be

11. *A Rake's Progress VIII: Bedlam* (William Hogarth)

The Rake, finally destroyed by his life of dissolution, lies manacled in Bedlam, surrounded by madmen. A religious fanatic inhabits the cell at left, while behind him a crazed astronomer makes calculations on the wall. The two ladies who have come to Bedlam to amuse themselves by watching the lunatics are both fascinated and repelled: one whispers to the other, pointing out a man urinating in the cell beside them, as her friend shields her gaze behind her fan.

arrested by Wild for his association with the Hawkins gang, 'went into Bedlam, where the many melancholy objects I saw there inspired me with a thorough sense of my own worse condition'.

The admission of visitors to Bedlam increased its revenues by over £400 a year; it was not until 1770 that the doctors realized that being stared at like animals in a zoo 'tended to disturb the tranquillity of the patients',[15] and closed the hospital to sightseers. In 1784 the poet William Cowper recalled visiting Bedlam as a boy:

In those days when Bedlam was open to the cruel curiosity of holiday ramblers I have been a visitor there. Though a boy, I was not altogether insensible of the misery of the poor captives nor destitute of feeling for them. But the madness of some of them had such a humorous air, and displayed itself in so many whimsical freaks, that it was impossible not to be entertained, at the same time that I was angry with myself for being so.

Dissolution

Owen Wood's home, where Jack Sheppard lived and worked during his apprenticeship, was in Wych Street, just off Drury Lane in Covent Garden – 'that receptacle of sharpers, pickpockets, and strumpets'.[1] All the sins of London were concentrated in Covent Garden. Here painted whores plied their trade, desperate gamblers tried to save their families' fortunes, gentlemen of the road lost the profits they had made earlier in the night on the highway, and drunks stumbled randomly from one dank, smoky coffee-house to another. The main fruit, flower and vegetable market of central London was situated in the piazza, but according to the journalist Ned Ward, even the flower-girls 'stank so of brandy, strong drink and tobacco, that the former overcame the fragrance that arose from their sweet herbs and flowers'.

Covent Garden had become fashionable in the seventeenth century when Francis Russell, Duke of Bedford, commissioned Inigo Jones to design and build a church and piazza on land his family had owned since the Reformation (hence the name: 'Covent' was derived from 'convent'), creating a residential area described by Bedford as 'fit for the habitations of gentlemen and men of ability'. But by the eighteenth century, Covent Garden was known principally for its gaming- and whore-houses, rowdy taverns and coffee-houses filled with loose women; whether the beau monde had moved west out of distaste for their new neighbours, or whether the empty houses had been filled with disreputable characters simply because their previous tenants had left, is unclear (illustration 12, page 90; Hogarth's *Morning*).

12. *Morning* (William Hogarth)

A genteel lady walks to Mass early on a winter's morning across Covent Garden, passing Tom King's Coffee House on her way to Inigo Jones's St Paul's Church. Her icy disapproval of the amorous couples outside the coffee-house reflects the chill of the morning air. At her waist is a pair of scissors or a nutcracker shaped like a human skeleton.

Gaming-houses, like brothels, abounded in the piazza, with names like Pharaoh's Table, called after the card game faro. Gambling was an eighteenth-century passion. In one night, Sir John

Bland lost £32,000 at the hazard table. Colonel Charteris financed the brothels he owned with his gambling winnings, which he preferred to take in land than cash. Charteris was utterly unscrupulous, determined to win at any cost: he once nearly cheated the Duchess of Queensberry of £3,000 by placing her in front of a mirror in which he could see her cards. The gaming-room of White's Chocolate House, which became White's Club, was used by Hogarth in Scene VI of *A Rake's Progress* (illustration 13, page 92). The club was destroyed by fire in 1733, and Hogarth shows the hold the cards had over the gamblers, so intent are they that they are unaware of the fire licking the walls. He depicts as well the relative egalitarianism of gambling: a highwayman sits, desolate, by the fire, and a usurer in Shylock's mould skulks around 'Old Manners', the brother of the Duke of Rutland, who was one of the most successful gamesters of his generation.

People of all classes gambled over dice, cards, sport — anything with an undecided outcome. A man fell down outside White's one day and inside, bets were taken on whether he was alive or dead; when a passer-by suggested he be bled, loud shouts erupted from inside. The outcome of the wager might be affected by this concern! Huge sums were placed on ridiculous competitions: a race to Tyburn of six chimney-sweeps mounted on asses, or women in hooped petticoats (a new fashion) racing one another. A thousand pounds was wagered on a competition between a Mr Gage and the Earl of Lichfield, that Gage's chaise and pair would beat Lichfield's chariot and four; Lichfield won. Lotteries, linked to loan or debt conversion, had been run by the government since 1694. Occasionally they were used by individuals or local authorities to raise funds for specific projects, for instance for Westminster Bridge, built in 1750.

The high life of Covent Garden — drinking, whoring, gambling and carousing — was an ideal which attracted many young men like Hogarth's Rake, but ultimately its rewards were hollow. Tom Rakewell 'is able to find mistresses and men of business and dancing masters easily enough, but he finds no friends'.[2] He ends up alone, spent and barren, because he has sought happiness in a transitory

13. *A Rake's Progress VI: In a Gaming House* (William Hogarth)
This scene, set in White's Chocolate House on St James's, shows the total absorption of the gamblers in their game. A usurer is lending money on the left of the scene, while on the right a highwayman sits by the fire, perhaps planning to rob the winners later on that night to recoup his losses.

world, where pleasure is the ultimate illusion and any hopes of true contentment are doomed to failure. The scene at White's, where Tom plays on, oblivious to the fire blazing on the other side of the room, draws a parallel between Tom and Nero, fiddling while Rome burns, and society collapses and dissolves, eaten away from within by the vice inherent in its nature.[3] The morbid melancholia of the English was a noted national characteristic: suicide was known on the continent as hanging *à l'anglaise*.

Tom King's Coffee House was the most famous Covent Garden establishment of its time. A 'rude shed immediately beneath the portico of St Paul's church', it was 'well known to all gentlemen to whom beds are unknown'.[4] Tom King, the owner, had attended

Eton College as a boy. He and his wife, Moll, welcomed a variety of customers, treating everyone, be they lord, rake, flower-seller or pickpocket, as an equal. 'Noblemen and the first beaux after leaving Court would go to her house in full dress with swords and in rich brocaded silk coats, and walked and conversed with every person.'[5] After Tom died in 1737, Moll carried on alone but two years later was convicted of keeping a 'disorderly house' – a whore-house in eighteenth-century euphemistic language – and retired to the country.

Coffee-houses and particularly taverns were primarily frequented by men. Ladies might go to chocolate-houses during the day, but only women careless of their reputations would go to taverns. Many doubled as whore-houses or, at the least, venues for soliciting, marked by subtle signals that would have been blatantly obvious to the initiated. The 'Sign of the Star' outside a coffee-house was said to indicate 'every lewd purpose'. Cesar de Saussure discovered that many coffee-houses were also 'Temples of Venus. You can easily recognize the latter because they frequently have as sign a woman's arm or hand holding a coffee-pot.' The evidence in court of one Susan Brockway shows how taverns might be used:

This man took us to the tavern and offered us a crown apiece to strip ourselves naked, and show him postures. He gave Mary Gardner money to fetch a penny-worth of rods, for him to whip us across the room, and make us good girls; and then for us to whip him to make him a good boy: but we told him it was neither a proper time nor place for any such thing, for it was Sunday night, and others might over-look us in the room we were in.

Taverns were far more rough-and-ready than coffee-houses. Cesar de Saussure described them as full of 'common people' drinking heavily 'because of the thickness and dampness of the air'. He was shocked that the English never seemed to drink water. Englishmen of all classes drank heavily, and took a great deal of pride in their ability to do so. To be considered a good drinker, and earn the respect of one's peers, one had to be at least a 'three-bottle' (of wine) man; Sheridan and Pitt the Younger were both very highly rated for being reckoned six-bottle men. Viscount Bolingbroke,

14 and 15. *Gin Lane* and *Beer Street* (William Hogarth)

The destructive effects of gin, as opposed to the health-giving benefits of beer, are clearly illustrated in this pair of prints. The pawnbroker in Gin Lane is doing a roaring trade, encouraging his customers in their dissolution, while in Beer Street, it is only the pawnbroker's shop that is exempt from the general air of prosperity and activity. In each print, a female figure takes the central position: the drunken

slattern, ignoring her illegitimate child in the centre of Gin Lane is mirrored by the virtuous maid in Beer Street, who holds a key, the symbol of her virginity, as a protection against the advances of the man behind her. In the background of Beer Street, the fat old woman squeezed into a sedan chair is balanced by the sight in Gin Lane of a young girl's dead body being lowered into a coffin.

Walpole's Secretary of State and Sally Salisbury's lover, used to go to work in the morning straight from the dinner table, with a wet napkin wrapped around his head to sober him up. Sir Robert Walpole spent £1,500 a year on wine alone. William Hickey's attitude towards drinking seems to have been fairly typical: 'I was always ambitious of sitting out every man at the table when I presided.'[6]

In 1750, of the 12,000 quarters of wheat sold in London, 7,000 of them were converted into alcohol. Beer-drinking was seen as healthy and virtuous, while gin-drinking was seen as pernicious and damaging to society. The dichotomy between the effects of beer and of gin is shown by Hogarth in his prints *Gin Lane* and *Beer Street* (illustration 14, page 94, and illustration 15, page 95). The beer drinkers are hale and hearty, their fat contented faces indicating their material satisfaction. The gin drinkers, on the other hand, are pinched and drawn, desperation etched clearly in the lines of their faces.

The Rose Tavern, on the corner of Drury Lane and Russell Street, was the background for the debauched tavern scene in Hogarth's *A Rake's Progress* (illustration 16, page 97), and was noted for the criminals who frequented it. The porter, Leathercoat, who also featured in Fielding's play, *The Covent Garden Tragedy*, was a well-known eccentric: for the price of a drink, he would lie down in the street and let a carriage run over his chest – and stand up again unharmed. (He was dissected after his death, and the surgeons found his chest to have been of incredible muscular strength.) He stands at the rear of the print, carrying a pewter plate on which the girl undressing in the foreground is about to pose. The duel in which the Duke of Wharton and his opponent Lord Mohun were killed was arranged in the Rose. The area around the tavern was so noted for the unsavoury and dangerous characters that peopled it, that it was said that a man could not walk from the door of the Rose to the piazza, a distance of perhaps fifty yards, without twice venturing his life. It was in this area, among characters like these, that Jack Sheppard spent his formative adolescent years.

At twenty, Jack was a slight young man, only 5 ft. 4 in., with a deceptive strength and suppleness revealed only in his hands, which

16. *A Rake's Progress III: The Tavern Scene* (William Hogarth)

The Rake, so drunk he is unaware that he is being robbed by his female companions, sits in the midst of a scene of total debauchery. He has been in a scuffle of some sort outside the tavern, because his sword is unsheathed. The woman undressing on the right in preparation for 'posturing' wears beauty spots, like Mother Needham in Plate I of *A Harlot's Progress*. Almost everything in the room is broken or disintegrating, conveying a sense of chaos: the mirror on the wall behind Tom, the lantern at his feet, the table precariously tilted towards the viewer.

were large and capable but tapered like an artist's. His face was pale and his large eyes dark; his mouth was wide and his smile disarming in its quick charm and innocent expression of honesty. He stuttered a little, not awkwardly but endearingly. In repose, he could be detached and watchful; but his expression was animated, and his wit made him popular in the taverns around Drury Lane.

The Black Lion, off Drury Lane, was a tavern, like many in the area, pervaded by an 'atmosphere of uninhibited pleasure and haphazardly controlled violence'.[7] It was owned by Joseph Hynd, a button-mould maker (a trade coiners were often trained in), who introduced Jack to Elizabeth Lyon, 'this She-Lyon'. Edgworth Bess, as she was known, was a blowsy Buttock-and-File who 'lived a wicked and debauched life'.[8] Defoe ascribed the 'foundation of his [Jack's] ruin' to Bess, 'that vile strumpet', of whom 'our young carpenter' was quickly enamoured. Jack also met Jonathan Wild at the Black Lion, and Joseph 'Blueskin' Blake, his future accomplice and companion.

Soon, Jack 'had given himself up to the sensual pleasures of low life, drinking all day, and getting out to some impudent strumpet at night'.[9] Mr and Mrs Wood, with whom he had lived for over five years, became frustrated at his insubordination and disobedience. Like the young Jonathan Wild in Wolverhampton, Jack had become 'weary of the yoke of servitude'.[10] He was restless and dissatisfied; he had learned his trade, and was good at it, but had two more years' service before he was free to practise it. If Wood was not as talented a carpenter as Jack, he would have been unable to continue to keep him interested in his work. Thrill-seeking in the fleshpots of Drury Lane offered Jack the only challenge and excitement he could find. Mrs Wood set him a curfew, and if he was out any later she locked him out of the house; but the agile Sheppard had no trouble climbing up to his window and slipping unnoticed into his bed after long nights of excess.

Edgworth Bess soon became Jack's mistress, but she continued to ply her old trade. In the spring of 1723 she took a man home with her and stole a ring from him. He had her arrested, and she was sent to St Giles's Roundhouse, in Soho. As soon as he heard, Jack went straight there and forced the beadle, Mr Brown, to give him the keys so he could set her free. At about this time Sheppard began to steal. He stole two silver spoons while he was on a job for Mr Wood in the Rummer Tavern, Charing Cross, and was undetected. His confidence boosted, and encouraged by Bess and her friends, he became bolder and at the end of July 1723 stole a large bolt of fustian cloth from Mr Bains, a piece-broker in White Horse Yard; the next day, on the advice of Poll Maggot, another woman he knew from the Black Lion, he went back and stole a further £30 in cash which he gave to Poll.

Jack hid the fustian in his trunk at the Woods' house, but his master, tipped off by the other apprentice who worked for him, searched Jack's belongings and found the bolt. When Sheppard heard that Wood had found it, he broke into the house to steal the cloth back. Meanwhile, Wood informed Bains that he had found some fustian, and Bains, missing a piece of cloth of that description, agreed that Jack must have been the thief. Sheppard threatened Bains with a prosecution for scandal, alleging that he had been given the fustian by his mother, who had bought it for him in Spitalfields. Bains spoke to Jack's mother who, to protect her son, insisted that his story was true, although she could not remember exactly where she had bought the cloth. Bains, frustrated, dropped the matter.

On 2 August Jack left Owen Wood for good, with only seven months of his seven-year indenture left. He moved first to Fulham, where he and Edgworth Bess lived together as man and wife at Parsons Green. Then he moved to the top end of Piccadilly, lodging in the house of a Mr Charles and working as a journeyman to a carpenter called Panton who lodged there as well. During this period, he took silver cutlery, gold rings, suits, linen and cash from his landlord, but was never formally accused of any crime. Throughout the winter of 1723–4, Jack continued his association with Bess, drinking and gambling away the money he stole (illustration 17, page 100). He also joined forces with his brother Tom, who had recently been burned on the hand for stealing carpenter's tools from his master. The brothers robbed an alehouse in Southwark, and Jack let Tom keep the proceeds as well as lending him a further 40s. The goods were sold through William Field, one of Wild's minions.

In February 1724 Tom was tried for robbing Mary Cook's linen shop in Clare Market and, to save his neck, gave evidence against Jack and Bess, who had been his accomplices. Jonathan Wild took it upon himself to find this impudent young robber who had as yet refused to have anything to do with him directly. Jack, recounting

17. *Industry and Idleness III: The Idle 'Prentice at Play in the Church Yard* (William Hogarth)

Tom Idle sits outside a church, gambling with a group of ne'er-do-wells instead of praying. He is cheating, using his hat to hide the counters they are playing with. Although Tom lies on top of a coffin, with skulls on the ground beside him and a gravestone behind him, he does not notice these *memento mori*, so consumed is he by his lust for pleasure.

his life story to Defoe while in Newgate, declared that he had never had any dealings with a thief-catcher:

I was indeed twice at a thief-catcher's levee, and must confess the man treated me civilly; he complimented me on my successes, said he had heard that I had both a hand and a head admirably well-turned to business, and that I and my friends should always be welcome to him: but caring not for his acquaintance I never troubled him, nor had we any dealings together.[11]

Later, he was to condemn thief-takers roundly – and bitterly: 'they hang by proxy, while we do it in person'.[12]

In April Wild sent James Sykes, alias 'Hell-and-Fury', to capture Jack. Hell-and-Fury Sykes had been a running footman to the notorious Duke of Wharton until 1720 and was one of the fastest and most celebrated athletes of his day; he also used his experience in one of England's grandest ducal households to help train Wild's Spruce Prigs. Playing on Jack's love of games, Sykes challenged him to a game of skittles at a tavern near Seven Dials, and led him straight into the arms of a waiting magistrate.

Although skittles was relatively sedate, most eighteenth-century recreational activities were based on and glorified violence, uproar and cruelty (illustration 18, page 102; Hogarth's *The First Stage of Cruelty*). In 1663 Samuel Pepys described the atmosphere at a cock-pit he visited as being pervaded with a 'celestial spirit of anarchy and confusion'. Wrestling and boxing, known as the 'British Art', were popular at all levels of society. John Broughton, the famous pugilist, inventor of boxing gloves (or 'mufflers', as he called them) and founder of the Academy of Boxing, was blinded by a single blow between his eyes in a match in 1750 in which he had been backed to the tune of £10,000 by his patron, the Duke of Cumberland.

Women also participated in public fights. The *London Journal* of June 1722 carried the following advertisement:

I Elizabeth Wilkinson, of Clerkenwell, having had some words with Hannah Highfield and requiring satisfaction, do invite her to meet me on the stage and box with me for three guineas, each woman holding half-a-crown in each hand, and the first woman that drops her money to lose the battle.

This challenge is interesting because of the masculine, duelling overtones implicit in the wording. The women held coins in their hands to prevent them from scratching each other's eyes out, ensuring they hit cleanly. Sword-play competitions were also popular, a form of eighteenth-century gladiatorial competition, with surgeons waiting on the sidelines to stitch up the wounded warriors and send them back into the fray. Ladies as well as men were onlookers.

Even football games could be savagely violent, lasting all day, with sides of up to a hundred people using any means at all to get the ball past their opponents' goal-line. 'It is a leather ball about as big as one's head, filled with wind: this is kicked about from one to

18. *The First Stage of Cruelty* (William Hogarth)

This print displays the contemporary cruelty towards animals: a cat, with plates tied to its back to act as wings, is thrown out of a high window at the rear of the scene, while in the foreground dogs and cats are being tortured and a cock-fight is about to begin. Tom Nero, who stands holding the hind leg of a dog in the centre of the print, wears a badge on his sleeve that marks him out as the responsibility of the parish of St Giles; William Hogarth implies that Tom's sins are as much the result of his neglect by the absent ward officer as of his own nature.

19. *The Cockpit* (William Hogarth)

The central figure is a portrait of Lord Albemarle Bertie, a famous aristocratic patron of cock-fighting. On the left in the gallery is a French fop taking snuff as he surveys the scene. The Frenchman is balanced by a grimy chimney-sweep on the right of the scene, also enjoying a pinch of snuff. Their juxtaposition emphasizes the egalitarianism of the sporting world. On the left, at the edge of the ring, is a professional cock-trainer, holding a bag with a cock in it; his face is hardened and impassive.

t'other in the streets, by him that can get at it, and that is all the art of it.'[13] It was a dangerous game to walk near, since the players took 'a great deal of pleasure in breaking windows and coach glasses if they see any'.[14] Gay describes passing 'the furies of the Foot-Ball War' taking place in Covent Garden.

Bulls and dogs were baited viciously; in Pepys's words, 'a very rude and nasty pleasure'. There was a famous bear garden in Marylebone Fields, near Soho Square. Cock-fighting was a passion, involving elaborate training that could take years and highly specialized methods of looking after the cocks. Individual animals were famous for their victories (illustration 19, page 103; Hogarth's *The Cockpit*). Cock-fighting slang is still used in modern English: words and phrases like 'cocky', 'cock-sure', 'ruffle one's feathers', 'well-heeled' and 'turn tail' all derive from the terminology of cock-fighting. These recreations could cut across class lines because they were based on a meritocracy of specialized skills and esoteric knowledge: a lord and a labourer would meet as equals when cocks they had bred and trained fought each other. There was a 'strange variety of people' at cock-fights, all laying heavy bets. 'Great wagers are laid; but I'm told, that a man may be damnably bubbled, if he is not very sharp.'[15] The Royal Cockpit was in Birdcage Walk, and there was another cockpit in a cellar in Drury Lane near the Black Lion.

Instead of his anticipated game of skittles with Hell-and-Fury Sykes, Jack was thrown into a cell on the top floor of St Giles's Roundhouse, from where a few months before he had rescued Bess. Within three hours he had broken through the roof, his only tool an old razor, using the feather bed in his cell to muffle the sounds of masonry falling on to the floor as he bored through the ceiling. He lowered himself down the outside of the building with a blanket and sheet tied together, and lost himself in the crowd that had gathered, attracted by the sounds of falling tiles and the pros-pect of witnessing a gaol-break. Still wearing his irons, he tapped one of the throng on the shoulder as he pushed his way through the mob, and pointed up at the prison roof: 'Look! Up there behind the chimney! Isn't that him?' The unsuspecting man shouted out, and Jack slipped away unnoticed as the crowd scanned the roof for any sign of him. He was pleased with his success and new-found notoriety: 'I was well enough diverted with the adventure.'[16] Jack was indicted for the robbery in Clare Street, but avoided trial be-cause he had escaped; his brother was tried for the same robbery in May, convicted and transported to America.

His afternoon in gaol had not filled Jack with any sense of trep-idation about continuing his life of crime. In mid-May he and a friend, Benson, were walking through Leicester Fields when they saw a man arguing with a woman, holding a gold watch out in front of her which he was apparently accusing her of stealing. It was too good an opportunity to miss; Benson grabbed the watch, and he and Jack ran into the crowds. The cry was raised, and Jack was caught and taken to St Ann's Roundhouse in Soho. Edgworth Bess visited him there the next morning, and was thrown into prison with him when it was found she had brought him the spike of a halberd as a tool. They were taken to New Prison, Clerkenwell, where they were recognized as man and wife, and allowed to share the same cell.

Visiting friends smuggled tools in to them, and Jack planned their escape. He sawed through his heavy iron fetters, and then set about the iron bar and nine-inch-thick oak bar at the window. He tied their clothes and sheets together to form a rope as he had done when he escaped from St Giles's Roundhouse, and first Bess and then Jack lowered themselves twenty-five feet out of the window. To their dismay, they were not free, but merely in the yard of the neighbouring Bridewell, or House of Correction. Using the locks and bolts of the gate for footholds, Jack, carrying Bess, scaled the Bridewell Yard's twenty-two-foot wall and dropped down to safety on the other side.

This feat was hailed as the most miraculous escape in history. Jack's determination, bravery and chivalrous treatment of his lover made him a hero as much as his insouciant disregard for incarceration. His achievement was doubly remarkable because while Jack was slim and small, Bess was a big, buxom woman; helping her out of the window and then over the wall had been a real challenge for Jack, Bess 'being more corpulent than himself'.[17]

'Like a dog to his vomit',[18] Jack returned to the area around Wych Street. His fame was celebrated by his peers: in *The Quaker's Opera*, a popular musical based on his life, a young boy approaches him and asks to be taken on as an apprentice in thievery. Jack replies, 'Ours is not a trade, it is a calling.' His company was hotly sought out by his peers. 'Jack was now become so eminent, that there was not a prig in St Giles's, but thought it an honour, as well as an advantage, to be admitted to his company.'[19]

Several weeks after his escape, he robbed a master tailor called

William Barton who lodged in the house of Henry Carter, a mathematical-instrument maker living near St Clement's Church. Carter's apprentice, Anthony Lamb, and Charles Grace, a cooper who needed money for his 'extravagant whore', were Sheppard's eager accomplices. They stole about £300 worth of cloth and cash; Jack, with a keen eye to his appearance, took a suit of Italian silk for his own use. Only Anthony Lamb was tried for the burglary; he was convicted and transported to America.

Lamb took advantage of the opportunities available in the New World to transform his fortunes. His son, John Lamb, learned his father's trade of instrument-making and then went on to earn a comfortable living selling liquor in New York. He was one of the founders of the American radical group the Sons of Liberty, formed in 1765 during the first stirrings of nationhood, and was an activist for eleven years before America achieved her independence. After 1784, when peace was finally made, he remained an important politician.

John Lamb's career shows the gradual change from old-fashioned flouting of authority, exemplified by Jack Sheppard's life, to a more focused, active movement for reform. Sheppard railed against the bonds that restricted him, but had little awareness of the power of his example to others, and was unformed by any political education and indeed unconscious of his own latent insurgence. His resistance was manifested in a glorification, through his own life, of living outside society's constraints. But Lamb was not content with mere defiance, and had the advantage of living in a time and place that allowed him contact with others who felt as he did; he and his companions were able to change the very fabric of their time.[20]

Although both Jack's accomplices, his brother Tom and Anthony Lamb, had recently been arrested, he himself was still free. He began stealing with Joseph 'Blueskin' Blake, another acquaintance made at the Black Lion. Blueskin had had an 'early inclination to roguery'; he had been involved with crime since his childhood. 'Nothing pleased [Jonathan Wild] more than to see a child or youth of promising genius, and that such never wanted his encouragement.'[21]

Blueskin was one of these promising youths who from an early age had been singled out by Wild. His nickname was derived 'from his dark countenance'; but might also have been a neat play on words. One of his closest friends from childhood, another thief in Wild's circle, was called William Blewitt – hence 'Blew'-witt and 'Blue'-skin – which would have been appreciated by the wits of the East End.

Blueskin's life was typical of a man brought up in hardship on the streets of London. He was in and out of prison from the age of fifteen. Although he had had 'no aptitude for learning' while he was at school, he was said to have robbed a Cambridge scholar of his suitcase, and given him £4 for it – 'so great a regard had Blake to learning'. If in no other subject, Blueskin was diligent in his application to crime. He was 'one who studiously took the paths of infamy, in order to become famous'. Just as for Wild and Sheppard, for Blueskin the only way to escape the drudgery, want and frustration of his life was through criminal notoriety.

Although he was described as fat and lazy, if only a tenth part of the stories about Blueskin are true, he seems to have had enormous success with women. On one occasion, he took a fancy to a servant girl who loved music, and promised her if she went with him to the Turks' Head Tavern he would show her a merry dance. The girl arrived and,

finding him alone, enquired where the fiddle was; 'It will be here presently,' saith he, 'Sweetheart, and you will have a great deal of pleasure, but you must take some pains yourself,' and then began to kiss and snuggle her, till the girl fell in a swoon, but when she recovered out of her trance she asked him if he had done already, for she was never so well pleased in her life, it was the finest music she thought she had ever met with. After this they took an opportunity at home almost every day to have another tune, the girl thinking she should never have her belly full . . .

Sometimes he had to fend women off, so eager were they for his charms. His landlady in Islington 'fawned upon him like a spaniel' and pestered him to let her come to his bed. One night he consented, knowing her husband was asleep downstairs. In the meantime, he invited a party of countrymen visiting London into his chamber for a drink, saying that he could not sleep for fear of the ghosts that haunted his room – but that he suspected it was only the maid trying to frighten him. He asked them to buy some rods, and whip her soundly when she entered his room, 'that she may never come again', which rejoiced the rustics as much as if they had been invited to a wedding. They rushed off to buy the rods, and came back to lie in wait. When the landlady crept quietly through the door, looking forward to her assignation with Blueskin, the men fell on her, taking up her dress and flogging her so soundly that her screams wakened her husband. Not knowing where the sounds came from, he began looking around downstairs while she sneaked back to bed. Meanwhile the landlord had reached Blueskin's room, where the rustics fell upon him as they had upon his wife, but he fought back and knocked one of them down. The terrified men, taking him for a hobgoblin, ran away. Blueskin came out of hiding, and his landlord, much shaken up, told him his room was haunted and advised him to gather his things together and leave as soon as possible . . . which Blueskin speedily did.

Another story about Blueskin shows his love of practical jokes. He was just outside London when he passed the home of a man 'noted for having more money than brains', and thought he might be able to take advantage of the situation. He saw a ladder leaning against the house and climbed up it to look through the window and see if there was anything to steal. To his surprise, he saw the squire 'at play with his lady', saying to her that 'he would give £500 to have her "Tow-Vow" set an inch higher'. The following day, having waited until the squire had gone out, Blueskin presented himself at the door as a 'Tow-Vow Setter', sent by the squire to set his lady's Tow-Vow, for which she was to pay him £500.

'Well do your work as well as you can, and I'll give you the money,' which she did, after he had performed it to her satisfaction, and then turning her smock over her face, he charged her to lie in that posture about two hours, without speaking a word. Her maid, seeing what was done, offered him forty pounds to rectify her Tow-Vow, which he did at the head of the stairs and left her in the same posture, which the cook-maid perceiving, gave him ten pounds to mend her kettle too, which he had no sooner done but throws her clothes over her head and clasps the end of a calf's tail into her Tow-Vow, charging her not to stir for two hours, lest she spoil the operation, and then marched off with his booty.

The squire returned unsuspecting, but finding the cook-maid looking as if she was about to give birth to a calf, and the maid prone at the top of the stairs, he thought they had both been possessed by the devil. He rushed to his wife's chamber but she begged him not to disturb her as the two hours had not yet elapsed, because she had had her Tow-Vow reset according to his order. The squire, enraged, rode off in pursuit of the impostor. Passing Blueskin on the road he asked him if he had seen anyone running away. Blueskin said a man had just raced past him into the wood; the squire handed him his horse, asking him to take it back to his house for him, and set off into the wood after the supposed villain. Blueskin carried on his way, on horseback, feeling very well satisfied with himself.

Despite his apparent willingness to take advantage of the female sex, Blueskin did draw the line at prostitution. Mother Wisebourne was returning from Hampstead in her coach with a young girl whose virginity she had just sold for twenty guineas when Blueskin held up the coach, and asked for her purse. Mother Wisebourne, furious, swore she recognized him, and that she would see him hanged for robbing her. Blueskin calmly replied,

'You double-poxed salivating bitch, you deserve hanging more than I, for ruining both body and soul of many a poor man and woman, whom you procure to work iniquity for your own profit; there is nobody your friends, but the beadles and justice clerks who for a bribe may work your peace with [their] masters: Come, no dallying, deliver your money, or else your life must be a sacrifice to my fury.' At which she delivered her money, calling him a thousand names . . . and for her sauciness [he] stripped her stark naked.[22]

The year before he met Jack Sheppard, Blueskin had testified for Jonathan Wild against his partners in a robbery. He expected a share of the cash reward for turning evidence, but on learning that he would receive only his liberty (because he had been an involuntary witness) he flew into a violent rage, wounding himself in his frenzy, and was arrested again and taken to Wood Street Compter. During his stay there, Jonathan Wild paid him a weekly allowance of 3s. 6d. as well as paying for the treatment of the cut Blueskin had inflicted on himself. It is not clear why Wild paid Blueskin this salary. Blueskin might have been acting as Wild's agent in gaol, or the money may have been a recompense for failing to secure Blueskin a share of the reward. Either way, it is clear that Wild valued him in some way, and that he in part at least owed his survival to Wild.

Blueskin Blake met Jack Sheppard soon after he was released from Wood Street and the two men started working together, fencing the goods they stole through William Field, one of Jonathan Wild's assistants, whom Jack and his brother Tom had used the previous year as a fence. Field was the model for the oily Filch in *The Beggars' Opera*. He had started his career as one of Charles Hitchin's Mathematicians, and carried on working for Wild when he went into business on his own. Wild had saved him from the gallows in 1720 and Field had earned his protection: he impeached in turn everyone with whom he worked, hanging perhaps thirty people during the course of his career. Jack called him 'a fellow wicked enough to do anything, but his want of courage permitted him to do nothing but carry on the trade he did'[23] – fencing stolen goods and informing on the people who brought them to him.

On 12 July 1724 Sheppard and Blueskin, and possibly Field, robbed Mr Kneebone's house in the Strand, taking goods worth £50. Kneebone, determined to recover his belongings, went straight to Jonathan Wild, who promised him he would find out what he could. Jack and Blueskin stowed their booty in a hired warehouse near the Horseferry in Westminster, and offered it, as usual, to William Field to sell for them. Field went to their warehouse, removed the cloth they had stolen from Kneebone, and brought it to Wild as evidence against them. Defoe, speaking for Jack, wrote that Field's act was 'one of the greatest of villainies that could be acted, for another to come and plunder them of things for

20. *Industry and Idleness IX: The Idle 'Prentice Betrayed by his Whore and Taken in a Night Cellar with his Accomplice* (William Hogarth)

Tom Idle sits with his accomplice in one of eighteenth-century London's notorious night cellars, used by criminals to plan robberies and spend their loot on wine, women and gaming. Cards and pistols lie on the floor, and a body is being secreted down a trapdoor to the right of Tom and his friend. Tom's whore stands at the door, pointing him out to the thief-taker and his men as she receives her reward for informing on her lover.

which they had so honourably ventured their lives'. Meanwhile Sheppard and Blueskin turned their talents to highway robbery, holding up a coach on the Hampstead Road on 19 July, and robbing an attorney nearby the next day.

Wild knew, through Field, that it was Sheppard he wanted for the Kneebone robbery; so he sought out Edgworth Bess, knowing that she would lead him to Jack. He took her to a tavern and plied her with drink. (This incident was used by Hogarth for Plate IX of *Industry and Idleness*; illustration 20, above.) Bess soon let slip that Jack was staying at Blueskin's mother's brandy shop in Rosemary Lane, and the following day, 23 July, Wild sent Quilt Arnold there to arrest him. Jack 'snapped a loaded pistol, and designed the present of the plumb that was in it for Arnold, for his good intentions',[24] but the pistol – or 'popp' in cant terminology – 'miss'd fire', and Quilt arrested him easily. Jack was taken to Newgate to await his trial.

Jack's arrest was noted by the press, whose interest in him had been excited by his escape with Bess from New Prison, Clerkenwell. But as yet they knew very little about him and confused the facts they had, mixing Jack up with his brother Tom. 'Yesterday [24 July 1724] one Shepheard, who lately made his escape from New Prison, and had impeached his own brother, was committed to Newgate, having been re-taken by Jonathan Wild; he is charged with several burglaries, &c.' On the same day, the Covent Garden madams Mothers Needham and Bird were arrested for having 'two women in bed with two gentlemen of distinction' in their houses; the 'gentlemen were bound over to the Sessions [let go until their trial], and their mistresses were sent to Tothill Fields Bridewell to hard labour'.[25] Only the whores were considered guilty; the men who had paid for their services were exonerated.

On 13 August Jack Sheppard was tried for three robberies. He was acquitted of breaking into the houses of William Phillips and Mary Cook and robbing them, because of insufficient evidence. The third count was an accusation of stealing 108 yards of woollen cloth, worth £36, and sundry other goods, from William Kneebone's house in the Strand. Kneebone took the stand first, identified Jack, and said that he had visited him in Newgate, 'and asked him, how could he be so ungrateful as to rob me, after I had shown him so much kindness? He confessed he had been very ungrateful in doing so, but said he had been drawn into it by ill company.' Kneebone sounded more disappointed in Jack than angry with him; he had been fond of him.

Both Jonathan Wild and William Field gave evidence against Sheppard, as they later did against Blueskin in October that year. Wild corroborated Kneebone's evidence, adding only that he had persuaded Field to confess, knowing he had been involved, in order to procure Sheppard's capture and conviction. William Field testified that Jack had approached him and Blake and told them he knew a 'ken worth milling' (a house worth robbing) and had taken them to Kneebone's house. He said that he and Blueskin thought the job might be too difficult, but Sheppard assured them that because he had once lived there he knew the house inside-out, and would enter it alone if they would keep a watch out. This he had duly done. Jack was convicted of a capital felony on this evidence, and condemned to death. Asked if he had heard he was to be hung, he replied, 'Yes, so my great Lord and Master says, but, by God, I'll do my best endeavours to prove him a false prophet.'[26]

Both Sheppard and Blueskin refused to admit at any point that Field had been involved in the burglary until they approached him and asked him to fence their loot for them, although they both confessed to robbing Kneebone. They said they had told Field all about the robbery when they had bumped into him outside Mrs Blake's brandy shop a few days later, and that Field had used their words in evidence against them in court, perjuring himself in Wild's service. Had Field not produced an eyewitness account of the robbery, and acquired the stolen items for evidence, it would have been far more difficult for Wild and Kneebone to pin the crime on Jack and Blake in the courts.

Although Sheppard was undoubtedly guilty of robbing Kneebone, this trial was a set-up, engineered by Wild to rid himself of a cocky upstart who refused to toe the line he had drawn. Jack insisted until his death that Field had had no part in the robbery, and Defoe shows sympathy to him on this point. He records Jack saying,

I declare upon the word of a dying man, that Will Field was not concerned with Blueskin and myself in the breaking and robbing of Mr Kneebone's house, although he has sworn the same at our respective trials . . . But he has done the work of his master, who in the end no doubt will reward him, as he has all his other servants. I wish Field may repent and amend his wicked life, for a greater villain there is not breathing.[27]

PART THREE

In fine, his business in all things was to put a
false gloss on things; and to make fools of mankind
(which was his own expression).

H. D. (DANIEL DEFOE),
*The Life of Jonathan Wild from his
Birth to his Death,* 1725

Business

In 1717 the second Transportation Act was passed. Its most important elements concerned not transportation, but receiving of stolen goods. Provoked in part by Wild's successes, it was the first law to make receiving a capital felony.

And whereas there are several persons who have secret acquaintance with felons, and who make it their business to help persons to their stolen goods, and, by that means, gain money from them, which is divided between them and the felons, whereby they greatly encourage such offenders, be it enacted by the authority aforesaid, that wherever any person taketh money or reward, directly or indirectly, under pretence, or upon account of helping any person or persons to any stolen goods or chattels, every such person, so taking money or rewards as aforesaid, (unless a person doth apprehend such felon who stole the same, and give evidence against him) shall be guilty of felony and suffer the pains and penalties of felony, according to the nature of the felony committed in stealing such goods, and in such and the same manner as if the offender had himself stole such goods and chattels in the manner, and with such circumstances, as the same was stolen.

This act was aimed at the heart of Jonathan Wild's emerging empire: it was known colloquially as 'Jonathan Wild's Act'. Defoe saw it as an unequivocal warning,

so directly aimed at Jonathan's general practice that he could not be ignorant enough not to see it . . . [But] he that was hardened above the baseness of all cautionary fear, scorned this advice, and went on in his wicked trade, not warily and wisely, as he had formerly done, but, in short, with more impudence and shameless boldness than ever, as if he despised laws, and the governors, and the provoked justice of the nation.

In practice, however, the act made very little difference to Wild's business. After it became law, Wild merely made sure that he never handed over stolen goods himself, always sending a messenger to exchange the item for money at a place and time he had arranged. Increasingly he did not accept a fee for his service, relying instead on the money he made in selling the goods back to their original owner – money that the person paying assumed was going straight to the robber. These precautions kept his hands clean, and the worst offence he could be charged with if he was caught was a minor common law misdemeanour.

From 1718 he consolidated his control over London's crime world and boldly attempted to use his power within it as a passport to respectability. It was almost as if he saw the law as a challenge to his perverse genius; as Defoe said, 'good advice to Jonathan Wild was like talking gospel to a kettle-drum, bidding a dragoon not plunder, or talking of compassion to a hussar'.

During the last years of the 1710s he became the acknowledged (if unofficial) Thief-taker General, using this title to mark himself apart from his rivals. One reason for his increasing dominance was his ability to appear as a quasi-servant of the law, despite his close alliance with pickpockets and highwaymen.

He acquired a strange, and indeed unusual, reputation for a mighty honest man, till his success hardened him to put on a face of public service in it, and for that purpose to profess an open and brave correspondence among the gangs of thieves, by which his house became an office of intelligence for inquiries of that kind, as if all stolen goods had been deposited with him in order to be restored.[1]

Ironically, as Defoe noted, it was the appearance of integrity he cultivated that made his intimacy with London's rogues and villains acceptable to his clientele.

He was much in demand. 'As soon as anything is missing, suspected to be stolen, the first course we steer is directly to the office of Mr Jonathan Wild.'[2] All this attention made Wild believe he was vastly important.

Jonathan Wild's house about eight a clock in a morning was as full as if it had been an Exchange [stock exchange], gentlemen and ladies from all parts resorting thither, to desire Mr Wild's interest to recover their lost things; who never vouchsafed to come out of his chamber till his emissaries told him his levee was full; and then like a Prime Minister, he dispatched all away with good words, though many of them had aching hearts at the same time.[3]

From 1721 Wild conducted his business in a large house in Great Old Bailey, but many small traders worked out of a coffee-house or tavern, as he had done when he first set up his own office in Mrs Seagoe's Blue Boar tavern.

The nascent stock exchange was in Cheapside, near the Royal Exchange, and was essentially a group of coffee-houses that bought, sold and traded stock and information on ventures like the South Sea Company, which crashed in 1721. The hustle and bustle of London's Royal Exchange made 'this Metropolis a kind of emporium for the whole earth'.[4]

Lloyd's Insurance was founded in the 1680s in Tower Street by Edward Lloyd. In 1692 it moved to Lombard Street, where four years later it first published Lloyd's News, the precursor of Lloyd's List and Shipping Gazette, and in 1712 it moved again to Pope's Head Alley. The Jerusalem and Jamaica coffee-houses were frequented by people involved in trade with China and the Indies – merchants, sea-captains and brokers. Grigsby's, in Threadneedle Street, was a coffee-house specializing in foreign news. Bankers went to Garraway's, in Cornhill, or to Jonathan's or the Amsterdam in Temple Bar. In 1723 the Bank of England moved to Threadneedle Street, where many of the early trading companies were based. Private banks were formed by the dozen in this period, including Hoare's and Child's, which are still in existence – but many others were less successful. Each bank was allowed to issue its own notes so any investment was a high-risk business: if a bank went bankrupt, there were no independent guarantees that its notes would be honoured.

In 1700 there were about 500 coffee-houses in London, either in the city or near the Strand. 'You have all manner of news there: you have a good fire, which you may sit by as long as you please; you have a dish of coffee; you meet all your friends for the transaction of business, and all for a penny.'[5] They were warm, noisy, bustling places, with a large fire burning at the far end of the room on which pots of coffee steamed. Ned Ward described coffee-house customers thus: 'Some going, some coming, some scribbling, some talking, some drinking, others jangling, and the whole room stinking of tobacco like a Dutch barge or a boatswain's cabin.' Many coffee-houses had billiard tables, although cards and dice were forbidden, as was swearing, for which a fine of a shilling was exacted. If a fight broke out, the instigators had to buy coffee for the rest of the customers. In addition to coffee and tea, one could buy liquor and snuff; at some, even toothpastes, beauty creams, lozenges and medicinal elixirs were available. Batson's, in Cornhill, was used by surgeons as a consulting room.

By 1700 there were three weekly deliveries of mail into and out of London; people used coffee-houses as addresses, when their actual address may have been less permanent. Swift had his post directed to him care of the St James' coffee-house. Advertisements were posted on the walls, not only for products, but also for a lost pet, or relating personal messages such as a husband looking 'for his beloved better half, who has abandoned him in order to follow her sweetheart'; or another husband warning shopkeepers not to sell anything to his wife on credit.

The main attraction of these places, however, was not the refreshments, but the news. Eighteen weekly newspapers were published in London in 1709. 'All Englishmen are great newsmongers,' commented Cesar de Saussure. 'I have often seen shoeblacks and other persons of that class club together to purchase a farthing paper.' Probably 60 per cent of male Londoners could read in 1750 (the rates were slightly lower for women), but if one couldn't read, the papers were read aloud throughout the day. Another foreign observer called London's coffee-houses 'the seats of English liberty'. Everyone, whatever his rank or fortune, had 'the right to read all the papers for and against the government'.[6] Coffee was called

'Politician's Porridge', because of the freedom of discussion on all topics in coffee-houses.

It was not only educated men such as Swift who commented on the corruption of Walpole's government. Illiterate men and women also understood and enjoyed political satire. The South Sea Bubble, which swelled in 1720 and burst in 1721, laid bare the corruption and greed of Walpole's administration, much to the scorn of the common Londoner. Roving players at St Bartholomew's Fair, which was held annually at Smithfield and was frequented by the dregs of London society, put on a performance of *The Broken Stock-Jobbers: Or, Work for the Bailiffs* just a few weeks after the Bubble burst. In it, Mr Pluckwell, the director of a bank, and his assistant, Mr Transfer, swindle first Lord Equipage, then down through the ranks of society to Sir Frippery Upstart, Dr Sinecure, and finally Headless, before losing everything themselves as well.

Further signs of the increasing rates of common literacy were the government's attempts, from the end of the seventeenth century, to keep subversive ideas out of popular hands. Previous methods of censorship had concentrated on the educated élite, because it was thought that the mass of the population would not understand radical ideas, even if they were to hear them read.

The old medieval emphasis on the church as the centre of the urban community was shifting to coffee-houses, political clubs, dissenting chapels, and reformation societies. The old system of parishes had been outgrown by the changing geography and population of London since Tudor times. In 1711 the London Churches Act assigned money for fifty new churches, but only ten were actually built. This was probably due to a combination of factors: a preference for fewer, grander places of worship than many smaller, perhaps more useful, ones, combined with the growing irrelevance of parish churches to London society. These impressive new constructions, including Nicholas Hawksmoor's Christ Church Spitalfields and St George's Bloomsbury, were built for the rich, with imposing box pews that left little space for a humbler congregation (illustration 21, page 122; *A Rake's Progress V* shows the in-

21. *A Rake's Progress V: Marriage* (William Hogarth)

The Rake is eyeing up the pretty bridesmaid even as he marries her aged mistress for her money. The shabbiness of the church's interior is a comment on the desecration of the institution of marriage by Tom in his shameless quest for fortune and sensual pleasure.

terior of a London church). Many of the poorest people in London only entered churches to steal from the wealthy worshippers lost in prayer. Charity also assumed a new secular, philanthropic air, with private, non-religious donations providing the funds for hospitals like Guy's, founded in 1725.

As the church lost its role as a focus for urban society, it was replaced by clubs for hobbies, moral improvement, sport or politics – indeed, for almost anything. The Society of Gardeners was a group of twenty nurserymen who met at Newhall's coffee-house in Chelsea. In 1717 the Spitalfields Mathematical Society was founded, with a proviso that membership must not exceed forty-nine members, or seven squared. In 1750 the novelist Edward Kimbar estimated that 20,000 men met nightly in London's social clubs. The high concentration of people gathered together, exchanging ideas, made the city a forum for political and social discussion. London's emergent middle class was challenging the aristocratic culture that had dominated the metropolis for so long. The coffee-house was its habitat, clubs and newspapers the means of expressing its views, Defoe's novels, Gay's plays and poems, Hogarth's engravings, its life.

Because most Londoners, except the very rich, lived in rented rooms, almost everyone ate their meals in a coffee-house or tavern. Pontack's Eating House, in Abchurch Street, was reputed to serve the best food in London. Fast food was also available. Some bakeries and pie shops had open shopfronts, and passers-by could take what they wanted and throw a penny in to pay for it. Bread cost a penny or two a pound. Food on the streets was plentiful as well, with hawkers selling anything from sausages to mussels, hot cross buns to peaches and plums.

Dinner was the main meal of the day, still at midday for most people – a habit regarded as odd by the French observer Henri Misson: 'Gluttony at noon, and abstinence at night.' The beau monde ate dinner increasingly (and fashionably, in the continental style) later, thus creating space during the day for new meals, luncheon and tea, to fill the gap while one waited to dine. Supper was a snack after a ball or the theatre.

Elaborate dishes were prepared in the houses of the aristocracy, such as salmagundi, a salad of meat, eggs and fish that was piled into a pyramid. The common man ate more usual tavern fare – pigeon pie, roast meats with home-made pickles and chutneys, salmon with fennel sauce – accompanied by vegetables 'well peppered and salted, and swimming in butter', washed down with beer, weak ale or wine, and followed by fruit tarts or jellies. In 1732 the painter William Hogarth and some friends journeyed to Kent for a 'peregrination'. A typical meal, described in the diary of one of Hogarth's companions, Ebeneezer Forrest, consisted of 'a dish of soles and flounders with crab sauce, a calf's heart stuffed and roasted, ye liver fried and the other appurtenances minced, a leg of mutton roasted, and some green pease, all very good and well-dressed, with good small beer and excellent port'. Henri Misson was fond of English puddings: ' "To come in pudding-time" [a common saying] is as much to say, to come in the most lucky time in the world!' But he was less impressed by the table manners of the English.

. . .Belching at table, and in all companies whatsoever, is a thing which the English no more scruple than they do coughing and sneezing. This is as strange to us, that come from a country where custom has ordained that belching should be a privilege reserved to hogs, as it is natural and usual among them.

Meals were bountiful, and as Misson noticed, people ate enthusiastically, all digging into a central platter with their own knife and fork. 'The goose is a silly bird,' wrote Samuel Ogden in the middle of the century, 'too much for one, and not enough for two.' Fielding's Tom Jones ate at one sitting 'three pounds at least of that flesh which formerly had contributed to the composition of an ox'.

But Wild, who had gained so much in importance since his release from Wood Street Compter, no longer had to work in a public house among all this gluttony. His methods of business were highly organized and efficient. He received his clients in a respectable office, but according to contemporary rumours he had another house nearby which he used for meeting robbers and sheltering fugitives. During rebuilding in 1844, the Red Lion tavern in West Street, Clerkenwell (called Chick Lane in Wild's time), and the chandler's shop next door to it were excavated. Human remains were found there, as well as instruments of torture and a knife engraved with the name 'J. Wild'. The two buildings were a tortuous maze of narrow staircases and twisting passages, with an underground opening leading on to the Fleet Ditch, a sewer that flowed into the Thames. A flight of rickety stairs led to a huge cellar, used by Wild as a store-room for stolen goods, and a workshop for his men forging coins and altering loot for resale. There were hiding-places for men Wild was sheltering from the law, trap-doors and secret exits to foil their pursuers, and possibly even a tunnel to Newgate Prison.

It was sometimes called Jonathan Wild's house, and the 'Old House in West Street'. From its remarkable adaption as a hiding place, with its various means of escape, it was a curious habitation. Its dark closets, trapdoors, sliding panels, and secret recesses, rendered it one of the most secure places for robbery and murder. It was here that a chimney-sweep, named Jones, who escaped out of Newgate about three years before the destruction of the house [1841], was so securely hidden for about six weeks that, although it was repeatedly searched by the police, he was never discovered until his lair was divulged by one of its inmates . . . It was here that a sailor was robbed, and afterwards flung naked through one of the convenient apertures in the wall into the Fleet [Ditch] . . . A skull, and numerous human bones, were found in the cellars . . . the place looked as if many a foul deed had been there planned and decided on, the sewer or ditch [with which it was connected] receiving and floating away anything thrown into it. . .[7]

The Fleet Ditch was London's main sewer. Immortalized by Swift in 'A Description of a City Shower', it was full of

> Sweepings from butchers' stalls, dung, guts and blood,
> Drown'd puppies, stinking spratts, all drench'd in mud,
> Dead cats and turnip tops come tumbling down the flood.

This was the worst of London, the stench of dead animals and rotting food and silage and waste, to which all the drains in the city flowed and where anything too disgusting to be disposed of in the street was taken. Drunks, typically, stumbled into it in the dead of night. Because of the stinking, fetid atmosphere of the areas around Fleet Ditch, they were inhabited by none but the most desperate. Some of the most notoriously dangerous, filthy, poorest and most crime-infested areas in London were within smelling distance of the Fleet Ditch – Smithfield, Clerkenwell, Whitefriars, Holborn, Fleet Street, Lincoln's Inn Fields – and the city's four main prisons, Newgate, Ludgate, the Fleet and Bridewell, were also very close to it.

A medical report written in 1838 detailed some of the causes of disease in London: imperfection or want of sewers and drains; uncovered and stagnant drains and ditches; undrained marsh-land; accumulation of refuse in streets; exhalations of cesspools, slaughterhouses and burial-grounds; gross want of cleanliness; and keeping hogs in dwelling-places. Most historians of London agree that matters of health and hygiene in the city had improved, albeit only slightly, over the eighteenth century, so the conditions which allowed this verdict must have been even worse the century before.

No one knew for certain who owned the Red Lion tavern, even when Wild was alive. It was one of many 'flash houses' in London at this time, 'flash' being a cant word for a successful criminal. Two of the most notorious and celebrated criminals of the eighteenth century – Jack Sheppard, the house- and prison-breaker who was to become the instrument of Jonathan Wild's fall from power, and Dick Turpin, the legendary highwayman – frequented the Red Lion. Flash houses were academies of vice, where criminals lodged, planned robberies, gambled, drank and whored. The landlord was often a fence, and might also run a sideline business storing and altering the goods he bought from thieves. In this respect Wild's flash house differed little from any other in London during the eighteenth century.

William Harrison Ainsworth, the nineteenth-century novelist, made Jonathan Wild one of the central characters in his 1839 novel *Jack Sheppard*. He told a story, based on rumours still circulating over a century after Wild's death, of how the fictional Sir Rowland Trenchard had visited Wild on evil business. After Sir Rowland had been shown into his office Wild signalled to his assistant, Abraham Mendez, who was waiting behind a cupboard. Mendez sprang out from his hiding-place and flung a cloth over Trenchard's head. Picking up a staff, Wild beat his head until the cloth covering it turned red, but Sir Rowland struggled vigorously and pulled off the cloth to reveal his pulped and bloody face. Even Wild and Mendez, the hardened murderers, were shocked by this terrible sight. Through a sticky crimson haze, Trenchard saw an open door and rushed for it, hoping to make his escape, but Wild struck him hard with his bludgeon. The injured man fell through the door into a pool of slimy water at the bottom of a brick well. Holding a candle down into the well, Wild and Mendez saw him struggling to stay afloat and get a firm grip on the slime-covered walls. Mendez, horrified, cried, 'Shoot him! Shoot him! Put him out of his misery!'

But Wild coldly replied, 'What's the use of wasting a shot? He can't get out.'

Ainsworth also created a fictional 'Museum' belonging to Wild, full of exhibits in glass cases, meticulously organized and labelled·

On this side was a razor with which a son had murdered his father, the blade notched, the haft crusted with blood; on that a bar of iron, bent and partly broken, with which a husband had beaten out his wife's brains . . . In front of them lay a large and sharp knife, once the property of a public executioner, and used by him to dissever the limbs of those condemned to death for high treason; together with an immense two-pronged flesh-fork, likewise employed by the same terrible functionary to plunge the quarters of his victims in the cauldrons of boiling tar and oil.[8]

The idea of a museum of criminal tools was derived from Wild's 'armoury of all kinds of instruments used in thievery'[9] from which he would choose according to the job at hand. The wild speculation that emanated from these stories about Wild no doubt pleased him. He 'delighted in investing himself and his residence with mystery, encouraged and perhaps originated these marvellous tales'. His reputation for cruelty and utter ruthlessness can only have bolstered his standing in the eyes of the men and women who worked for him and were ruled by their terror and distrust of him.

Wild's control over his 'Corporation of Thieves' often began from their childhood. Like Mother Wisebourne, the famous Covent Garden madam, Wild trawled the streets of London in search of children or down-and-outs whose hunger and loneliness made them willing to sign their lives away to him.

To see him, I say, pick up an unthinking youth in the streets, covered with dirt and rags, and willing on any terms to get out of his misery, to see this superlative wretch pretend charity to the child, and tell him he would provide for him, and thereby engage the lad to him, as a man sent from heaven to do him good, and provide for him; but instead of doing all this, he takes him by the hand and leads him to Hell Gates, and after that like a true devil thrusts him in: for first to tempt, and then to accuse, is the very nature of the devil.[10]

Joseph Blueskin Blake, Jack Sheppard's companion and accomplice, reportedly said that 'Jonathan first made him [Blueskin] a thief and then hanged him.' Defoe called these youngsters Wild's 'foster children', whom 'he has himself caused afterwards to be apprehended and hanged for the very crimes which he first taught them to commit'.

Some of the best sources of desperadoes were the 'bastard sanctuary' areas scattered around London, notorious hotbeds of thieves, debtors, prostitutes, down-and-outs and escaped criminals and transportees. They had been the sites of monasteries which, when they were dissolved in the 1530s, had retained their ancient liberties, one of which included sanctuary from the law. Constables and marshals, even the militia, dared not enter these areas. While only the Mint in Southwark, named for the Royal Mint it housed, officially retained its old freedoms (until 1723), other areas such as 'Alsatia', officially Whitefriars, between Fleet Street and the Thames, were still known to be populated almost exclusively by criminals. The most famous of these old bastard sanctuary areas was Thieving Lane, in Westminster, but they also included Smithfield, parts of Holborn, much of Covent Garden, and the Savoy.

Wild would have crossed the Thames to reach Southwark, probably by ferry. It cost tuppence to 'cross the river direct' in 1741 and might cost up to a shilling depending on how far downriver or upriver the destination was, and how seaworthy or crowded the boat. On land there were two forms of transport, apart from walking: the coach, either private or hackney, and the sedan chair. In London in 1739 there were nearly 2,500 private carriages, and just over 1,000 hired carriages, their iron-bound wheels clattering noisily over the cobbled streets. Some thoroughfares had post-and-rail fences separating pedestrian traffic from horse-drawn vehicles but many more did not.

A man of importance would have owned a coach-and-six, with liveried footmen clinging precariously on to its swaying back, or might drive himself through St James's Park in an open chaise, drawn by two prancing steeds, the better to bow graciously and skilfully to ladies. One of Wild's first purchases once he had achieved the wealth and importance he desired was a coach-and-six. The rest of the population had to settle for a seat in a hackney coach, the eighteenth-century equivalent of a black taxi. These cost 1s. 6d. for an hour's hire, and the same for a journey of average distance, say from Royal Exchange to Drury Lane, and were far less comfortable than a private carriage. They were dark and musty inside, their windows blocked up with perforated tin to keep the mud of the streets from splashing on to the passengers, and the drivers were notoriously truculent and aggressive about fares, and competitive with each other, to judge by a description in the *Spectator*: 'the coachmen make signs with their fingers as they drive by each other, to intimate how much they have got that day'. Roads were rough and uneven, and most carriages, even the best-made and most expensive, were badly sprung. The blue stocking Elizabeth Montagu, shaken by her travels, began 'to think from my frequent overturns a bone-setter a necessary part of my equipage'.

Sedan chairs, like carriages, were either private or hired. The bearers of hired chairs had to deposit a relatively large amount of money before being allowed to register as chair carriers, to ensure that they didn't get too excited at the thought of rich pickings from a well-dressed client. Private chairs borne by liveried footmen, like private carriages, could be incredibly luxurious and comfortable, usually sporting the coats of arms of their owners on the sides. Sedan chairs were raced through the streets, often a danger to passers-by who had to be constantly alert for the cry of 'Chair!' that warned them to move out of the way. The onslaught of thundering carriages, sprinting sedan-carriers and overladen carts and wagons made London's streets perpetual obstacle courses.

In the early eighteenth century the Thames was still the hub of the city. London was not only the central market of England, but a thriving seaport receiving goods from all over the world. These were the years of the consumer revolution, which turned England

22. *Marriage à la Mode VI* (William Hogarth)

This print shows the sober, functional interior of a London alderman's home. The furniture, clothes and food are plain and simple. On the window the arms of the City of London are proudly displayed.

into the proverbial nation of shopkeepers. Silks, spices, cottons, wine, porcelain, timber, tobacco, furs – all these and more came into London from China, the Indies, the Americas, Africa and Europe, to be haggled over and despatched again. Swaggering bronzed sailors regaled packed taverns with tales of Oriental mysteries and African monsters; black captives were sold as slaves to fashionable ladies and wiry Lascar deck-hands had their first hesitant glimpses of a modern European city.

Until Westminster Bridge was built in 1750, the only bridge across the Thames was London Bridge. It looked a little like Florence's Ponte Vecchio, piled high with ramshackle buildings, shaking slightly as its perpetual burden of laden carts and wagons thundered over the river. It can be seen in the background of Plate VI of Hogarth's

Marriage à la Mode (illustration 22, page 130). Most lands south of the river were still fields and marshland; Southwark was the only built-up part of the area except for Lambeth, the palace of the Bishop of London, directly across the water from Westminster. The whole of Southwark, not just the Mint, was a disreputable area, and had been so since Shakespeare's time.

In the winter of 1718–19 Jonathan Wild visited the Mint. He kept his horses nearby, at the Duke's Head, in Red Cross Street, and one of his warehouses was in Newington Butts, in Southwark, so he was often south of the river conducting business. His quick wit, obvious wealth, and concerned interest made him a popular figure in the Mint, allowing him to pick and choose among the rogues he befriended according to what he needed them for. On several occasions he met a young (unnamed) cheesemonger from Oxfordshire who was in hiding from his creditors, and according to his usual practice he bought him some food and beer, lent him a little money, and offered to put some work his way if he was interested. Wild flattered the young man by implying that he thought him too good for mere robbery, and offered to set him up as a highwayman, with a horse and pistols, if he would share his profits with him. An offer like this was every young man's dream, and the cheesemonger leapt at the chance to join the criminal élite.

Highwaymen, or 'Snafflers', were seen, and saw themselves, as 'Gentlemen of the Road'. Tales of their gallantry abounded. Some begged to be excused for being forced by dire necessity to rob; many refused to point their guns at ladies, or search them, and chivalrously insisted on returning to them items of sentimental value; others took only some of the goods they found. One highwayman held a man up, and took his watch. His victim politely asked him if he would be willing to accept two guineas and a promise that he would not turn him in to the authorities, instead of his watch, of which he was particularly fond. He suggested that they ride to his home so he could get the money for him. The highwayman agreed, they rode off together, the exchange was completed, and 'after the drinking of a bottle of wine, with mutual civilities they took leave of each other'.[11]

The highwayman's traditional love for his horse was another aspect of his romantic image. Dick Turpin's beloved Black Bess, who, according to legend, collapsed and died carrying him on his celebrated ride to York in 1739, was renowned as a symbol of the devoted love of an animal for its master. William Spiggot, who was tried in 1721 for highway robbery, refused to plead in court unless his horse was returned to him, and as a result faced *peine forte et dure*, a torture involving being weighted down until one could bear it no longer, and submitted to the demands of the court. Spiggot lasted half an hour with a weight of 350 lb. on his chest, and gave in and agreed to plead only when another fifty pounds were added. As a mark of the admiration for his valour, after he was hanged his body was carried off by the mob and hidden.

This example of physical courage was typical of highwaymen. They were at their most bravely defiant on the scaffold, facing death. One of them, James Maclean, kicked off his shoes and jumped into the air holding his knees to his chest, to hasten his death, like a child doing a cannonball jump into a swimming pool. Dick Turpin's coolness on the scaffold was betrayed only by the trembling of one leg, which he tried to quell by stamping his foot repeatedly. Like Maclean, he refused to wait for the cart holding him to move away, and flung himself off the platform. The more a criminal showed his defiance of the authorities, the more he was respected by his peers.

Such stories lent highwaymen an allure that captivated the reading public – particularly the female side. Claude Duvall was one of the best-known highwaymen of the late seventeenth century – a heart-throb, as famous for his lovemaking (he was French) as for his wit, generosity and wild lifestyle. One of the most often told stories about him recounts how he held up a couple and asked the gentleman for permission to dance with his beautiful young wife, which the man could hardly refuse. Duvall helped her out of the coach and danced a minuet with her on the roadside. 'Scarce a dancing master in London, but would have been proud to have shown such agility in a pair of pumps, as Duvall showed in a great pair of French riding boots.' His epitaph read,

> Here lies Duvall, Reader, if male thou art,
> Look to thy purse, if female, to thy heart.[12]

Sophie von la Roche, a German visitor to England in 1786, had heard of a respectable young man forced to take to the road because of his gambling debts (quite a common motivation); he was reformed, and reclaimed for respectability, by the generosity of an association of his lady victims, who had collected 150 guineas to give him to save him from ruin. In 1709 Mrs Crackenthorpe of the *Female Tatler* mocked the fantasies of middle class women dreaming mistily of being held up by a masked highwayman who kisses their sweaty palms as he takes their husbands' money, and gallops off into the distance, his cloak streaming out behind him.

Mrs Mary Fanciful, having heard a world of stories about highwaymen, has a curiosity to see one. She sets out for the bath, on Monday next, with ten guineas (not hid in the privat'st part of her coach) therefore, if any of these gentlemen please to clap an uncharged pistol to her breast, only that she may know how it is to be robbed, they shall receive the ten guineas with a sincere promise never to be prosecuted for the same. Her sister, Mrs Sarah Fanciful, wants mightily to see a ghost.

Of all types of criminals, highwaymen most clearly fitted the public's idealized vision of an honourable outlaw. The idea of the noble highwayman was a fusion of several different concepts. Most obviously, the accomplishments of the ideal highwayman were essentially those of a gentleman: horsemanship, courage, the ability to handle weapons well, wit and eloquence with which to disarm his victims, a certain insouciance, a sense of honour. Men of gentle birth turned to the road rather than to other forms of crime because it glorified these qualities, and allowed them to take pride in their actions. Even if they were of common birth, as most were, these qualities exalted their crimes. A highwayman could be as famous for his charm as for his bravery. Because he had a fast horse, and time to ride off before an alarm could be sounded, his chances of escape were high, while a footpad or pickpocket, desperate to avoid recognition and escape untouched could not afford to treat his victims with respect. Highwaymen also made a lot of money from their trade, because carriages and stagecoaches offered rich pickings. They could afford to be discriminating about whom they robbed, or to give money back to someone if they discovered they were poor.

Highwaymen were often trained footmen. Claude Duvall had been a footman in the French court of Charles II and had come in his entourage to England in 1680. Footmen were hired as much for their looks and presence as their skills, because they were meant to display their masters' magnificence; their arrogance and unruliness were legendary. They saw the luxuries of their masters and to some extent shared them – dressing in rich liveries, eating fine foods left over from their employers' meals, watching balls and plays while they waited to take them home, driving behind high-stepping horses – but were paid a pittance. The magnificence of the lifestyle they were denied was daily displayed to them in all its glory. They used the manners they had learned to rob the very people who had exposed them to these riches.

Obviously, not all highwaymen fell into this category, but the popular conception of these outlaws was such that any highway robber could imitate the manners of the aristocracy, priding himself on his chivalry and honour. One noted eighteenth-century highwayman had begun his career on a hired mount. While some came from very poor, labouring families, others came from a middle-class background. James Maclean, a country parson's son, financed his apartment in St James's (one of the smartest areas of London; neighbouring St James's Square housed six dukes in 1721), in which he lived with his mistress, by nightly excursions – including, famously, holding up and shooting at Horace Walpole in Hyde Park in 1752, his bullet grazing the side of the great man's head. He was a well-known society figure, who was believed to live off the income from his extensive (imaginary) estates in Ireland. Idleness, called by Defoe the 'mother of mischief', was seen by much of eighteenth-century society as the 'badge of gentry'. The financial freedom their lives of crime gave highwaymen and thieves also brought them an aristocratically idle way of life, described in the 1724 ballad, 'The High-Pad's [highwayman's] Boast':

> I keep my horse; I keep my whore;
> I take no rents; yet am not poor;
> I travel all the land about,
> And yet was born to ne'er a foot.
>
> With partridge plump and woodcock fine,
> At midnight, I do often dine:
> And if my whore be not in case,
> My hostel's daughter has her place.
>
> The maids sit up and watch their turns;
> If I stay long, the tapster mourns;
> Nor has the cookmaid mind to sin,
> Tho' tempted by the chamberlain.
>
> But when I knock, O how they bustle;
> The Hostler yawns, the geldings jostle:
> If the maid be sleepy, O how they curse her,
> And all this comes of, 'Deliver your purse, Sir!'[13]

The ambiguity of the relationship between gentlemen and highwaymen was summed up at the end of *The Beggars' Opera*: 'It is difficult to determine whether (in the fashionable vices) the fine gentlemen imitate the gentlemen of the road, or the gentlemen of the road the fine gentlemen.' Macheath sends his men off with a chivalrous, 'Success attend you!' The whores with whom he dances address each other as 'Dear Madam', punctuating their speech with polite phrases such as, 'I would not for the world . . .' In Captain Alexander Smith's eighteenth-century biography of Robin Hood, he says that two legends exist as to Robin's background: that he was either the illegitimate son of the Earl of Huntingdon – and thus, in the romantic tradition of an aristocrat who turned to robbery to restore his fortunes; or that he was a butcher, a profession which, like that of a footman, was common among highwaymen. Thus in the retelling of a centuries-old story the duality of the romantic idea of a highwayman was expressed.

Sympathy with the Jacobite cause was another mark of the high-wayman's romanticism. Claude Duvall was a royalist who had served Charles II; his dashing style was intimately bound up with his links to the glamorous court-in-exile. One of the original members of the Hawkins gang was an Irish soldier, Captain Leonard, who turned to highway robbery during a visit to England to raise money and men for the Pretender's cause. He was arrested by the King's Messengers (a private royal force) in 1718. Ralph Wilson, tried in 1721 for highway robbery, was accused in court of 'drinking a health to the devil, and damnation to King George, and success to King James the Third (as he called the Pretender), and swore that, if he was in the field, he would fight for him against King George'.

Despite their reputation as gentlemen, if crossed highwaymen could be cruel to their victims. They might shoot or hamstring horses to prevent the coach travelling any further, or murder coachmen. In 1721 an old woman, witness to a highway robbery, shouted out to the victims that she recognized one of the thieves, and could inform on him; her tongue was cut out. Any sign of re-sistance or lack of respect could cause a highwayman to fly into a violent rage, and kill or injure the perpetrator of the insult.

The life of these outlaws was seen as one free from the restric-tions and struggles of day-to-day existence. A biography of the seventeenth-century highwayman and royalist James Hind held that 'the virtue of the brave . . . made him scorn to be a slave'. Implicit in their rejection of 'normal' societal roles was their glorification of their own courage, wit and nobility. Ballads celebrated life on the road, outside conventional society, free from entanglements and complications. Many songs held up the life of the Gypsies as an ideal of independence and liberty; the Gypsies, in their turn, made heroes out of criminals, for example frequently naming their chil-dren Dick after Dick Turpin, whom they thought of as one of their own. Highwaymen were neither shackled by service, nor living off the poor, and as such they inspired popular adulation. Common people lived vicariously through the defiant adventures of their he-roes, and identified with their defiance of conformity precisely because they themselves would never have dared to throw off the chains that bound them as these men had managed to do.

Highwaymen were seen as the ideological descendants of Robin Hood. Thomas Easter, a Norwich butcher turned outlaw, held up a carriage on Putney Heath. 'Why, I took you for an honest man!' exclaimed the man inside. 'So I am,' replied Easter, 'because I rob the rich to give to the poor.'[14] A ballad called 'Turpin's Appeal to the Judge' typified the common idealization of these noble robbers, living by a code of honour but refusing to be shackled by society's restrictions.

> He said, the Scriptures I fulfilled,
>   Though this life did I lead,
> For when the naked I beheld,
>   I clothed them with speed:
> Sometimes in cloth and winter-frieze,
>   Sometimes in russet-grey;
> The poor I fed, the rich likewise
>   I empty sent away.[15]

Largesse was considered an essential attribute of a gentleman of the road, and it served a vital dual purpose. Not only did it satisfy an altruistic desire to redistribute the wealth of the rich among the poor, but it also secured support for the highwayman within the local population, ensuring they would protect him against the forces of law, and supply him with food, information, horses or hiding-places when necessary.

Highwaymen worked all over the country, taking advantage of the vast development of the road network across England since the first toll roads were created in the 1660s. These improvements had made travel easier in England than on the continent. It took only four days to go from London to York or to Exeter by stagecoach. The better-paved toll roads favoured highwaymen, too: both by tempting more travellers on to the road, and by making escape easier for the robbers. While some highwaymen, most notably Dick Turpin, were rural brigands, most lived in London and worked on the main arteries leading into and out of the city. They had within easy access the large London network of safe houses and receivers, as well as a concentration of the richest pickings. Ralph Wilson described the successes of the Hawkins gang, of which he was one of six members:

One morning we robbed the Cirencester, the Worcester, the Gloucester, the Oxford and the Bristol stagecoaches, all together; the next morning the Ipswich and Colchester, and a third morning perhaps the Portsmouth coach. The Bury coach has been our constant customer; I think we have touched that coach ten times.

The cheesemonger Jonathan Wild had approached in the Mint, down on his luck, was well aware that he could transform his fortunes by taking to the road as a highwayman. He accepted Wild's offer gratefully, began working around London, and for a time did very well. But soon he started to resent Wild's control over him, particularly his insistence on taking over half his earnings, and disappeared with the horse and guns Wild had given him.

Wild was furious, but powerless until he could discover where his errant associate had fled. In the spring of 1719 he received news that a young highwayman was making the roads around Oxford almost unpassable, and knew he had his man. He obtained a warrant, and 'stuck round with pistols, as thick as an orange with cloves',[16] he set off to Oxford to make an example of this truant. He chased the former cheesemonger across country until he caught up with him and challenged him. The young man said that he wanted to change his ways and lead an honest life, but Wild, who was determined to have his blood, and anyway would never have accepted that excuse for his betrayal, shot him, and took the body to the local magistrate, expecting to be fêted for ridding the area of a known criminal. But the young man, who had grown up near Oxford, was well known there and Wild was arrested for murder. He was released after putting up his bail, 'it having been thought not reasonable to imprison an honest man for killing a rogue',[17] but the whole incident was embarrassing to all concerned: to the authorities, who had unwittingly arrested the man reputed to be the greatest thief-taker in the land; and not least to Wild, whose personal dignity and public reputation, so carefully guarded, were a little tarnished by the unhappy affair.

Wild was always quick to make an example of any villain who thought he could get away with not working for him. One such was John James, a successful highwayman, who, working with his partner Nathaniel Hawes, had been able to support very comfortably a wife, three children and two mistresses. Wild clearly had no option but to get rid of him; it would never have done for the highwaymen who worked for him to see how rich they could be if they didn't have to share their profits with him. Therefore he had persuaded Hawes to inform on James and had secured a warrant for his arrest. Bursting through the door of John James's lodgings in Monmouth Street with the warrant, Wild surprised the outlaw in bed with one of his mistresses.

Another highwayman Wild apparently hunted down successfully was Benjamin Child. Like many of his peers, he was known for his womanizing, gambling and drinking, but he seems also to have been genuinely concerned with the plight of others. On one occasion he freed all the debtors in Salisbury gaol with profits he had made from his robberies. According to his biographer, he made a fortune from his career in crime despite his expenditures: he was reported to have left over £10,000 in his will. Wild was desperate to have the honour of being the man to bring him to justice because he knew the government wanted him caught: Child's actions highlighted the injustice endemic in English society, and his presence encouraged an attitude of defiance.[18] It is not known whether or not Wild actually had a hand in his arrest, but John Hawkins, another highwayman later hanged by Wild, swore he would be avenged on the man who had impeached Child; many believed that man to be Wild.

From 1718 Wild cleared London of all the major gangs working there, either appropriating their members into his Corporation, or making examples of them by sending them to the gallows. He was responsible for the breaking-up of William Spiggott's gang of eight highwaymen, of John Hawkins's gang of six, and Shaw's and

Carrick's gangs of about fifteen footpads each. A measure of his control over London's criminal population was the fact that there were no arrests of highwaymen from 1723 until his death. It was no wonder that his power was unchallenged by any other thief-taker, or that his assumed authority was not squashed by the state, because he was in fact ridding the city of the gangs that had terrorized it for the previous few years.

Wild's control extended beyond London, but it is unclear whether an arrest in a provincial town, credited to him, would have been carried out by him in person, or by one of his agents. He was responsible in some way for capturing criminals in Bristol, Portsmouth, Oxford, Maidstone, Gravesend, Dover and Southampton. Arrests in port towns were usually of returned transportees who had not served out the seven or fourteen years in America to which they had been sentenced.

The 1719 Transportation Act increased Wild's control over the men and women who worked for him. The government extended the system of rewards to include £40 to anyone who could discover and convict a returned transportee. Thus Wild, who previously had indebted people to him only by playing on their poverty or fear, was able to wield his power over a new group of criminals. As well as debtors such as the cheesemonger, who depended on him to live, he had a new set of desperate runaways who depended on him, quite literally, for their lives. Felons who had been transported and returned illegally to England already had experience working in crime, having been tried and convicted of at least one offence, but could not begin an honest life because they had to hide from the law. If they were caught by the authorities – or were given up to them – their lives were forfeit. Working for a man like Wild was their only means of survival because they could remain underground, unnoticed; but Wild could turn them in whenever he pleased, maybe to make an example of them to their peers, or perhaps merely to claim the reward. To him, they were disposable assets, to be used to increase his power and discarded when they were no longer needed.

The two exceptions were Quilt Arnold and Abraham Mendez,

Wild's closest associates. Respectively Clerk of the Northern Road and Clerk of the Western Road (theoretically to control crime on the main arteries into and out of London; in reality, they patrolled these areas as thieves themselves), Wild depended heavily on both men. They acted as deputies when Wild was unavailable, and accompanied him as strong-arm bodyguards when he was on a dangerous thief-taking mission.

Wild's very public assistance to the government in its ineffectual fight against crime, by preying on men and women whose last resort was the life of dependence and parasitism that Wild offered, only enhanced his reputation as a master thief-taker. His ostensible service to the public disguised his lust for power.

And thus by taking some of his own gang now and then, because they disobliged him, and apprehending others because they were not part of his gang, and hanging them . . . he was reckoned a very useful man, and was often called upon by the court to look at the prisoners, and give them characters [references]; which seemed to have great weight at the time.[19]

The authority with which Wild was credited by the courts greatly enhanced his fame, both among his clients and among the criminals. He is mentioned frequently in the popular published accounts of trials, either giving evidence against men he had decided to sacrifice or defending his loyal servants. Wild let it be known that he was on terms of intimacy with London's magistrates, often leaving word at his office that if anyone called for him, he could be found in such-and-such a tavern with Justice So-and-so.

Wild was a past master in the art of self-promotion, creating an image that appealed at once to the respectable middle and upper classes who relied on him to restore their stolen property to them, and to the members of London's criminal underworld who were effectively his servants. He was close not only to justices of the peace, but also to the officials at London's prisons. The Ordinary, or chaplain, of Newgate, as a perk of his job was entitled to publish very popular and very profitable first-hand descriptions of the last days of condemned men — many of whom had been brought to their end by Wild. These accounts showed Wild as a determined thief-taker who always got his man.

By 1720 Wild had become a celebrity. He was recognized wherever he went. For the first time newspapers were now being read by a broad section of London's society, and they contributed immeasurably to Wild's fame and success by portraying him in a positive light. Not only did his use of advertisements keep his name in the news, but his movements were also frequently reported by the London daily and weekly papers, just like those of the aristocracy. His successes were celebrated, and he lost no opportunity to announce them to the world at large.

On Sunday morning, Mr Jonathan Wild had apprehended a gang of about ten persons in Southwark, supposed to be guilty of several robberies on the highway; they were examined before Justice Machen, Marshal of the King's Bench, and most of them committed to the county gaol.[20]

Grub Street was the centre of London's newspaper and broadsheet publishing. In his 'Letter to a Young Poet', Jonathan Swift wrote, 'Everyone knows, Grub Street is a market for small-ware in wit, and as necessary considering the usual purgings of the human brain, as the nose is upon a man's face.' Henry Fielding, like Swift, looked down on Grub Street and its populist attitude towards literature, reflecting the new power and self-confidence of the urban middle class: he said the world of letters as epitomized by Grub Street was becoming 'a democracy, or rather a downright anarchy'.

The term 'hack' originated in this period, derived from the verb to hack, or to turn hackney or prostitute, 'to traffic commercially in something fundamentally admirable, and thus to sully it'. Grub Street was seen as a corrupting influence on literature, doing for the art of writing what prostitution did for sex. One writer decried Grub Street as 'Thou fruitful nursery of tow'ring genius!', using the word 'nursery' deliberately: it was common slang terminology for a brothel.[21]

Johnson's description of his friend the notorious Richard Savage, could be applied just as easily to some hacks today:

He spent his time in mean expedients and tormenting suspense, living for the greatest part in fear of prosecutions from his creditors, and consequently skulking in obscure parts of the town, of which he was no stranger to the remotest corners. But wherever he came, his address secured him friends, whom his necessities soon alienated; so that he had, perhaps, a more numerous acquaintance than any man ever before attained, there being scarcely any person, eminent on any account, to whom he was not known, or whose character he was not, in some degree, able to delineate. To the acquisition of this extensive acquaintance every circumstance of his life contributed. He excelled in the arts of conversation, and therefore willingly practised them. He had seldom any home, or even a lodging in which he could be private; and therefore was driven into public houses for the common conveniences and supports of nature. He was always ready to comply with every invitation, having no employment to withhold him, and often no money to provide for himself; and, by dining with one company, he never failed to obtain an introduction into another. Thus dissipated was his life, and thus casual was his subsistence; yet did not the distinction of his views hinder him from reflection, nor the uncertainty of his condition depress his gaiety.

Despite the harshness of this judgement and the image the name 'Grub Street' conjures up, it was in parts at least a vital industry. It nurtured writers such as Defoe and Swift, who wrote for a middle-class London market enjoying for the first time its own literature and philosophy independent of the élitist world of court and aristocracy. Much of the new literature was based on crime, and Wild was in an ideal position to benefit from this contemporary fascination with criminals and their world.

He also used his appearance to augment his authority in the eyes of the public. Defoe described the figure Wild cut at the height of his power: 'He now became very eminent in his profession of thief-catching, and made a considerable figure in the world, having a silver mounted sword, and a footman at his heels, and scarce an Assize passed but Jonathan slew his man.' This sword, a remnant of his days with Hitchin, was a symbol of nobility. Members of the middle classes who aspired to leave their humble backgrounds behind them wore swords to signify their gentility.

Another similar manifestation of the social aspirations of the lower classes was their insistence on fighting duels. The *Westminster Journal* reported in 1735 that a duel had been fought

behind Montagu House between two journeyman laceweavers . . . One of the parties discharged his pistol, the ball from which took away part of the sleeve of his antagonist's coat, and then like a man of courage without waiting for the fire being returned made the best of his way off the field. The quarrel began at a public house about the mode of cooking a dish of sprats, one insisting on having them fried and the other on having them boiled. With the assistance of some friends, the sum of 3s. was raised to procure the use of pistols to decide this important contest.

As late as 1812, Lord Chief Justice Ellenborough, fed up with dealing with cases involving merchants and tradesmen challenging each other to duels, announced that 'really it was high time to stop this spurious chivalry of the counting-house and counter'.[22]

Wild's weapons served a dual purpose, adding to his image both as a ruthless catcher of ruffians who would stop at nothing to capture his quarry, and as a man of style and gentility.

The people had a notion that his presence frightened away the thieves; and, to countenance this belief, he went doubly and trebly armed, and often wore armour under his clothes, which he took care to show in all companies; being attended by three or four, and sometimes half a dozen, terrible looking fellows by way of *garde du corps.*[23]

Wild went often to fairs with his entourage, conducting business and displaying himself to the criminals who congregated at them. Fairs (illustration 23, page 145; Hogarth's *Southwark Fair*) were well known as centres for distribution of stolen goods and meeting places for criminals. Amid the 'coffee-houses, taverns, eating houses, music shops, buildings for the exhibitions of drolls, puppet shows, . . . mountebanks, wild beasts, monsters, giants, rope dancers, etc.'[24] roamed an indiscriminate gathering of thieves, whores, receivers, swindlers and outlaws, all alert to the opportunity that might present itself at any moment. The hawkers, acrobats, jugglers, quacks and clowns provided a colourful background for this activ-

23. *Southwark Fair* (William Hogarth)

This fair was abolished in 1762 because of the high rate of violence and vice it attracted. Shown here are representatives of London's itinerant population: clowns; strolling players; a bagpiper in the bottom left-hand corner, next to a dog in fancy dress and a table of arguing gamblers; a pretty drummer in the centre; a broadsword fighter ready to meet all challengers on the far right; and a fresh-faced young girl with a look of the young Harlot about her watching him.

ity. Cesar de Saussure visited St Bartholomew's Fair, at Smithfield, but didn't enjoy it much. 'The noise and uproar is so continuous and overwhelming, besides which you run a perpetual risk of being crushed to death, and also of being robbed.' May Fair, which took place annually between Piccadilly and Oxford Road (now Oxford Street), was banned in 1708 because of the 'drunkenness, fornication, gaming and lewdness' that occurred at it.[25]

Wild was seen everywhere, at races, fights, conducting business at coffee-houses, watching the opening of Parliament, as well as at fairs. He attended the hanging of the Waltham Blacks at Reading in 1723, although he had played no part in the capture of any of the miscreants. His connection with the Blacks was probably limited to an involvement with the black market trade in venison in London, although one of the Blacks, Aaron Maddocks, was known by the nickname 'Wild's Man', because he had worked for Wild in London before joining a band of maverick poachers in Enfield.

Wild always carried a silver baton on these expeditions, 'to gain credit with the ignorant multitude',[26] which he claimed represented the authority he had been invested with by the government. The City Marshals (like Hitchin) carried similar silver maces; Wild's appropriation of this symbol of power is evidence not only of his ambition but also of his arrogant egotism. His success was due in part to his creation of 'a public persona as servant of the state' despite his continuing private status.[27] His assumption of this official role, and his image as a government-sanctioned thief-taker, only made it more difficult for the state to challenge his authority or try to curb his ever-growing dominion.

Aspiration

But Wild was not wholly content with his unofficial role as 'Thief-taker General'. Although he had virtual immunity from the law because the service he provided was considered so valuable, his achievements had not been officially recognized. In 1720 he was consulted by the Privy Council about the increase of crime in London. Wild, hoping to augment the income he derived from thief-taking, suggested that the government offer higher rewards to those who turned in wanted criminals. The Council duly instituted a temporary £100 reward for villains apprehended within the London area.

Although Wild benefited economically from this new measure, he still had not been singled out for what he liked to portray as his service to London society. What he wanted above all was professional recognition and social acceptance. In order to accomplish this aim, Wild applied for the Freedom of the City of London late in 1723. He claimed admission because 'Your petitioner has been at great trouble and charge in apprehending and convicting divers felons . . . [and] has never received any reward or gratuity for his service.' His application got as far as a reading in front of the Court of Aldermen on 2 January 1724 but was finally refused, with no reason given.

Wild, undeterred, continued to aspire to bourgeois respectability. He insisted that the work he did was for the benefit of society rather than himself. Is it not possible, he would ask, that a man can serve his country without suspicion? Did not the number of arrests and deaths he had brought about prove his worth to society? Was his office not the only place to go to recover stolen property? Did he not as often as not refuse to accept a fee for the service he provided?

His air of injured innocence when he was accused was part of the front of respectability he assumed hoping that, one day, others would accept it.

Lord Chesterfield, one of Wild's clients, called him *deliciae sui temporis*, but had reservations about the manner in which he conducted business:

His levee was crowded with personages of the first rank, who never regretted any expense or imposition that gave them the opportunity of paying court to so illustrious a man. Jonathan was a merry facetious fellow, had a very dextrous volubility of speech, yet received them rather with an awkward familiarity, than with that submission and civility which he owed to his superiors.

Wild 'kept a country house [in Dulwich], dressed well, and in company affected an air of grandeur'.[1] In the eighteenth century, for a tradesman – for presumably that is how Wild hoped to pass himself off – to own a country house was the first step towards gradual infiltration of the rural gentry and, eventually, he hoped, the aristocracy. A merchant's children would be brought up as the children of a gentleman were, in the country, educated at the same schools, wearing the same clothes, reading the same books; and with the added attraction of a vast fortune might marry well. This tradition of accessibility to the upper echelons of society, usually over a few generations, was well established in England and it was a far easier ladder to climb there than elsewhere in Europe at that time. Defoe quipped,

> Wealth however got, in England makes
> Lords of mechanics, gentlemen of rakes,

but there remained a vast gulf between England's well-off gentry and merchant classes, and their lords.

The English aristocracy lived at this period in a strange mixture of intense formality and almost barbaric crudity and perverse eccentricity. Their clothes, houses, art and manners seemed perfect on the outside; but the metaphorical petticoats under their delicate silk

24. *Vauxhall Pleasure Gardens* (Anon.)

Londoners of all classes spent their leisure hours watching each other as they strolled around the city's public gardens.

gowns were stained. Dining rooms with pale panelled walls, edged in finely carved gilt detailing, held chamber pots so that conversation wouldn't be broken up if anyone needed to relieve themselves during dinner. Ladies' shoes were not only used as champagne glasses, but on one occasion in 1747 a party ate a pair of shoes, sliced and fried in butter, 'to testify their affection for the lady [Fanny Murray, the most beautiful courtesan of her generation]'.[2] Female sexuality was frowned on as unladylike, yet ladies' lapdogs – shock dogs – were-trained to sit under their skirts licking their mistresses' 'love grottoes'.

The urban middle classes reinforced the aristocracy's cultural hegemony by emulating their lifestyle. Merchants' wives stopped working behind the counter, and instead sat in a parlour reading magazines or novels; children were sent away to boarding-school to improve their manners; men and women of all classes dressed up to walk around London, window-shopping, strolling through the parks, just showing off. Fashionable urban recreations were linked not to the seasons, as they were in the country, but centred on what the city had to offer: shopping, going to Bedlam to look at the lunatics, walking 'in whole shoals' through the pleasure gardens of Vauxhall or Greenwich (illustration 24, page 149; engraving of people strolling in Vauxhall Gardens). Perhaps most important, these pursuits were accessible to all sections of society, and the rights to enjoy them were jealously protected by the lower classes. When Queen Caroline asked Robert Walpole how much it would cost to make Hyde Park a royal park, he replied, 'Only three crowns.'

The *Female Tatler* in 1709 recorded a conversation in which

a general complaint was made that the prosperous vulgar take so much upon them in dress, air, equipage and visiting, that people of rank are hardly distinguished from upstart pretenders . . . If they once get a knack of pleasing their betters with novelties, the business of whose life is amusement, and can tongue-pad themselves into a reputation, they immediately get estates, and pretend to look folks in the face. We have our quality midwives that keep coaches, quality mantua-makers that carry home jumps [bodice stays] in [sedan] chairs, nay even quality waiting women that won't stir without a Hackney and a footman.

This preoccupation with social rank extended to all levels of society. 'How contemptibly a cutler looks at a poor grinder of knives, a physician in his coach at a farmer on foot, and a well-grown [St] Paul's churchyard bookseller upon one of the trade that sells second-hand books under the trees at Moorfields.'[3] Even among criminals these distinctions existed. A highwayman considered himself infinitely superior to a house-breaker; a house-breaker realms above a mere pickpocket.

While on one side the poor looked up to and imitated their masters, at the same time many of them deeply resented the privileges and airs they assumed. The poet John Gay in *Trivia*, his account of 1720s London, describes the downfall of a man of fashion at the hands of an embittered dustman.

> I've seen a beau, in some ill-fated hour,
> When o'er the stones choked kennels swell the shower,
> In gilded chariot loll, he with disdain,

Views spattered passengers, all drenched in rain;
With mud filled high, the rumbling cart draws near,
Now rule thy prancing steeds, laced charioteer!
The dustman lashes on with spiteful rage,
His pond'rous spokes thy painted wheel engage,
Crushed is thy pride, down falls the shrieking beau,
The slabby pavement crystal fragments show,
Black floods of mire th'embroidered coat disgrace,
And mud enwraps the honours of his face.

The resentment and scorn with which some members of the lower classes behaved towards their superiors was far more prevalent in London than in the counties; and this disrespect encouraged a parallel disrespect for the law, the purpose of which was to shield the upper classes from the rest of society.

While some of the population belittled the aristocracy, and others emulated it, an articulate, self-conscious middle class was emerging in London in the early eighteenth century. Hogarth and his circle of friends were typical of this new layer of society. His wife was the daughter of Sir James Thornhill, Serjeant Painter to the court of George I; other close friends included an attorney who also wrote a popular ballad-opera, and a merchant adventurer. They were professional men, whose comfortable lives were unmarked by the desperation of the lower classes or the icy refinement of the upper classes.

The changing social order was reflected in the novels that were being written for this new class. Defoe's protagonists are essentially middle-class figures seeking improvement, both material and social. Robinson Crusoe ignores his father's moderate advice, and leaves his home and family to seek his fortune, driven by a 'secret burning lust of ambition for great things'. Moll Flanders's life is devoted to the quest for financial security. Swift's Lemuel Gulliver, a common sea-captain, carries in his pockets spectacles and a pocket telescope, instruments of discovery and learning, as well as the usual eighteenth-century accoutrements of a snuffbox and pocket-watch. Gulliver is from a middle-class background, but wears a sword and carries a pistol, both marks of gentility.

The plots of eighteenth-century novels, while sometimes fantastic, are grounded by attention to physical detail and day-to-day concerns. 'The heroes and heroines of the age are cobblers and kitchen wenches,' commented Lady Mary Wortley Montagu. The extension of the reading class was altering the nature of literature. New sections of society, down to apprentices and servants, were learning to read – and, living in their masters' houses, often had access to novels and free time in which to read them. Their aspirations, attitudes and values were increasingly reflected in the literature directed at them. Together with the widespread dissemination of news through coffee-houses and newspapers, and the efficiency of the new postal service, novels helped create and mould a self-conscious urban middle class.

Men such as Wild who sought to raise their social standing, aspired to this new respectability. This was exemplified in the distinctive dress of the professional classes (lawyers, clergymen and doctors), that was imitated by tradesmen to create an illusion of gravitas and dependability. Their clothes were costumes, elaborate and intended clearly to denote the profession of the wearer. Wild also cultivated an importance of manner. His pride was evident in all his dealings. He treated all his clients as his equals, which was almost revolutionary for the period. He boasted inordinately. He refused to allow people to allude to his alliance with London's underworld, demanding to be accepted as an honest businessman.

The flip side of the new middle-class respectability was, in the view of observers such as John Gay, the emergence of new vices: avarice, masked by hypocrisy. The characters he used in *The Beggars' Opera* to embody these traits, Peachum and Lockit, are consumed by their desire for money, power and social acceptance; for them, as for Jonathan Wild, the means by which they gain these ends are immaterial. As long as the façade they created to conceal their true motives remained intact, they cared not about the consequences of their greed.

Part of Wild's façade, and of the fictional Peachum's, was a duplicitous emphasis on honour. While highwaymen liked to believe they were carrying on a noble, chivalrous tradition as 'Gentlemen of the Road', Wild chose to portray himself as a gentleman of business, carrying out his work to benefit society rather than himself. For this reason, he made a point of always ensuring goods people paid for in advance, before he had located them, were found and returned at the appointed time. The best example of this is the return of the Duchess of Marlborough's sedan chair. Wild was left ten guineas by her frantic footmen, whose negligence had given the thieves time to spirit the chair away. He assured them that the chair would be left outside Lincoln's Inn Chapel at a certain time, and so it was. Later, he prided himself on his handling of the incident as proof of his 'honourable' practices.

On another occasion a grand silk merchant arrived at Wild's office in a state of panic. A bolt of his finest bespoke damask had been stolen as it waited for collection; it was to be made into a suit for the king's birthday party, and the merchant feared for his business if he failed to deliver it in time. In his desperation, he offered to pay thirty guineas to recover the missing fabric that day, but declared he would pay no more than half the sum if it took longer – implying that Wild knew where to get hold of it. Wild, bristling, affronted, insisted nothing could be done in less than a week. A minute later, a man came into his office and asked to speak to Wild in private. After five minutes Wild returned, all smiles, saying, 'I protest, Sir, you're the luckiest man I ever knew!' He said the man who had just come to see him had news of the silk, and he told the draper where to go to collect his goods for only twenty guineas. Wild feigned reluctance to accept the other ten guineas the grateful merchant tried to press on him: ''Tis satisfaction enough, Sir, to an honest man, that he is able to procure people their goods again' – but did accept in the end. Wild emphasized his integrity and desire to serve, while glossing over his connection with thievery; he swallowed the insulting assumption that he was somehow involved with the crime in order to increase his reputation, with a public display of miraculous efficiency.[4]

A newspaper report of May 1724 shows the heights of hypocrisy Wild was prepared to scale to cultivate an image of respectability.

On Sunday last (whilst the family were all at church), the house of Mr Kirby, in Bridgewater Square, was robbed of gold and diamonds to a considerable value: it is supposed that entrance was made by false keys, for, 'tis said, a servant in the neighbourhood saw a person open the door in church-time, whom he took to belong to the family. Jonathan Wild was consulted that evening on this occasion, but he, good man! was pleased to tell those that applied to him, that he did no business on the Lord's Day.[5]

Wild was also susceptible to demonstrations of arrogance that he could not disguise. A certain Lady M. had a diamond buckle stolen from her while she was staying at Windsor Castle, so she came to Wild's office and offered twenty guineas for its recovery. 'Zounds, Madam, you offer nothing – it cost the gentleman who took it from you forty for his coach, equipage and other expenses to Windsor!' he replied. The thief was one of Wild's specially trained Spruce Prigs whose ease in polite circles allowed them to circulate unnoticed in the grandest of company.[6]

Despite his insistent self-importance, Wild was also capable of humour. A group of his Spruce Prigs challenged a bell-ringing club to a competition to see who could ring the loudest.

There were a parcel of rich citizens who took a singular pleasure in ringing bells. One day each week they met and dined together, and passed the rest of the day in ringing; in summertime they travelled from place to place wherever they heard of a good ring of bells, in order to divert themselves with ringing and to try to find where were the sweetest bells. One of our gentry found means of getting into their company; and one night, when they were getting pretty warm with wine, and boasting of their great excellence in ringing, our spark offered that he and five more he would bring should ring with them for two hundred guineas, provided he was to name the bells. They took him up immediately, and entered into articles under a forfeiture of £100 to those that should fail . . .

The prig named Lincoln Cathedral as the venue, and accordingly once the bell-ringers had taken off their coats and wigs, and got into their ringing clothes – drawers, a waistcoat and a cap – Wild's men carried off all their goods and their horses, as well as the money for the wager. 'I saw £300 besides watches, snuffboxes, tobacco-boxes, clothes and periwigs,' Wild declared proudly.[7] But he never dropped the mask of respectability he cultivated so assiduously: however he might seem to mock himself, however he was able to swallow his pride for the sake of his profit, he was always playing the part of a wealthy, respectable businessman.

Lord Chesterfield believed Wild's ambition was due in part to the court paid him by members of the aristocracy.

Condescension of people of a high rank has often an adverse effect upon those in a low one. This was evident in the case of Jonathan Wild. He grew insufferable [sic] arrogant: he had his levee-days, and would only be spoke to upon those days. The rest of the week was given up to his pleasures, his thieves and his mistresses.

Wild's 'wives' also aspired to bourgeois splendour. His association with Mary Milliner had ended in the mid-1710s, and he took up with Elizabeth, or Betty Mann, another Buttock-and-File. She was suddenly overcome with disgust and horror at the life she led, and converted to Catholicism, and died soon after, probably in 1718. This piety touched Wild deeply, and he was devoted to her memory, asking to be buried by her side. 'He loved her above the other women he had taken for wives, and lived publicly with her, which he did not with any of the rest . . . Jonathan retained such an impression of the sanctity and goodness of this wife that he never forgot it as long as he lived. . .'[8]

Three other women who 'supplied the place of wives' followed (or ran parallel to) Betty: Sarah Parrin; Judith Nunn, on whom he had fathered a daughter in about 1715; and Mary Brown, his last 'wife', a noted beauty of the underworld. When Wild set his sights on her, she was married to a robber called Scull Dean, who made it publicly known that he would brook no interference with his wife from Wild despite his position. Wild had him arrested, and sent to the gallows – rather more quickly than was usual – and then took up with Mary. There is no record of their marriage although early accounts of Wild's life say they wed in February 1719. This may have been a sly dig at Wild, for the account states they were married by the Ordinary (pastor) of Newgate; in any case, he still had a legal wife in Wolverhampton, and to marry so publicly would have been blatant bigamy. Except for his attachment to Betty Mann, Wild cherished his independence. 'Thank God I have no wife to follow me to an alehouse; that I can say, I am master of my self, and am not afraid of a bawling daughter of Eve, or tied to anybody's honour but my own.'

Whether or not they actually were married, however, Mary Dean was considered Wild's wife. She was known rather unflatteringly as 'Benefit Jonathan' but took pride in being pointed out as 'Madam Wild'. Mary's pretensions of grandeur were equal to Jonathan's. 'When Madam Wild appeared abroad, she always took the wall of her neighbours [a term for assuming precedence in the street, because taking the wall meant walking away from the mud and splashes of the gutter] with a footman at her arse, with a fine laced livery.'[9] Livery and costume were abiding preoccupations of aspirants like Wild and Mary. People were fascinated by fashion because clothes so clearly defined the wearer's status – but also because the leisured classes took pride in the sheer frivolity of consumption, in which the latest styles in clothing played a large part. Mrs Crakenthorpe, writing for the *Female Tatler*, described her visit to a fabric shop in Ludgate Hill, at the north-east end of Fleet Street, in 1709. Shopping was

as agreeable an amusement as a lady can pass away three or four hours in; the shops are perfect gilded theatres. The variety of wrought silks, so many changes of fine scenes; and the mercers are the performers in the opera, and instead of 'Viviture Ingenio' ['Long Live Genius'; a reference to the inscription above the door] you have in gold capitals 'No Trust by Retail'. They are the sweetest, fairest, nicest dished out creatures, and by their elegant address and soft speeches, you would guess 'em to be Italians. As people glance within their doors they salute 'em with: 'garden silks, ladies, Italian silks, brocades, tissues, cloth of silver, or cloth of gold, very fine Mantua silks, any right Geneva velvet, English velvet, velvets embossed' – and to the meaner sort – 'fine satin threads, both striped and plain, fine mohairs, silk satinets, burdets, perfianets, Norwich crepes, auterines, silks for hoods and scarves — any camlets, drudgets, or sagathies; gentlemen, night-gowns ready made, shalloons, durnaces and right Scotch plaids'.

The variety of materials available shows the overwhelming significance attached to clothes by London's middle classes. Fashions disguised the wearer, making human forms mere mannequins. Hair was pomaded and powdered, faces painted and rouged, busts thrust up, waists cinched in, legs hidden under huge hoop-skirts. But blinding desire to keep up with the latest fashions sometimes led to sartorial mistakes. 'I have often counted fifteen patches, or more, upon the swarthy wrinkled phiz [face] of an old hag three-score and ten, and upwards. Thus the English women refine upon our fashions,' commented the Frenchman Henri Misson.

The ostentatious display of dress that marked eighteenth-century fashions stemmed from the same source as Jonathan Wild's professional arrogance: a constant desire to better oneself in the eyes of the world, to rise a step higher, to leave the old life behind and prove oneself in the new.

[Wild had only to keep] his compting house, or office, like a man of business, and had his books to enter everything in with the utmost regularity . . . [and he might have] carried on such a commerce as this, with the greatest ease, I do not say honesty, in the world, if he had gone no further . . . So that in a word, Jonathan's *Avarice* hanged him.[10]

Fame

On 9 October 1724, the day before Thomas Sheppard was transported for the robbery in which he had impeached Jack and Edgworth Bess, Blueskin Blake was arrested by Jonathan Wild, Abraham Mendez and Quilt Arnold. All three appeared at his trial five days later and gave evidence against him. Mendez testified that he had gone with Wild to arrest Blake,

and, as we were coming by the prosecutor's house, Mr Wild said to the prisoner, 'There's the ken [man; victim]!' and he answered, 'Say no more, Mr Wild, for I know I am a dead man; but what I fear is that I shall be carried to the Surgeons' Hall and anatomized.' [Dissected; it was a common medical practice to dissect the bodies of criminals in front of students.] To which Mr Wild replied, 'No, I'll take care to prevent that, for I'll give you a coffin.'

Quilt Arnold followed Mendez:

I went with Abraham and Mr Wild to apprehend the prisoner, and, going to his chamber door, I bid him open it, but he swore he would not, and so I burst it open. He drew a penknife, and swore he would kill the first man that came in: 'Then I am the first man,' says I, 'and Mr Wild is not far behind, and if you don't deliver your penknife immediately, I'll chop your arm off.' Then he threw the knife down and I apprehended him. I afterwards heard Mr Wild promise to give him a coffin.

Then William Field took the stand. He gave his evidence as he had done at Sheppard's trial, but the tone of his testimony was altered slightly to implicate Blueskin further than he had done at Jack's trial, where his (and Wild's) main aim had been to ensure

Jack's conviction. He started by saying that he did not know Jack well, except through Blueskin – but Jack had been fencing his takings through him since before he started working with Blake. Field said that Blueskin, on his own, asked him to join with him and Jack to rob Kneebone's house – though at Jack's trial, Field had said that Jack had persuaded both Blueskin and himself, at the same time. In the evidence he had given at Jack's trial, Field had said that as soon as he and Blake agreed to join in the burglary, Jack had led them to Kneebone's house and then robbed it alone. Now, at Blake's trial, Field said that he accompanied Blueskin to find Jack, and then they went together to Kneebone's house. Once there, he continued, all three of them entered the house to carry off the loot. At Jack's trial, he had insisted that Sheppard had gone in alone while he and Blake kept watch outside. Field was obviously following Wild's orders; and Wild was determined that both Jack and Blueskin should go down for good.

Blueskin, like Sheppard, maintained that Field had not been with them when they robbed Kneebone, but had merely found out about the robbery from them later. Listening to Field's false evidence, he must have realized that Wild was finally casting him off. In the baildock after the trial, Blake begged Wild to help get his sentence changed from hanging to transportation. Like everyone who had worked for Wild, Blueskin thought there was nothing Wild couldn't accomplish if he wanted to. Knowing that Sheppard was going to die for the crime, he thought it possible that as an accomplice he might get off more lightly if Wild spoke on his behalf. 'You may as well put in a good word for me as for another person,' he ventured. Wild replied, 'You are certainly a dead man, and will be tricked upon very speedily.'

On hearing this, with his hopes of survival shattered, Blueskin suddenly drew a clasp penknife and lunged forward, cutting Wild's throat. Blood spurted out from the wound, and he collapsed and was carried off to a surgeon. Blueskin later explained his motivation:

None prompted him to that assault, but a sudden thought entered that moment into his mind, or else he should have provided a better knife, which would have cut off a head directly; adding, that he had so acted, because, that person, as he thought, could have obtained transportation for him; as one man, Sheppard, was condemned for the same offence before.[1]

When the judge asked Blueskin how he dared attempt to commit murder in court, he said 'he was only sorry that he had not done it, for never did such a rogue as Wild live, and go unpunished so long'. Later, he publicly apologized for not killing the 'Viper', saying,

he should be hanged with pleasure if Wild did but die before him . . . Blueskin being examined at what induced him to do so base an action after Mr Wild had supported him at his own expense while he had been in Newgate, declared, 'That he had fully determined to murder him, and that his intention was to have cut off his head and thrown it into the Sessions House yard among the rabble,' and cursed with many bloody oaths both his hand and his knife, for not doing it effectually.[2]

Jack Sheppard, sitting in the security of the Castle, heard the news of Blueskin's attack with glee. Newgate was in an uproar, its inhabitants divided between those who depended on Jonathan Wild for their survival, and those who hated him for bringing them to justice. 'Blueskin's Ballad', attributed to Swift, was published soon after this incident.

> Ye fellows of Newgate, whose fingers are nice
>   At diving in pockets, or cogging of dice;
> Ye sharpers so rich, who can buy off the noose;
> Ye honest poor rogues, who die in your shoes;
>   Attend, and draw near,
>   Good news you shall hear,
> How Jonathan's throat was cut from ear to ear;
>   How Blueskin's sharp penknife hath set you at ease,
> And ev'ry man round me, may rob, if he please.

That night, Jack's gaoler asked him if he needed anything else, because he would not be able to come back to check on him before morning. Jack bade him come as early as possible the following day, well knowing that the confusion that had ensued after Blake's celebrated attack would last the night. As soon as the keeper left Jack set to work. It was the best chance for escape he would get. 'When a man works for Life, 'tis natural to suppose, he'll put the best foot foremost; so did Sheppard; and about twelve o'clock he worked out his Redemption with dexterity of hand and magnanimity of heart. . .'[3]

He had no candle to illuminate his work, but holding in his teeth a crooked nail he had found on the floor and secreted on his person, he picked the locks of his handcuffs. He left his leg irons on, but was able to twist and break the links holding them to the staples in the floor; he used the scraps of metal later as tools. Using a thick iron bar he pulled out of the chimney, he climbed up through the chimney and broke through a wall into another strong-room, called the Red Room, which had not been used for seven years, since the last of the Jacobites was executed. Jack wrenched open the locks and forced his way in. He went through five other strong doors, breaking all the locks and bolts in his way, and into the chapel. Using one of the iron spikes on the wall, he got himself out on to an outside wall which sided on to a neighbouring house. Here he realized that he had no way of letting himself down and crept back the way he had come to collect his blanket from his cell. He rushed back to the wall, and climbed slowly down in the early hours of the morning, using his blanket as a rope, narrowly avoiding waking the sleeping inhabitants of the house next door. They heard him moving and called out, but when there was no reply he heard them assuring each other that it must have been only a cat, or a door slamming in the wind.

London exploded in shock and excitement. Jack's escape was, unusually for a crime report, the opening feature in many newspapers. 'Nothing contributes so much to the talk of the town at present, as the frolicksome and desperate adventures of the famous house-breaker and gaol-breaker John Sheppard.'[4] On 20 October the first biography of Jack Sheppard was advertised in the *Daily Journal*; *The History of the Remarkable Life of John Sheppard* was published by John Applebee, and was most probably written by the ageing Daniel Defoe who worked closely with Applebee throughout his career on Grub Street. 'I don't remember any felon in this kingdom, whose adventures have made so much noise as Sheppard's,' stated the recorder of the *Annals of Newgate*.

Still in his irons, Jack hid in a cowshed near Tottenham Court Road for two days. He told a passing journeyman shoemaker he had been put into a house of correction for fathering a bastard child, and gave him 20s. – well over a week's wages – to bring him tools to rid himself of his shackles. Jack 'tied a handkerchief about [his] head, tore [his] woollen cap in many places, as likewise [his] coat and stockings'. Disguised as a beggar, he set off into the city. Disguise was a crucial element in Jack's successful escapes. After the last one he and Page had dressed as butchers to leave London unnoticed; and he continued to use his ability to appear to be someone else to roam anonymously through the city as he pleased.

The next day, I took shelter in an alehouse of little or no trade, in Rupert Street, near Piccadilly. The woman and I discoursed much about Sheppard. I assured her it was impossible for him to escape out of the kingdom, and that the keepers would have him again in a few days. The woman wished a curse might fall on those who should betray him [did she recognize his diminutive figure and wry smile?]. I continued there till the evening, when I stept towards the Hay Market, and mixt with a crowd about two ballad singers; the subject being about Sheppard. And I remember the company was very merry about the matter.[5]

Was he pleased to hear his name on the lips of everyone he met? Did he long to throw off his ripped cap and shout out that he was the genius whom they were all applauding? Or did he fear for his life, knowing that his capture was worth £40 to anyone who recognized him? Speculation about when and if he would be recaptured ran wild. One newspaper reported that Sheppard had 'been seen two or three days ago, begging some wort [drink] of the stoker at Tate's and Nichol's Brewhouse in Thames Street. If he is so poor as not to be able to purchase drink, an account may soon be expected of his being retaken.'

25. *Industry and Idleness VII: The Idle 'Prentice Returned from Sea and in a Garret with a Common Prostitute* (William Hogarth)

Tom and his whore lie in bed in an attic, the door bolted and blocked, pistols on the floor beside the bed. While the girl greedily examines their loot, Tom, fearful of capture, is startled by a cat jumping down the chimney. The medicine pots, wine bottle and glasses are testaments to the debauched life they have been leading.

Despite the risk of being recognized, he did not wish to wander the streets of London alone. He hired a garret in Newport Market (illustration 25, above) and sent for a 'sober young woman [probably Kate Cook] who for a long time had been the real mistress of my affections, who came to me and rendered all the assistance she was capable of affording'. Edgworth Bess was in gaol for helping Jack escape from Newgate in August, but he had tired of her anyway and instead sought out Kate Cook and Kate Keys, with whom he lived for a few days in Cranbourn Alley, near Leicester Fields. His feet-locks and handcuffs were found in their room after his recapture. Although Bess had always been the foremost among Jack's female acquaintances, he had never tied himself to her. Like Macheath in *The Beggars' Opera*, he enjoyed the company of many women: 'A man who loves money, might as well be contented with one guinea, as I with one woman.' In December 1725 Kate Cook was tried for possessing stolen silver cutlery which she said she had had 'from Jack Sheppard'. It was common for thieves to use their girlfriends and wives as fences; Jack had used both Edgworth Bess and Poll Maggott in this role before he was arrested. At her trial Kate added, 'with a vulgar double entendre, that she was Jack Sheppard's washerwoman, and had many a time washed his three pieces betwixt her legs'.

But like all good criminals, Jack loved no woman more than his mother. Several days after his escape, she visited him in the garret he was sharing with the two Kates, 'begging on her bended knees of me to make the best of my way out of the kingdom, which I faithfully promised; but I cannot say it was in my intentions heartily to do so'. Distraught, his mother went to St James's Palace to petition the king for mercy. 'Some are of the opinion, that the intercession of some great personages in that unhappy man's behalf, may prevail for the same.'[6]

Some of the published lives of Jack Sheppard include copies of the letters he was supposed to have written during this period of freedom. One was addressed to his warden at Newgate, Mr Austin, signed 'from your fortunate prisoner, Jack Sheppard'. He taunted him about the success of his escape: 'But pray not be angry about the loss of your irons; had you not gave me them, I had not taken them away; but really I had left them behind me, had convenience a-served.' He reputedly also wrote to Applebee, the publisher of his biography, commiserating with him for the loss of profits he would suffer by not being able to publish Jack's 'Last Dying Speech' at his execution; he delivered this missive himself, disguised as a porter.[7]

On the night of 29 October he broke into a pawnshop in Drury Lane belonging to two brothers named Rawlins. When he was inside, he realized that they heard him 'rifling their goods as they lay abed. And though there were none to assist me, I pretended there was, by loudly giving out directions for shooting the first person through the head that presumed to stir.' He took a black silk suit, a silver sword, some diamond rings, snuffboxes and watches, a wig and some cash: all he needed to equip himself for a night on the town. The following day, attired in his new clothes, he recounted:

I made an extraordinary appearance; and from a carpenter and butcher was now transformed into a perfect gentleman; and in company with my sweetheart aforesaid, and another young woman of her acquaintance, went into the city, and were very merry together at a public house not far from the place of my old confinement.

Jack and the two Kates spent a happy day together as Jack boldly revisited the haunts of his misspent youth. Unrepentant, he revelled openly in his freedom, knowing all the while his captors would be edging closer and closer to their prey.

At four that same afternoon we all passed under Newgate in a hackney coach, the windows drawn up, and in the evening I sent for my mother to the Sheers alehouse in Maypole Alley near Clare Market (where she lived) and with her drank three quarterns of brandy; and after leaving her I drank in one place or another about that neighbourhood all the evening, till the evil hour of twelve, having been seen by many of my acquaintance; all of them cautioning me, and wondering at my presumption to appear in that manner.

Despite the dangers, Jack enjoyed flaunting his freedom in front of his old cronies. At the end of the evening, he and Moll Frisky were roaring drunk in a public house when its owner, a constable, ordered his arrest.

At length my senses were quite overcome with the quantities and varieties of liquors I had all the day been drinking, which paved the way for my Fate to meet me; and when apprehended, I do protest, I was altogether incapable of resisting, and scarce knew what they were doing to me, and had but two second-hand pistols scarce worth carrying about me.

He was taken off to Newgate in a coach, calling out, 'Murder! Help for God's sake! Rogues! I am murdered, and am in the hands of bloodhounds, help for Christ's sake. . .' *Parker's London News* reported that Jack was arrested, equipped in every way like a gentleman, having on a peruke [wig] worth six or seven guineas, a diamond ring on his finger, with a cornelian, and two other plain gold rings, a gold watch, and snuffbox in his pocket, nine guineas, and some silver. He was dressed in a very genteel suit of black, having furnished himself therewith on Friday morning last, by breaking open a pawnbroker's shop on Drury Lane . . . When he was brought back to gaol he was very drunk, carried himself insolently, and defied the keepers to hold him with all their irons, art and skill.

Jack was loaded with 300 lb. weight of irons in the Middle Stone Room, next to the Castle, the room from which he had last escaped. It was 1 November 1724, barely eighteen months after his first robbery, and he had become the most notorious criminal in the country. But he had neither killed nor injured anyone in the course of his career; the burglaries he committed were usually impromptu, haphazard; his work had, in fact, been marked more by his sense of humour than by violence or greed. From the moment he distracted the crowd's attention on to the Roundhouse roof, after his first break from gaol, to his calling of directions to imaginary accomplices as he robbed the Rawlins's pawnshop the day before he was recaptured, his wit had entranced the people of London.

While Jack was in Newgate, he was 'always cheerful and pleasant to a degree, as turning almost everything as was said into a jest and banter'.[8] Even Mr Kneebone, whom Jack had used so ill, could not bring himself entirely to condemn him.

Although his crimes were audacious and many, yet the boldness in his attempts, and the presence of mind he always had to release himself out of difficulties, made him pitied even by his enemies, and those very persons whom he had injured, could not but say, it was a pity such an ingenious fellow should be a thief.[9]

Sheppard was visited by over a thousand people in the first week after his recapture, each paying 4s. a visit – a shilling more than the usual fee; the turnkeys made a fortune. He was given money by his visitors, too, but because he was so tightly tied up, he had no use for it, and so he gave what he had to other prisoners who were worse off than him. Although he must have felt like an exhibit in a zoo, he enjoyed the attention he received, and strove to make his visitors feel they had their money's worth.

Jack 'usually sent the company away, who came to see him, with as much pleasure as admiration: for although he was so strictly chained down to the floor, which must needs be a pain to him, yet he took as much delight in giving people answers, as they did in asking him'.[10] He had an opinion about everything, and took a particular delight in justifying his crimes. If his robberies were 'ill in one respect, they were as good in another; and that though he cared not for working so much himself, yet he was desirous that others should not stand idle, more especially those of his own trade, who were always repairing of his breaches'.[11]

Sir James Thornhill, tutor and father-in-law of the young Hogarth and Serjeant Painter to King George I, came to Jack's cell to paint him, emphasizing the strength and delicacy of the thief's hands, and his childlike face. The painting does not survive, but a mezzotint engraving taken from the portrait still exists (illustration 26, page 168). Verses addressed to Thornhill in the *British Journal* implied that it was only in painting Jack Sheppard that Thornhill's fame would rest; that, having made Sheppard immortal – 'Thy pencil brings a kind reprieve/And bids the dying robber live' – Thornhill guaranteed his own artistic reputation. The king himself sent for 'two prints of Sheppard showing the manner of him being chained to the floor in the Castle at Newgate'; James Figgs, the prize-fighter, visited him in his cell; the Lord Chancellor, the Earl of Macclesfield, made a point of meeting him when he was resentenced at the King's Bench on 10 November.

A letter dated 6 November from Walpole's Secretary of State, the Duke of Newcastle, ordered the Attorney General to bring Sheppard before the King's Bench to be sentenced again to death, 'to the end that execution may without delay be awarded against him'. Because of his popularity, Jack was regarded as highly dangerous, potentially incendiary. It was not the threat he posed as a thief that made it necessary to hang him as quickly as possible; it

26. *Jack Sheppard* (engraved by G. White from a painting
by Sir James Thornhill)

was what he represented. If he escaped again, if he succeeded in
slipping the shackles of authority once more, he would demonstrate
to the poor of London that the state's control over them was little
more than illusory.

Jack went to court for the last time on 10 November, and was
told that if he would inform on his accomplices – and thus tar

himself with the brush of betrayal and diminish his honour by informing on his friends – he could save himself from the gallows.
Jack replied that the judges knew all his accomplices in his robberies already: his brother Tom, who had just been transported; Blueskin Blake, who was awaiting execution; William Page, who had
been arrested with him at Finchley Common; and Edgworth Bess,
who had been arrested at Wild's instigation after helping Jack escape through the window of the condemned cell. Jack insisted that
his only accomplice in his last escape had been 'God Almighty'.
The shocked judges berated him for his profanity; if he had been
assisted by supernatural intervention, they believed it was the devil
who had come to his aid, not God. But Jack steadfastly refused to
name any accomplice, offering as proof of this statement to display
his skills by extricating himself from his handcuffs if the judge
would have them put on him. Although a man and a woman had
been found with some of the goods Jack had stolen from the Rawlins's pawnshop in Drury Lane, and arrested, he refused to implicate them, and they were let go.

As Justice Powys could get nothing out of Jack, he was resentenced to death as the Duke of Newcastle had decreed. He was
taken back to Newgate, and put into the condemned hold to await
his execution. A constable trying to keep back the waiting crowd
that surged forward to see Sheppard as he was taken from Westminster Hall to Newgate had his leg broken in the crush.

Back in his cell at Newgate, Jack expounded on his theory of loyalty. 'If all were such Tight-Cocks as himself, the reputation of British thievery might be carried to a far greater height than it had been
done for many ages, and . . . there would be but little necessity for
gaolers and hangmen.'[12] He remained utterly loyal to Page and to
Blueskin Blake. In the autobiography published by Applebee, Jack
adds a revealing postscript to his life story: 'After I had escaped
from the Castle, concluding that Blueskin would certainly be decreed for death I did fully resolve and purpose to have gone out
and cut down the gallows the night before his execution.'

Meanwhile, Blueskin, who had fallen dangerously ill in October (he had not been expected to survive to be hanged), had recovered. He and his cell-mate, Abraham Daval, a forger, were caught trying to saw through their irons. Two days later, on 11 November, the day after Sheppard's trial, they were hanged.

Blueskin, being delivered by the Keepers of Newgate, and put into the cart at the foot of the stone steps, a great quarrel arose among the sheriff's officers concerning Daval's going in a coach; during the disorder, Blueskin with his teeth got his handstrings off, and was endeavouring to loose the halter with which he was tied, and to have escaped out of the cart, the crowd countenancing the attempt by a profound silence, &c. But the heat being over, the officers found out what he was doing, and prevented his design.[13]

Blueskin turned to drink to still his terror as he faced death. It was vitally important to put on a brave face before one died, as the words to a seventeenth-century ballad showed: 'His heart's not big, that fears a little rope.'[14] Despite these brave sentiments, many condemned to the gallows went to their executions incapable of walking unsupported, weeping uncontrollably, screaming and fainting. Though Blueskin 'drank deeply to drive away fear, yet at the place of execution he wept again, [and] trembled'.[15] He was remembered as the man who had nearly killed Jonathan Wild. 'Joseph Blake alias Blueskin was notorious for many things, and only famed for one, that is, in attempting to cut Jonathan Wild's throat, which he not doing effectually, was the only thing that grieved him. . .'[16]

PART FOUR

'The fury after licentious and luxurious pleasures
is grown to so enormous a height, that it may be called
the characteristic of the age.'

HENRY FIELDING,
Charge to Westminster Grand Jury, 1749

Law

Although there was a well-established legal system in eighteenth-century England, with an equally well-established popular tradition of using that system to settle disputes, there was as yet no modern police force to enforce the nation's laws. The tired system which existed was based on medieval structures which had long been outgrown, particularly in London where the centuries had effected more change than in slow-moving rural areas.

In England's counties, justice emanated down from a royally appointed Lord Lieutenant, who in turn appointed unpaid justices of the peace, or magistrates, who played both administrative and judicial roles. These men, like Lord Lieutenants, were usually chosen because of their wealth, land and birth; from 1732 JPs had to own lands that brought them over £100 in income per annum. Some were active, and had a working knowledge of the law; many more accepted the position for the 'credit and title in their county' that accompanied it, but stopped short of 'giving themselves the trouble of doing the duty'.[1] In 1714 only three-quarters of the newly appointed JPs in Kent took the optional oath to play an active role; still more swore to do their duty, but failed. The reasons for this inertia were manifold. Many of the magistrates' tasks were boring administrative ones – they were responsible for the regulation of wages, distributing Poor Relief, settling local disputes and mediating in local rivalries. These duties took up a lot of time, and, if properly done, were expensive. The magistrate's office had once been seen as an honour, a patriotic duty; but it had become a burden that few were willing to shoulder. In 1751 the reforming JP, Henry Fielding, dismissed the majority of the justices for being 'as regardless of the law as ignorant of it'.

Many areas fell between the city's confused boundaries: St Giles bordered the municipalities of both London and Westminster but was included in neither – possibly because neither borough wanted to claim such a poor slum area. In addition, very few rich gentlemen in London were willing to take on the responsibilities of the magistracy, because of the high incidence of crime in the city and the onerous burdens of the duties they would be expected to undertake. Therefore, London JPs were often what was known as 'trading justices', who used their offices for personal gain, rather than in the traditionally paternalistic spirit originally envisaged by the system. Fielding's description of Justice Thrasher's ignorance and corruption in *Amelia* was typical of London magistrates in this period: 'To speak the truth plainly, the Justice was never indifferent in a cause, but when he could get nothing on either side.' Law in London was becoming a 'bureaucratic lottery'.[2]

While magistrates were supposed to handle the judicial and administrative sides of county affairs, sheriffs, also ostensibly under the guidance of the Lord Lieutenant, dealt with the military concerns. They mustered and trained the local militias, and in cases of emergency, such as a food riot or a Jacobite rising, led them against the rebels. If a murderer was on the loose, or a convict had escaped, the sheriff or JP – or, indeed, any responsible citizen – would raise 'hue and cry' and the *posse comitatum* (literally, power of the company; every adult male in the county) would ride out to capture the miscreant. This system was woefully badly organized; until 1735 no officer was specifically responsible for raising the cry. In London the sheriff used the gaolers of Wood Street Compter as his official armed escort. They were known as 'Javelin Men' and their duties included marching alongside the condemned men on their way to Tyburn (see illustration 30, page 218).

Parish watches and constables were responsible for keeping the peace on a day-to-day basis. This system dated back to the thirteenth century and was, by 1700, completely inadequate for the needs of a large city like London. Parish laws, which included provisions for street lighting (each house was required to have a lantern hanging by its front door) and for pavements (it was the duty of the house-holder to build and maintain a pedestrian path along his house-front), had, by the eighteenth century, outgrown the areas they were meant to control. The laws were based on the principle that householders should share the responsibility for the protection of their properties. In practice, these regulations were far better heeded in some areas than in others, according to the wealth of the tenants: richer house-holders could afford to pay for well-lit streets, wide pavements and efficient watchmen, while the poor did not have the luxury of choice.

Every year, each parish elected constables from its men whose duty was to patrol the night-time streets, stopping suspicious-looking individuals and questioning them as to their intentions, keeping their eyes open for any wrong-doing. Constables were ap-pointed, unpaid, for the term of a year, but to properly perform their parish duties they often had to neglect their normal business. Thus most appointees chose to pay a deputy constable to act in their place. Because the constable-elect had to pay for his deputy himself, he tended to hire the cheapest, and often, therefore, most incapable, man available. They were

chosen out of those poor old decrepit people who are, from their want of strength, rendered incapable of getting a livelihood by work. These men, armed only with a pole, which some of them are scarcely able to lift, are to secure the persons and houses of his Majesty's subjects from the attacks of gangs of young, bold, stout, desperate and well-armed villains.[3]

Because of their extreme poverty, which had obliged them to take this thankless job in the first place, constables were particularly sus-ceptible to bribery.

There was obviously a little confusion as to exactly what the con-stables' duties were, as this 1724 advertisement shows:

Just published, *The Complete Constable*, directing constables, headboroughs, tithing-men, church-wardens, overseers of the poor, surveyors of the high-ways, and scavengers, in the duty of their offices, according to the power allowed them by the laws, wherein the constable's duty, relating to the passing of rogues, vagabonds, and sturdy beggars is fully set forth. To which is added, abstracts of an act for preventing riots, &c.. Act for punishing robberies committed in houses. Act for preventing mischiefs by fire. Printed for and sold by Tho. Norris at the Looking Glass on London Bridge. Price bound, one shilling.[4]

The difficulties of the deputy constable's job were compounded by his lack of any official powers. He did not wear a uniform that would distinguish him from other passers-by, or lend him authority in their eyes. He was not allowed to search or forcibly enter any property. He could not pursue a criminal beyond the boundaries of his parish, or arrest the perpetrator if he was as little as one step outside his jurisdiction. (In London, parish areas were tiny: there were 676 in the City of London alone.) His powers of arrest were limited, and he could be held personally accountable for a wrongful arrest, or if someone he had arrested later escaped. It was far easier, and safer, for him to keep his eyes to the ground, and accept a penny or two to keep his mouth shut if by chance he happened to see something he shouldn't have. Furthermore, the people scorned the efforts of their constabulary to maintain order or enforce restrictions. When William Vanderman's Covent Garden gambling-house was raided in 1722, he shouted rudely, 'A turd on your proclamation! I don't give a fart for it!' at the constables.[5]

In 1655 Oliver Cromwell had set up a *gendarmerie* on the French model, but it proved so unpopular that within eighteen months he was forced to abolish it. The British considered their lack of an effective police force a matter for national pride. (The word police as we use it now is anachronistic; it was not in use in England until the nineteenth century.) In the eighteenth century a police force was a standing army. The French name for policemen, *gendarmes*, was derived from the word for soldiers, *gens d'armes*, because the first policemen were soldiers left idle in peacetime. In England, soldiers were more likely to be criminals, tempted to fight for king and country by the offer of two guineas and a new suit of clothes, than crime-fighters.

Despite the increase in crime, and the perpetual threat of popular risings, the English staunchly refused to form a standing army or a permanent police force, believing it would infringe on individual liberties. They believed a police force might be corrupted into a network of government spies, or still worse, a private state army. Vagrancy had plagued English governments since Elizabeth I's time, but imprisoning beggars *en masse*, as the French had done since the seventeenth century, was seen as too drastic a step (although individual cases had always been punished by incarceration). Relative stability such as that enjoyed by France was too high a price to pay for the loss of freedom. Liberty was the birthright of every free-born Englishman (this meant male landowners only; women, children and servants were excluded).

There is nothing an Englishman can value himself upon beyond any other subject in the world, so much as the enjoyment of liberty; a Frenchman, a Spaniard, or an Italian, may boast of a finer climate, a sweeter air, and a soil productive of greater delicacies for the uses of life, but wanting liberty, they want that which must give a value to all the rest.[6]

The idea of an Englishman's birthright, determined not by his station in life but by his nationality and individual freedom, permeated political thought at this time. The revolutions of the seventeenth century, although not (strictly speaking) popularly inspired, had shown Englishmen of all classes that their views could affect the government of their country. Despite the supremacy of the Whig aristocracy, their domination of property and law, every Englishman believed he had certain inalienable rights: freedom of speech and conscience, freedom to own property, freedom from foreign rule and domestic tyranny, freedom from arbitrary government. Although the philosophies that bolstered the position of the governing classes emphasized their exclusive right to rule, there was a prevailing belief that rich and poor were born and died equal, regardless of how fate had determined their rank or fortune. Jonathan Wild, who refused to kowtow to his aristocratic clients, and Jack Sheppard, who defied the rigid structures of eighteenth-century society, were living proponents of this new democratic world-view.

It was not just people at court or directly involved in politics who held strong opinions on public affairs and argued them volubly. Joseph Addison commented of this period that 'There is scarce any man in England of what denomination soever, that is a free-thinker in politics, and hath not some particular notions of his own . . . Our nation, which was formerly called a nation of saints, may now be called of statesmen.' This egalitarianism shocked some foreign visitors, who were used to seeing the lower classes cowed and beaten; but it excited others, such as Voltaire, who saw in it the realization of their ideals of democracy and individual freedom. The right to protest, while often annoying to governments and sometimes threatening, was also a cause for pride. 'Better to be governed by a mob than a standing army.'[7] 'I love a mob,' said the Duke of Newcastle, Secretary of State under Robert Walpole. 'I headed one once myself.'

Generally speaking, popular risings were highly localized, and resulted from specific grievances. They were cathartic, providing an outlet for pent-up frustration almost more than actively seeking reform: once their grievances were aired, the rioters usually dispersed. Despite the élite's fears of popular radicalism, most mobs sought to defend an existing situation against proposed changes. The Black Act of 1723 provoked perhaps the most important uprising of the early eighteenth century. New penalties against poaching, a crime seen by the landowners as a form of rebellion against their authority, provoked violent resistance. A virtual 'woodland war' broke out in some areas, most notably Waltham Forest in Hampshire. Poachers with blackened faces (hence their name, the Waltham Blacks) fought gamekeepers to defend what they saw as their traditional rights, which were being usurped by selfish landlords.[8] This situation exemplified the gradual extension during the eighteenth century of laws to protect individual property. Crime was being defined in new ways, and what had once been considered acceptable – for example, an estate worker helping himself to the occasional stag – was increasingly defined as illegal.

Smaller risings were common. In 1720 7,000 journeymen tailors struck in London, and were forbidden by Parliament to 'combine' in the future. Factory workers, frustrated by their lack of control over their lives, took to 'machine-breaking'; in 1727 smashing stocking frames was made a capital offence. The literature of these disputes often displayed a naivety and paranoia that reveal the ignorance of their organizers. 'To the damned eternal firebrands of Hell belonging to Odiham [Hampshire] and its vicinity. In other words to the damned villains of farmers that withhold the grain,' stated one manifesto. 'Both simple and gentle shall starve if any do,' averred another. Horace Walpole ascribed the mob's motivation to the dullness of their lives. 'The dreariness of provisions incites, the hope of increase of wages allures, and drink puts them in motion.' They were a 'sable shoal' with 'destinies obscure'. Because the mass of the population during this period had little notion of the future – they lived for the present, did not have savings or mortgages, worked when there was work and rested when there was none – risings generally erupted spontaneously, with little planning, and had short-term objectives.

One exception was an incident that took place in 1765, and was described by the *Northampton Mercury*. An announcement was placed in the newspaper on 29 July:

This is to give notice to all gentlemen gamesters and well-wishers of the cause now in hand, that there will be a football play in the fields of Haddon aforesaid, on Thursday the 1st day of August, for a prize of considerable value; and another good prize to be played for on Friday the 2nd. All gentlemen players are desired to appear at any of the public houses in Haddon aforesaid each day between the hours of ten and twelve in the forenoon, where they will be joyfully received and kindly entertained.

The next issue of the paper, on 5 August, carried the following report:

We hear from West-Haddon, in this county, that on Thursday and Friday last a great number of people being assembled there, in order to play a football match, soon after meeting formed themselves into a tumultuous mob, and pulled up and burned the fences designed for the enclosure of that field, and did other considerable damage.

This rising was probably planned, with the advertisement a pre-arranged signal; but it is typical of many others in that it was merely a demonstration that dispersed once its goal had been achieved. The reference to 'gentlemen players' in the initial announcement shows the aspirations of the protesters to gentle status – and thus, to the right to have their opinions heard. The social ambitions that marked these rioters were manifest also in Jonathan Wild's yearnings for respectability and acceptance by his betters.

Popular risings were part of a long-standing tradition in England, dating back to the Middle Ages. As was the case in many medieval rebellions, eighteenth-century mobs were often manipulated by powerful individuals to further their own ends. The Duke of Newcastle's remark about having headed a mob is significant not only because it shows the aristocracy's paternalistic pride in the courage and determination of the English lower classes, but also because he implies he used the force of a mob for his own purposes.

London was considered by contemporaries to be one of the most volatile cities in Europe in the eighteenth century. It was 'an insecure city where King Mob might at any time resume his reign after the briefest interregnum'.[9] But for all the terror the idea of a riot could inspire, the English ruling classes steadfastly refused to control the country by instituting methods that would endanger the traditional freedoms on which the nation prided itself, and which it believed were making England great.

Throughout the seventeenth century England had been weakened by civil war; diplomatically, she was still less powerful than France or Spain in the early eighteenth century, but both politically and commercially was emerging as an important force on the world stage. The eighteenth century was dominated by images of England's greatness: 'Rule Britannia' and 'God Save the King' were written, as were the songs 'The Old Roast Beef of England', Fielding's oral version of Hogarth's 1748 painting of *The Gate of Calais*, and 'Hearts of Oak'. Cesar de Saussure thought there was no nation 'more prejudiced in their own favour than the British people'.

The English were a 'self-conscious nation, openly proud of their virtues and secretly fascinated by their vices'.[10] They saw their virtues as solid good sense, independence, industriousness and honesty. 'As they have in all times been fond of liberty, they can't bear constraint. They are not given to talking, but when they speak, 'tis not so much to flatter a great man as to tell the truth,' wrote Baron Muralt in 1726. Seven years earlier, his countryman Henri Misson had agreed. 'The idea of the English is that civility (unlike on the continent) does not consist wholly of these outward shows, which very often are hypocritical and deceitful.' It is hardly surprising that the books of both Muralt and Misson, when published in England, were bestsellers.

England was the plucky, dogged defender of freedom, a David to the continental Goliaths of the Bourbon and Habsburg dynasties, who oppressed their peoples through a combination of 'popery and wooden shoes'. The French reply to this taunt was that they were 'as happy in their wooden shoes, as our people [the English] are with their luxury and drunkenness'.[11] Whereas Hogarth saw the English vices – a love of drinking, gambling and a preoccupation with violence and cruelty – as qualities that degraded them, many of his contemporaries took a perverse pride in them. Ironically, while the English prided themselves on their dissolution ('the ordinary amusements of the English are wine, women and dice, or, in a word, debauchery'), they believed that the source of their depravity was foreign. Hogarth's scathing portrayal of the country's aristocracy's preoccupation with Italian paintings, French cooks, fencing teachers and dancing masters, and German musicians reveals his disdain for the continental fashions that corrupted the native virtues of the English (illustration 27, page 182; *The Rake's Levee*). Despite this fascination with European fashions, the English remained un-ashamed of their jingoism. Cesar de Saussure was frequently splat-tered with mud as he walked the streets of London, and called 'French Dog!' He must have been consoled by the fact that it was the elegance of his attire that marked him out from the crowd.

27. *A Rake's Progress II: The Rake's Levee* (William Hogarth)

Tom Rakewell, wearing his nightcap in a fashionable state of *déshabillé*, is surrounded by a composer sitting at the harpsichord, a violinist who holds his bow in a gesture reminiscent of the fencing master behind him, a garden designer, and a jockey holding a cup won by the Rake's horse, Silly Tom. In the anteroom, a milliner and a poet wait to be admitted.

Their liberty entitled Englishmen 'to be as wicked as we think fit';[12] Misson believed that 'the excessive clemency of English laws gave room for abundance of ill actions that would not else be committed . . . There is much less danger in being wicked at London than at Paris.' Despite this light-hearted view of the English legal system, there was a great deal of pride in the nation's laws. England was 'not an arbitrary tyranny, but a land governed by a known and rational constitution'.[13] Laws had developed over the centuries according to the rights of its subjects, unlike in the autocratic governments of the European *anciens régimes*. They depended on trial by jury; other states, whose justice systems were based on Roman law, depended instead on autocratic control. The law was the 'cornerstone of English liberty';[14] and on this foundation rested the tenet that a police force would infringe on the personal liberty of England's citizens.

One of the great drawbacks of the parish system of watches was that it was completely separate from the county justice system of magistrates and sheriffs. Because there was no centralized form of policing, and the structures that existed were so appallingly inefficient, other, more rudimentary means of detecting and catching criminals were used. It was considered the duty of the victim of a crime to bring the perpetrator to justice, from apprehending the villain, to taking him to court and prosecuting him. Every man was responsible for the protection of his own property. If he needed help he could raise a 'hue and cry' and summon the sheriff's forces. He could hire a lawyer, but many people preferred to plead their own cases – that is, if the matter got to court at all. It was very expensive to bring a case to court, and until the 1750s neither witnesses nor prosecutors were repaid the costs of their involvement in a trial. The accused also had to pay for the privilege of being charged with a crime, a higher rate for pleading not guilty, and again when he was either convicted or acquitted. Going to court did not benefit the prosecutor, who might pay more in legal fees and loss of business during a trial than he had lost initially; nor the accused, who would not want to go to gaol if he was convicted but did not want to lose money defending his case even if he was innocent; nor the constable, who might be accused of wrongful arrest. If the matter could be settled out of court – as the young Jonathan Wild was able to do with the Wolverhampton man whose horse he stole – it was in everyone's interests to do so. Traditional methods of extracting compensation for a crime were enshrined in a law that gave any traveller robbed on the highway the right to claim damages from the inhabitants of the district in which the crime had taken place unless they could catch the perpetrator within forty days of the incident.

If, in the end, the criminal was condemned, his victim could relax and congratulate himself on putting a lawbreaker safely behind bars awaiting the gallows or transportation. And congratulate himself he did, for the government's regular reward to a man who facilitated the capture and conviction of a known criminal was £40, no insignificant sum in those days. In certain cases, the reward would be raised to compensate for the risk involved in intercepting so dangerous a villain; the reward offered for Dick Turpin, the most wanted man in the land in the 1730s, was £200. In addition, private individuals or companies, as well as the government, might offer rewards for the capture of specific miscreants.

The high rewards for thief-catching were almost a government sanction for thief-takers such as Jonathan Wild because only a professional could benefit from this system. A thief-taker had to have inside knowledge of the criminal underworld in order to track down specific villains, as Wild had found Mrs Knap's murderers. He had to wield power over criminals to make them betray one another; to gain this power, he had to be involved in their world. And the money he received was used to expand his empire, bribing magistrates and witnesses, paying spies, financing smuggling operations or hiring warehouses to store stolen goods – not to mention paying the high costs of bringing a case to court in the first place.

It was easier for the government to rely on thief-takers than to try to control crime; they encouraged the business of men such as Charles Hitchin and Jonathan Wild because they fulfilled a role, however underhandedly, that the government was unwilling to take on. Nothing less than a total overhaul of the existing system would have sufficed to reform it, as corruption had infiltrated every layer of officialdom in every department, from top to bottom. In 1720, in response to a public outcry in the capital about crime, the government – on Jonathan Wild's advice – merely issued a proclamation adding £100 to the existing reward of £40 for the prosecution and conviction of footpads within a radius of five miles of London and Westminster. By 1732 the government had begun to recognize its mistake: the act was revoked because the inordinately high rewards encouraged people to perjure themselves, or even to lead others into crime in hopes of giving them up to the law, for the sake of the money.

Thief-takers were supported by the incentives offered to criminals who informed on their peers. Royal pardons were granted to those who, like Isaac Ragg, revealed the identities of their accomplices to the authorities. Persuading men to impeach each other – no thieves' honour here – was one of Wild's most valuable skills. Using one man's evidence against another, he would create havoc among a gang of criminals by implying to each of them that the others were just about to turn evidence against the rest; often they would vie to be the first to betray their companions to ensure their own freedom.

As well as cash rewards and pardons, another incentive for informants was the 'Tyburn Ticket', instituted in 1699. This exempted the holder from liability for parish duties, including the hated night-watch. It was also transferable; in some parishes, such as Covent Garden, which was notoriously dangerous at night, and therefore a particularly difficult beat for a constable, a Tyburn Ticket could be sold for as much as £25. These rewards, incentives and threats encouraged and often forced people to become unwitting agents in the state's corruption. The government's need to appear to be controlling the rising tide of crime forced it to harness that which ostensibly it was trying to eradicate.

If criminals were celebrated for evading the law when they were free, it was much harder for them to do so in court. L. O. Pike, a nineteenth-century legal historian, deplored 'the old [eighteenth-century] attempts to crush a prisoner by invectives from the bench, to interpret everything to his disadvantage, and to deprive him, as far as possible, of a hearing'. Until 1731 Latin was still the official language of the court, although most oral proceedings took place in the vernacular. Therefore, legal advice was essential for a badly educated defendant or plaintiff. But legal advice was forbidden to defendants, although prosecution lawyers were permitted, because defendants were supposed to be under the protection of the judge. It is no wonder that prisoners spent most of their time in gaol conducting mock trials and reading law manuals.

The Old Bailey was the main criminal court in London. To protect the lawyers and judges from the vile diseases carried by the defendants, the quarter sessions were held, theatrically, in the open air in front of the main building. Crowds of people watched the trials, jostling each other and calling out to the prisoners. There was massive, almost obsessive, popular fascination with crime in the eighteenth century, which reflected a broadly based hostility to the government and its laws. Newspapers and magazines were full of accounts of crimes, arrests, trials and hangings. In the 1720s accounts of trials in the Old Bailey were published eight times a year. Broadsheets costing a penny or two carried invitations to the executions of particularly unpopular villains, or copies of the epitaphs of the convicted. Sellers of the last dying speeches of those about to be executed did a roaring trade on hanging days. Ballad-writers sang songs exalting the actions of the condemned. Bound copies of the lives and confessions of those about to die sold like wildfire for a shilling apiece.

In addition to the system's inherent prejudice towards the accused, lawyers were notoriously corrupt. Swift described them in *Gulliver's Travels* as 'a society of men . . . bred up from their youth in the art of proving by words multiplied for the purpose, that *white* is *black*, and *black* is *white*, according as they are paid. To this society all the rest of the people are slaves.' Witnesses could be bought for a penny or two: 'straw-men', so called because they stuck pieces of straw in the buckles of their shoes to identify themselves, walked up and down outside the Old Bailey waiting to be asked by crooked lawyers to come inside and perjure themselves for a price. 'A lawyer is an honest employment,' states Peachum in the opening scene of *The Beggars' Opera*, 'so is mine. Like me too he acts in a double capacity, both against rogues and for 'em; for 'tis but fitting that we should protect and encourage cheats, since we live by 'em.' Lawyers practised an esoteric craft, inaccessible to the outsider; they were looked on askance because their work, which so often seemed to benefit none but themselves, was carried on behind a veil of complicated language and specialized costume. Satirical prints throughout this period commonly portrayed lawyers as being in the service of the devil.[15]

Jonathan Wild, whose tortured genius extended to legal wranglings, was almost always successful in court, either defending his man or bringing down his opponent: criminals considered his backing essential for victory in a case. Lying and bribery were only the start of it. He thought nothing of plying witnesses with drink so that they were too drunk to stand in court and testify against his man, who would be acquitted through lack of evidence.

Although legal procedure favoured the prosecutor, it was still difficult to get a conviction. Witnesses were a vital part of every case, because conclusive forensic evidence did not exist, but often, because of the expense and inconvenience involved, they did not want to testify. Without eyewitness evidence, it was not easy to determine guilt unless a confession had been extracted. A great deal of evidence was required to convict someone of murder; infanticide, a common crime among poor young women, could be disproved by the defendant producing in court a little shirt she had sewn, which would show that she had been preparing for the birth of her baby – even if, unbeknownst to the jurors, she had made it the day before she appeared in court. This was where an effective arguer, like Wild, could be of use to people he wanted to save: providing alibis for them, or demonstrating the weaknesses in the prosecution's argument, or introducing technicalities that rendered a case null and void.

No person was tried at the Old Bailey, or anywhere else, if Jonathan was in court, but Mr Wild was consulted about the character of the criminal: which gave such interest among the thieves, that many of them really thought, if they could but keep in with Mr Wild they need not fear, let them commit what rogueries they would.[16]

In October 1723 Quilt Arnold, Wild's right-hand man and his official 'Clerk of the Northern Road', was accused of stealing a pair of silver shoe buckles from the house of one Martin Bellamy, a well-known thief who had forged Wild's signature to cash a note of hand in his name worth nine guineas. Wild told the court he had ordered Quilt to enter Bellamy's house (an illegal act in itself) and bring Bellamy to him. Quilt was unable to find Bellamy, but brought back to Wild Bellamy's shoes as evidence of having been there – hence their disappearance. In his testimony Wild emphasized how important Quilt was to him in his business of apprehending violent and dangerous criminals. Quilt was acquitted, but the judge reprimanded Wild for 'countenancing people to enter houses by no other authority than his orders'. Although the authorities were willing to turn a blind eye to Wild's pretensions of official status, the judge did not like this blatant flaunting of his power, and he was rapped on the knuckles.

The laws themselves did nothing to protect the innocent or oppressed. 'Laws grind the poor, and rich men rule the law.'[17] John Gay's *The Beggars' Opera* criticized the social system that allowed thieves to be judged and punished by men who also committed crimes, but prospered by them rather than being punished for them. Peachum, the character based on Wild, and Lockit, the turnkey, are compared by Gay to courtiers and politicians, specifically Robert Walpole, Chief Minister at the time. Both Peachum and Walpole gloss over their crimes – manipulation, selfishness and greed – with false sentiment. In some ways, they are less honourable than the thieves off whom they feed, because 'Macheaths' are forced to live by courage and wit, while the 'Wilds' of the world survive sustained by hypocrisy and deception.

In the words of John Locke, 'Government has no other aim but the preservation of property'; and those like Macheath or Jack Sheppard who threatened the sanctity of property ownership through crime were condemned to the harshest penalty. After the Glorious Revolution in 1688, a torrent of legislation raised the number of capital crimes from about fifty to over 200 by the turn of the nineteenth century. In place of the social infiltration and control that a police force would have imposed, crime was to be deterred by brutality, often incommensurate with the crime it was supposed to punish and sometimes inconsistent with punishments for comparable crimes.

This discrepancy was noted by Henri Misson. 'A man that is convicted of having forced a door, a window, or a pane of glass, with intent to steal, is guilty of burglary and condemned to death, even though he has taken nothing; whereas one that steals, finding the door is open, is punished less severely.' New statutes included the Shoplifting Act, in 1699, making shoplifting a capital offence. The first act against receiving stolen property was passed in 1691 (3 William & Mary c.9; section 4), making a fence an accessory after the fact. Until Jonathan Wild's Act, this was only a common law misdemeanour, punishable by branding the hand rather than by death.

However, while the number of capital crimes rose in this period, the number of villains actually executed declined. The ruling classes preferred to display their power by granting pardons, often apparently arbitrarily, to convicted felons, rather than by treating them with consistent and humane justice. The regularity of pardons 'allowed the class that had passed one of the bloodiest penal codes in Europe to congratulate itself on its humanity'.[18] The system created an artificially intimate relationship between the accused and the meter-out of justice. Once condemned, the prisoner was utterly dependent on the whim of the judge, or the mercy of the king, or the patronage of his protector, to save him from the gallows or have his sentence reduced to transportation instead of hanging. The theory behind this highly personal approach to punishment was that the judge should use his discretion to distinguish between crimes mitigated by circumstance and the nature of the crime itself. In fact, it was a means through which the highly personalized system of patronage and dependency was perpetuated, encouraging the reliance of the lower classes on the gentry who controlled most aspects of their lives.

Mercy and lenience did exist, despite the harshness of the laws. Many victims of crime were reluctant to press charges for a minor misdeed, like the theft of a silk handkerchief, because they knew that the miscreant would almost certainly be sentenced to hang. Stealing anything worth over one shilling was punishable with

death, but something worth less than a shilling merited only branding of the hand. Judges, too, were sometimes willing to undervalue
a piece of stolen property used as evidence to soften the sentence,
perhaps from hanging to transportation to the Americas, instituted
in 1719. First-time offenders were usually treated with mercy, as
were those driven to steal by necessity, or those who committed a
crime but were unarmed. Confession and returning what had been
stolen also helped a defendant's defence.

The new laws created in the early eighteenth century were intended either to encourage commerce, which included legislation
against forgery and smuggling, or to bolster property rights, such as
the Black Act of 1723, and the many new and revised acts against
robbery and receiving. It was not until the middle of the century
that the first hesitant steps towards a police force were taken under
the guidance of Henry and Sir John Fielding, half-brothers who
were successively magistrates of Bow Street in Covent Garden for
over a quarter of a century from 1749. Henry Fielding believed that
to live with the constant threat of assault and robbery was not liberty, but anarchy; he held that true liberty was each person's freedom to enjoy their life in safety, and that this could be achieved
only with the aid of a regular, uncorrupted band of law-enforcers.
It is ironic that in part he used Jonathan Wild's methods of thief-
taking as the basis for his Bow Street Runners.

Punishment

In eighteenth-century England the severest penalty was reserved for treason. The offender would be 'drawn to the place of execution on a hurdle',[1] and there hanged, cut down while still alive, disembowelled, castrated, beheaded and finally quartered. Compared to contemporary French punishments, which revelled in red-hot pincers and drops of burning oil, this was relatively humane. Petty treason – the murder of a master – like grand treason, was considered a direct challenge to society's moral order. It was punished simply by drawing the miscreant on a hurdle to the gallows and hanging him there. A woman convicted of murdering her husband, also petty treason, was burned. In many cases, the executioner would strangle the woman before the flames reached her, or ensure the hanged man died on the gallows before he was cut apart. Mercy was at the discretion of the individual; but barbarity was the state's decree.

For lesser offences, such as manslaughter, the court might sentence a malefactor to burning of the hand, which involved being branded by a hot iron. For a fee of 13½d., though, the brand would be dipped in cold water before it touched the skin, vastly lessening its effect. Public or private flogging was another common punishment, inflicted only on those considered not to be of gentle birth. The most common method was called being flogged 'at the cart's tail'. The prisoner would be stripped to the waist, tied on to the back of a cart, and whipped until his or her back was bloody as the cart travelled its charted route. This was the usual action taken against prostitutes.

Whipping and the pillory were very public humiliations, usually for crimes that offended society's norms in some way. Cheating at cards, fortune-telling, falsely accusing someone of fathering an illegitimate child, or of making 'sodomitical advances', were all punished by the pillory. One man was pilloried for saying that 'he hoped to see all Protestants fry in their own grease before Michaelmas next'.[2] When someone was pilloried, a description of his crime was clearly displayed above his head. He would be sentenced to stand for an hour or two, exposed to the wrath of the assembled crowds. Charles Hitchin, Jonathan Wild's old rival, died as a result of injuries inflicted on him when he stood in the stocks, as did Colonel Charteris's procuress, Mother Wisebourne. Sometimes, though, the people came out in defence of the accused party. A man pilloried at the Royal Exchange for speaking out against King George I was released by a sympathetic mob. In 1703 Daniel Defoe was pilloried in Cheapside and then in the Temple for sedition. He was covered with flowers as he stood in the stocks while all around him drank his health and sang his 'Ode to the Pillory'.

Defoe was unusual in that, though an educated man, he was punished as a commoner. Although the English prided themselves on the egalitarianism of their penal system, the majority of those punished by the law were young, ill-educated men, often apprentices from a poor background. Fewer women than men were found guilty of felonies; women were also more likely to avoid execution if convicted, 'pleading their belly', or claiming they were pregnant. If a condemned woman was found to be pregnant, and it was always easy to get pregnant quickly, especially in Newgate, her sentence would be deferred or reduced to transportation.

One early eighteenth-century Solicitor-General, Archibald MacDonald, estimated that of every twenty offenders executed in London at the time, roughly eighteen would be under the age of twenty-one. By this reckoning, Jack Sheppard was lucky to live to twenty-three. Forty per cent of Tyburn's victims were or had been apprentices, like Sheppard. The Ordinary of Newgate believed being 'bred to no trade' was a factor that contributed to the high numbers of young people dying on the gallows; young men like

Jack Sheppard, in fact more than half of all London's apprentices, who had left their master before completing their term of apprenticeship, fell into this category. Unable to succeed through the routes offered to them (learning a trade and then setting up their own business) they rejected convention and turned instead to crime, following the path down which Hogarth's Idle Apprentice slipped.

The moral dissolution of the lower classes, illustrated by Hogarth in his series of prints, *Industry and Idleness*, was exactly what the government hoped to reverse by its harsh penal code. The aim of punishment in the eighteenth century was to uphold the authority of the law, instilling in the common people a reverence for and obedience to the government. Hanging, in particular, was designed to be a demonstration of the power of the state over those who refused to conform to its rules. As the saying went, 'Men are not hanged for stealing horses, but that horses may not be stolen.' It had the dual purpose of ridding society of malefactors and serving as an example to others who might be tempted to crime. Death, the ultimate punishment, was also seen as the ultimate deterrent. Therefore, the more people who witnessed the state exercising its power to take the lives of lawbreakers, the greater the state's control over the bulk of the population. Public execution

is a ceremonial by which a momentarily injured sovereignty is reconstituted. It restores that sovereignty by manifesting it at its most spectacular . . . Its aim is not so much to re-establish a balance as to bring into play, at its extreme point, the dysymmetry between the subject who had dared to violate the law and the all-powerful sovereign who displays his strength.[3]

The criminal effectively challenged the state's power by committing a proscribed act; and hanging or burning was the state's chosen method of displaying its continued power and control over these threats to the order of society. For these purposes, men condemned to death who publicly confessed and repented on the scaffold were the government's ideal victims. Repentant sinners reinforced the legitimacy and authority of the government by asserting its rectitude while accepting their fate. If punishment is no more than a social ritual, then the victims of punishment who complied perpetuated the authority of the state through their deference.

But as the eighteenth century wore on, the accused increasingly refused to bow their heads and beg forgiveness for their sins. Fielding called the condemned men at Tyburn 'triumphant'. He continued, '[public executions] tend rather to inspire the vulgar with a contempt of the gallows rather than a fear of it'. Bravery on the scaffold was the felons' only way of defying to the end the laws and society that had been their downfall. 'Making a good end' was part of a criminal's code of honour: 'those that die merrily, or that don't at least show any great fear of death, are said to die like gentlemen'.[4]

Not only was the prisoner's personal honour satisfied by putting on a brave face in front of the crowds at Tyburn, but a vague sense of collective pride was felt by the crowd as they watched one of their number die with courage – or at least, with bravado. 'Of the ragamuffin class [at Tyburn] . . . many expressed their admiration of the fortitude, as they termed the hardness and stupidity, of one of the sufferers.'[5] At executions where the crowd showed its support for the criminal, the power of the state was ridiculed. The mob's strong identification with the condemned men they watched hang only reinforced their hostility to authority. People cried out, watching a hero die, 'hoping the L—d will deliver him out of the hands of his adversaries; meaning the laws of the country'.[6]

An element in the popular fascination with criminals, and especially the spectacle of their execution, might have been the way in which these hangings brought death close to people's lives. In a time when violent death and dreadful diseases were accepted facts of daily life, perhaps it was better to embrace the spectre of death than to try to avoid it. *Applebee's Journal* commented philosophically on the crowds who turned out to watch four men die at Tyburn.

And are they not all under an absolute indefeasible sentence? . . . and with this difference too, that many of the rest shall die in torture and terror, ten thousand times more grievous than those four. Nay, perhaps few of the thousands who will go to see these few people die shall get so easy a passage out of life.

The bulk of the population would not have had such a rational approach to hangings. Superstition still governed the lives of the common people. Hair was cut at the full moon; blood was let in springtime. The rituals surrounding the dead bodies of felons show what sway folk-magic still held over the inhabitants of what was arguably the most sophisticated city in Europe. Even the government subscribed to these traditional beliefs. If a condemned man committed suicide while awaiting execution, his body was not merely buried. A stake was driven through it to prevent his spirit becoming a ghost; he was then buried at night at a crossroads, which would diffuse the evil trapped in his body. Ironically, some of the mystique once attached to the crown had been transferred to criminals: the monarch had once touched people to rid them of the King's Evil (scrofula); by the eighteenth century the king or queen no longer claimed these healing powers, but the touch of a dead felon's hand was thought to cure the disease.

The educated classes scorned the masses' easy acceptance of their heroes' shows of defiance.

Most of them die like beasts, without any concern, or like fools, for having no other view than to divert the crowd . . . Though there's something very melancholy in this, yet a man can't well forbear laughing to see these rogues set themselves off for heroes, by an affectation of despising death.[7]

They saw the blustering disregard of the dying men as little more than a front designed to distract the crowd from their fear of death.

The terror of death inwardly excruciates him; but his fear of showing this, of being called a coward, and laughed at by his companions, has some command over his outward appearance . . . But his impudence would soon fail him, and his inexhaustible stock be but a weak match for the agonies he suffers, if he took not refuge in strong liquors.[8]

Jack Sheppard was not outwardly drunk when he died – he needed his wits about him if he was to escape, as he hoped until the very last minute to do. Blueskin Blake, however, was reeling drunk when he was hanged, his swagger a poor defence against the prospect of eternity, like Gay's Macheath, who drowns his worries in drink as he sits in his cell awaiting death.

> Since I must swing – I scorn,
> I scorn to wince or whine.
> But now again my spirits sink;
> I'll raise them high with wine.
> But valour the stronger grows,
> The stronger liquor we're drinking.
> And how can we feel our woes,
> When we've lost the trouble of thinking?
> If thus – A man can die
> Much bolder with brandy
> So I drink off this bumper – And now I can stand the test,
> And my comrades shall see, that I die as brave as the best.

Regardless of whether their show of contempt for death was real or not, the refusal of the dying men to submit meekly to the state's punishments lessened the impact of public executions. 'Ritual punishments depended for their effectiveness as a ceremonial deterrence on the crowd's tacit support of the authorities' sentence.'[9] If the crowd supported the man about to be punished, rather than the state as punisher, there was little the state could do to swing public feeling back behind it. The ceremony of death, intended to define and reinforce the state's authority, could become instead a celebration of resistance to that same authority. The crowd's support justified the criminal's defiance.

The government did its best to limit displays of resistance. Last dying speeches that challenged the Hanoverian succession, or denied the inviolability of private property, or flouted approved norms of behaviour were suppressed. So little could spark a curious crowd into a violent mob – such as the scuffle over Jack Sheppard's body, which caused riots that lasted throughout the night of his death – that the government was forced to become cautious.

Persistent popular resistance to authority on hanging days – verbal abuse, stones thrown at the executioners, guards and soldiers, and attempts to seize the condemned men – gradually changed the élite's views on public executions. Although some political thinkers, such as the anonymous author of the 1701 pamphlet 'Hanging: Not Punishment Enough', believed only harsher treatment would curb the rising incidence of crime, most were coming round to the idea of reform. 'Why should we delight in the intrepidity, though it was real, of a villain in his impiety?' The spectacle of hanging days clearly did not inspire either the dying man, or his supporters, with the proper respect for his impending doom and by extension for the authority that had meted out that doom. Bernard de Mandeville believed that far from deterring people from crime, public execu tions positively encouraged them to it:

The notions which the vulgar have of courage, as well as honour and shame, are full of dangerous errors. Compliments, as well as reproaches, when ill-applied, are often the causes of great mischief; and I am now persuaded, that the perverseness of opinion now reigning amongst us, both in applauding and discommending the conduct of criminals in their last hours, is an accessory evil, that very much contributes to . . . the frequency of executions.

The celebration of criminals like Jack Sheppard made the criminal lifestyle seem desirable – as indeed it probably was, for an able, frustrated man or woman living on the edge of survival. The inability of the government to control the exhibition of punishment reflected their parallel failure to accommodate a huge proportion of London's population.

'I will appeal to any man who hath seen an execution, or a procession to an execution,' wrote Henry Fielding in 1751,

Let him tell me when he hath beheld a poor wretch, bound in a cart, just on the edge of eternity, all pale and trembling with his approaching fate, whether the idea of shame hath ever intruded on his mind? Much less will the bold daring rogue who glories in his present condition, inspire the beholder with any such sensation.

The reform movement that had started with the institution of houses of correction and workhouses at the turn of the eighteenth century, impelled by the crusading zeal of the Reforming Societies, by the middle of the century turned its attention to punishment. Religious conviction fuelled this change of attitude. 'The greater provision we make for the souls and future happiness of these short-lived sinners, the less indulgence we should have for their bodies and sensual appetites.'[10] Genuine religious repentance was thought to be a better example to the populace than a showy public renunciation of moral and social values. The death penalty was still seen as the ultimate deterrent: but instead of making a public display of it several times a year, it was carried out before a restricted audience, and with humanity. Thus the automatic drop – intended to cause the neck to break at once, thus resulting in almost instantaneous death – was introduced in 1760; and after 1783, all executions took place just outside prisons. It was not until 1868 that they were performed without an audience, once public opinion had turned against the death penalty. The *Daily News*, covering the last public hanging in 1868, said that the ceremony 'made the law and its ministers seem to them [the public] the real murderers, and Barrett [the victim] to be a martyred man'.

The new view was that punishment 'should strike at the soul rather than the body'.[11] The 'certainty of being punished and not the horrifying spectacle of public punishment . . . must discourage crime'.[12] Imprisonment and transportation gradually replaced the death sentence as the penalties for most felonies. These new forms of punishment carried with them the hope of personal reform and regeneration. The state, which had been tainted by the cruelty it unintentionally revealed at public executions and in its arbitrary displays of mercy, hoped to exalt itself by punishing miscreants with humanity and reason.

This was a result partly of the new awareness of the injustice inherent in the existing penal system. In the eighteenth century a starving child who stole a shilling paid the same penalty as a murderer or an armed robber. A young girl in Norwich was hanged for stealing a handkerchief. Fifteen-year-old Joseph Harris, who had stolen two half-sovereigns and some silver, rode to Tyburn with his head in the lap of his weeping, desolate father. As late as 1833 a nine-year-old boy who stole two pennyworth of paint by poking a stick through a cracked shopwindow was hanged. Popular sympathy with the victims of cases like these was very high. Public executions had become the focus for disorder, unintelligible and irrelevant displays of tyrannical control. Even if it had wanted to retain the death penalty for robbery, the government would have been forced sooner or later to bow to public opinion and reform the penal code.

Dr Johnson believed the eighteenth-century uniformity of punishment led to criminals taking a nonchalant attitude towards their actions: 'If the penalty for robbery and murder is the same, the thief will think little of adding murder to his crime.' Because there was no difference between the penalties assigned to crimes, there was no moral evaluation of crimes. 'Death is *ultimum supplicium*, and is therefore intended only for crimes of the highest rank; but when it is indiscriminately inflicted, it leaves no room to difference the punishments of crimes widely different in their own nature.'[13] Dr Leon Radzinowicz suggests that the fact that eighteenth-century society made no effort to differentiate between the morality of different actions might reflect its overriding concern with the protection of property at the expense of social welfare.

Jack Sheppard, who turned to crime because all other avenues of opportunity were blocked in front of him, was a victim of this system. Plato believed that misery is the mother of crime; for Jack, and so many others like him, it was not misery that thrust him into a life of crime, but frustration. In court he claimed that he had turned to crime because he 'had no opportunity to obtain his bread in an honest way'. He was pooh-poohed by the judges, who saw any crime simply as a lack of discipline. But it was the impossibility of rising out of his allotted sphere, despite his talents, that forced Jack to seek an alternative route to the material rewards held up – just out of his reach – by society as desirable. So he chose to use the carpentry skills he had learned, but been unable to practise legitimately, in burglary. His undoubted talents had been thwarted, and he had taken the only option open to him: crime. In burglary, and particularly in prison-breaking, he discovered independence and self-respect for the first time in his life. And because he was loath to relinquish these new-found freedoms when Jonathan Wild demanded that he do so, he became a martyr to Wild's insatiable lust for power.

Gaol

After his trial Sheppard had been taken back to Newgate. The prison stood on the site of a Roman gatehouse, at the junction of Holborn and Newgate Streets, conveniently close to the Old Bailey. There had been a gaol there since about 1130. In 1422 Dick Whittington had left a bequest for the rebuilding of the gaol, hence its cant nickname, the 'Whit'. It had been rebuilt again after the Great Fire, and was finished in 1672. However, although the exterior had been adorned with pilasters, and illusory battlements and statues of the virtues had been added to the façade, the fifteenth-century interior was largely untouched. Like many other prisons built before the reforming movement that took place after 1750, Newgate had not been designed as a gaol. Restrictive measures were attempted – iron bars were set into the windows and crushed glass stuck on to the tops of walls – but gaolers had to rely on physical confinement to keep prisoners under control. In the absence of a large, alert staff or properly secured buildings, inmates of Newgate had to be chained up. They were collared, handcuffed, their feet put in irons and 'stapled' to the floor or walls.

But just as in Wood Street Compter, the debtors' prison Wild had inhabited in his younger days, relative freedom, and indeed comfort, were available within Newgate's walls – for a price. In *The Beggars' Opera*, Mr Lockit, the turnkey, offers Macheath a selection of irons in varying degrees of weight and discomfort, depending on how much he was willing to pay in garnish. 'We have them [fetters] of all prices, from one guinea to ten, and 'tis fitting every gentleman should please himself.' After paying an entrance fee, and buying his freedom from a ball and chain, a prisoner could begin to negotiate about where he stayed within the gaol.

Standard accommodation was in the 'Common Ward', where prisoners were packed like slaves or sardines into a vast room whose walls were lined with shelves that were used for beds. Bedding was available only if one paid for it; it would have been vital in the winter, since there was no heating. In 1709 a room with a window on the 'Master's Side' cost 22s. 6d. a week in rent, about double what was charged for the Common Side; the prisoner had first to pay a deposit of £500 for the cell and its furnishings. Those who could afford no rent at all were simply thrown into the 'Hole'. The best rooms in Newgate were in the Press Yard – a part, theoretically, of the keeper's residence, but available to the prisoners, like everything else, at an extortionate price. A single room in the Press Yard cost the same to rent as 'the best house in St James's or Piccadilly'. The prisoner could employ servants and chefs, bring his wife and children to live with him, and have a steady stream of visitors, all charged the standard rate of 3s. a visit.

Major Bernadini was a Jacobite arrested in 1688 just before William of Orange took the throne. He was not tried, because no evidence was brought against him, but was never released, because he refused to swear allegiance to the new king. By 1722, when he had been in Newgate for thirty-four years, he had been impoverished by the constant demands of the keepers on his finances. A sympathetic newspaper reported that he was 'reduced to such want, that [he has] nothing to live upon'. This article aroused the pity of a wealthy female, who married him, moved with him from the Common Ward to the Press Yard, and there bore him ten children.[1]

The conditions Major Bernadini endured during his years in the Common Ward were soul-destroying. There was no light, no ventilation; the air was fetid and damp because it could not circulate. There was no space for exercise. There was no heating, and no cleaning facilities; an open sewer ran through the middle of the ward. Some parts of Newgate were below ground-level and water covered the floor, sometimes up to six inches deep. Rats, cockroaches and lice plagued the prisoners. 'The lice crackling under their feet made such a noise as walking on shells which are strewn over garden walks';[2] many who could not afford shoes would only have worn rags tied around their feet to protect them from the vermin underfoot. Food was a thin soup made from bread and water; it was no wonder that in 1729 a Parliamentary Committee discovered 350 prisoners dying of starvation in Marshalsea Prison. In 1726 twenty-one felons from Newgate were hanged — and nearly four times that number, eighty-three, died in prison in the same year of hunger or illness. The stench of disease and filth was so disgusting that female visitors held vinegar-soaked handkerchiefs to their mouths and noses to prevent them retching, as well as to kill the germs the air might be carrying.

'Gaol fever' was a virulent form of typhus, possibly complicated by smallpox, that plagued Newgate and London's other gaols during the eighteenth century. It was 'a contagious, putrid and very pestilential fever, attended with tremblings, twitchings, restlessness, delirium with, in some instance, early frenzy and lethargy; while the victims break out often into livid pustules and purple spots'.[3] It was caused by the dreadful conditions in which the prisoners were forced to live, and exacerbated by the poor diet which provided them with no protein. In 1750 an outbreak of gaol fever for the first time infected people outside Newgate. 'The very air they breathed acquired a pestilential degree of putrefaction.'[4] The disease spread through the Old Bailey, the felons' only point of contact with the outside world. Sixty people died, including the Lord Mayor, jurors and lawyers. Panic ensued. Prisoners were washed with vinegar, a disinfectant, before being taken to court; judges breathed into a nosegay so as not to inhale the tainted air that clung to the prisoners. (This remains a tradition at the opening of each legal term at the Old Bailey.)

It was such incidents that frightened the public into acknowledging the dreadful state of gaols. From the start of the eighteenth century, an awareness that there was room for improvement within the penal system began to grow. Workhouses like those where Jack Sheppard and Dickens's Oliver Twist were sent, and houses of correction, like that into which Hogarth's Moll Hackabout was committed, were intended to scare the poor and destitute into obedience and diligence. They were meant to be agencies of social reform, transforming potential criminals into upstanding, industrious members of the community, cowed into accepting the low wages, hard work and harsh living conditions their rank dictated. These were institutions created to fill a void; previously, no controls had existed for the merely poor and destitute except laws against vagabondage.

But the existing prison system appeared adequate, and so what to do with actual criminals (as opposed to potential ones such as the youthful Jack Sheppard) was not really an issue until the late eighteenth century. Since most prisoners had committed crimes against property – sacred in the eyes of the Whig aristocracy and gentry who ruled the country – no conditions were thought to be too harsh for them. Cesare Beccaria, whose book *Crimes and Punishments* was first published in English in 1764, suggested in it for the first time that prisons might be used to reform their inmates, rather than acting as a deterrent to others, or simply restraining their charges before their trial and sentence. The first purpose-built gaol, Pentonville, designed to use incarceration as a punishment in itself, was not opened until 1842. Where Newgate had been disorderly, chaotic and uncontrolled, Pentonville was regimented, tightly constrained and inhuman. Criminals were scrubbed in a carbolic bath when they arrived, their heads shaved, their clothes and possessions burned, and they were given a number by which they were called, instead of their names, for the length of their stay. They lived totally isolated in their cells, all of which were overlooked by the wardens and a preacher in a central office. No communication at all was permitted, and prisoners wore masks when they were out of their cells for chapel or exercise to prevent them recognizing each other. Every year between five and fifteen out of the 450 inmates were taken to an insanc asylum, with the threat of returning to Pentonville if they 'recovered' hanging over them.

The difference between Pentonville and Newgate was that while internment at Pentonville was the punishment, Newgate was only a storage house for criminals waiting either for trial or punishment. Exceptions such as Major Bernadini did, of course, exist; and debtors were a different case because they remained in prison until they paid off their debts. Occasionally a gaol sentence would be given for crimes such as perjury or commercial fraud; Sally Salisbury was sentenced to a year in Newgate for assaulting and wounding John Finch but died before her term had elapsed. But the average prisoner stayed at Newgate for between a week and three months.

Jack Sheppard, because of his previous escape, was not an average prisoner. He was placed in the condemned hold, and shackled firmly within. In 1663 Samuel Pepys witnessed the hanging of Colonel Turner whom he visited in the condemned hold at Newgate. Pepys called it

a most fearful, sad, deplorable place. Hell itself in comparison cannot be such a place. There is neither bench, stool, nor stick for any person there; they lie like swine upon the ground, upon one another, howling and roaring – it was more terrible to me than [Turner's] death.

Howling and roaring were common words used to describe Newgate's uproar. The prisoners, both men and 'hell-cat' women, used to shriek obscenities at passers-by. They pissed out of windows and threw the contents of their chamber pots into the streets. But if the inmates were a disreputable, unruly mob, the keepers were no better.

The horrid aspects of turnkeys and gaolers, in discontent and hurry; the sharp and dreadful looks of rogues, that beg in irons, but would rob you with greater satisfaction if they could; the bellowings of half a dozen names at a time, that are perpetually made in enquiries after one another; the variety of strong voices, that are heard, of howling in one place, scolding and quarrelling in another, and loud laughter in a third; the substantial breakfasts that are made in the midst of all this; the seas of beer that are swilled . . .[5]

In the sweltering heat of the summer of 1724 Jack Sheppard concentrated on escaping his confines once more. Unlike Jonathan Wild, who was able to turn his time in prison to his advantage, captivity only made Sheppard more determined to be free. Whereas

Wild had learned the rituals of gaol, and clawed and scrambled up its intricate hierarchy, Sheppard resisted. For Wild, it was merely a case of establishing a set of rules by which he could live, and succeed, and dominate. Having not found his niche within the conventional, hardworking (if harsh and a little mundane) community at Wolverhampton, he had come to London. There he had discovered a new society, with its own laws, ones which he understood, and knew that he could manipulate to his advantage. He wanted to be a rich, respected member of the London mercantile class; but he cared not if he used the conventional route, or found his way there via an educational stay in the Wood Street Compter and an apprenticeship to a professional thief-taker. But for Jack Sheppard, independence was the ideal. He cared little for the rewards of crime, spending or giving away what he stole almost immediately. For him, having to conform to any rules, be they those of a modest carpenter in the City of London or those of a criminal in and out of Newgate, working in an organized gang, and informing on his friends when Wild asked him to or when his neck depended on it, were abhorrent. For him, liberty was everything.

Two weeks after Jack was condemned to death, on 30 August, Edgworth Bess and Poll Maggott, another 'loose woman' whom he knew from the Black Lion, and who had encouraged him to crime as Bess had, came to visit him in the condemned hold at Newgate. They brought a set of women's clothes, which Jack slipped into while the attention of the keepers, at the other end of the ward, was distracted. He had chosen his time wisely: the annual St Bartholomew's Fair was on at Smithfield, so the streets of London were full of vagabonds and strolling players, and the city's authorities had their hands full; the court was at Windsor, so the focus of government was outside the capital; and there were disciplinary problems within Newgate itself. The prisoners who helped the turnkeys with gaol administration had been caught stealing the charity money that was used to buy bread for the poorest inmates, and were refusing to let visitors bring beer into the prison. Sheppard had already loosened one of the iron rods in the internal window of his cell, in preparation, and after taking it out, the girls pulled him through the window into the open ward. Like Toad dressed as a washerwoman, he walked brazenly out of Newgate with Bess and Poll under the eyes of the keepers, once more a free man.

Although Edgworth Bess had betrayed him to Wild, nevertheless he went with her to 'lie down in softest pleasures the remembrance of dangers past'.[6] But from this time, he and Bess became alienated from one another. She had in the past been referred to as his wife, and had lived with him as such; but after her betrayal, he denied this hotly. 'There is not a more wicked, deceitful, lascivious wretch living in England. She has proved my bane,' he told the Reverend Wagstaff, the Ordinary of Newgate, before his death. 'She indeed rewarded me as well for it [helping her escape from New Prison], in betraying me to Jonathan Wild so soon after.' But Wild caught up with Bess only days after she had helped Jack escape.

Last Tuesday, Joseph Shepheard's [*sic*] wife, who assisted her husband to make his escape out of the condemned hold, was discovered and taken by Jonathan Wild the thief-taker and late on the same night, she was brought to Newgate, being charged with felony for the same; we are certainly informed, that the said Shepheard went off by water between 7 and 8 o'clock on Monday night, at Blackfriars Stairs, the waterman saw his irons under his nightgown, and was terrified thereat; he landed him at the Horseferry at Westminster, for which he rewarded him with 7 pence.[7]

The day after his escape, Jack met up with his friend William Page, a butcher's apprentice in Clare Market. Disguised as butchers in blue smocks with white aprons, they set out to Chipping Warden in Northamptonshire, hoping to stay there with Page's family until the furore over Sheppard's latest escapade had died down. But Page's relatives were poor, and although they were welcoming they could not afford to harbour the young men for long. The two friends also found the country a trifle dull. 'As life doe not consist in breathing the air, but enjoyment, he began to be tired of his inactivity and longed to be a part again in the busy world. . .'[8]

So Jack and Page returned to London after only three days. Almost immediately, they were recognized in Islington by a milkman who spread the word that they were back. London's shopkeepers, who had been on tenterhooks since Sheppard's escape, hired guards for their shops. The pair passed a watchmaker's on Fleet Street, foolishly left guarded only by a boy, and stole three watches. Later on, having drunk the proceeds from the sale of one of the watches, they found the milkman who had raised the alarm and drenched him in milk and cream from his pans. Knowing that they would soon be captured, they decided to go on a second 'rural expedition' and left London, heading towards Finchley Common, still dressed as butchers.

Finchley Common was one of the capital's many growing suburbs. Though they were being rapidly absorbed into London proper, in the early part of the eighteenth century they still retained their strongly rural feel. Meat, fruit, vegetables and dairy products were all supplied to the city from the suburbs, and sold in one of the large markets in town which traded six days a week. Smithfield, then as now, was a meat market, dealing also in live cattle, sheep and horses; Covent Garden sold fruit, vegetables and flowers; meat, poultry, game, eggs and hides were on offer at Leadenhall; and fish and coal could be bought at Billingsgate. Many of these goods came into town by river to be distributed around the capital: cheese from Cheshire, Gloucestershire and Warwickshire; fruit from Kent; coal from Newcastle. London was the largest market town in England, the centre for all English trade. Despite its size – it was ten times bigger than any other city in the country – in parts it still had the feel of a country market town, with milch-asses roaming the streets, sallow milkmaids delivering milk from the 'lactarium' in St George's Fields, just south of the river, horses everywhere and mud, straw and manure fouling the streets (illustration 10, page 81; Hogarth's *Evening*, which shows the rural nature of London's outskirts). When Sheppard and Page stumbled out of the city to Finchley in the early hours of the morning of 9 September 1724, with the rising sun dispersing the mists that covered the nearby fields, they would have passed graziers and hog-keepers minding their flocks and milkmaids and farmers busily preparing to take their goods into town to be sold.

Jonathan Wild was determined to reap the glory of recapturing Sheppard. He found Edgworth Bess almost immediately, but she didn't know where Jack had gone – or would not tell Wild. He sent a man to Stourbridge to look for Sheppard, but he was following a false trail. Wild was made to look a fool when the keeper of Newgate, at the head of a posse, caught up with the fugitives at Finchley Common and took them back to gaol. The keeper, like Wild, wanted to take the credit for bringing Sheppard back to justice. In the *Daily Courant* of 4 September 1724, he had advertised a twenty-guinea reward just for 'discovering' Sheppard: 'He is about twenty-three years of age, and about five foot, four inches high, very slender, of a pale complexion, has been very sick, did wear a light bob wig, a light-coloured cloth coat and white waistcoat, has an impediment in his speech, and is a carpenter by trade.'

Jack gamely tried to slip the keeper's grip as he got out of the coach at Newgate, but could not. He was taken to a cell known as the 'Castle', the innermost stronghold of the gaol, and fastened to the floor with double fetters.

From the time he escaped Newgate's condemned hold with the help of Edgworth Bess and Poll Maggott, the public could not read enough about Jack Sheppard. His exploits were all over the newspapers.

He [Sheppard] has hinted in dark terms, that he hath committed robberies since his escape, and denies he was ever married to the woman who assisted him therein, and who is now in the Compter for the same, declaring that he found her a common strumpet in Drury Lane, and that she hath been the cause of all his misfortunes and misery; he takes great pains in excusing his companion Page of being in any way privy to his crimes, whom he says only generously accompanied him after his escape.[9]

The *London Journal*, a weekly paper, mentioned Jack in almost every issue from 5 September 1724 until his death. Broadsheets were published depicting his adventures (illustration 28, page 210; *The*

28. *The London Rairey Shows or Who'll Step into Ketch's Theatre* (Anon.)
This broadsheet, which would have been sold for a penny or two, was published just before Jack Sheppard's last escape from Newgate. He is shown sitting behind the window on the middle floor above the gate; Jonathan Wild is collecting fees from those wanting to go in and see Sheppard; and Jack Ketch, the hangman, invites them to 'Walk in Gentlemen', from his perch above Wild on the left-hand battlement. Newgate's old-fashioned architecture is set against the neat row of Georgian houses on the left of the print.

London Rairey Shows or Who'll Step into Ketch's Theatre). More space was devoted to him in London's newspapers than to any other single news item: other stories might merit a sentence or a few lines, but there was always a long paragraph about Jack.

Practically as soon as he was re-incarcerated, Sheppard began planning his next escape. Within the week, he had a file smuggled in to him in a Bible; when questioned about it, he retorted, 'One file's worth all the Bibles in the world.' His irreverence shocked the middle classes, but must have appealed to his peers, to whom religion was a foreign territory, occupied solely by their pious, respectable betters. Jack refused to treat the divines who visited him to try to save his soul with respect, calling them 'gingerbread fellows' (cant for moneymen) motivated more by curiosity than by charity. In chapel one Sunday, one of the Lord Mayor's men asked to have

Jack Sheppard pointed out to him. Jack called out impudently, 'Yes Sir, I am the Sheppard, and all the jailers in the town are my flock, and I cannot stir into the country but they are all at my heels baughing after me.'[10]

A few days later, two files, a chisel and a hammer were discovered hidden in the rush matting of his chair. How he had got them is a mystery, but the inmates of Newgate were renowned for the ingenuity of their escape attempts. In 1735 a gang of highwaymen had pistols smuggled into their cell in 'smoking hot pies'. Jack was distraught at his plan being foiled. 'When he perceived his last effort to escape thus discovered and frustrated, his wicked and obdurate heart began to melt, and he shed an abundance of tears,' reported the *Daily Journal* on 17 September.

In early October Jack was found by his keepers walking freely about his cell, having released himself from the chains that had bound him to a staple in the floor. ' 'Twas troublesome to be always in one position,' he announced nonchalantly to the stunned turnkeys. *Parker's London News* reported,

They searched him from head to foot, but found not so much as a pin, and when they had chained him down again, the head keeper, and others, came up and entertained him to discover, by what means he had got himself free, he reached forth his hand, and took up a nail, and with that, and no other instrument, unlocked himself again before their faces. Nothing so astonishing was ever known! He is now handcuffed, and more effectually chained.

Jack obviously took great pleasure in showing off his skills to his dumbfounded keepers, but he played down his achievement: 'Though people have made such an outcry about it, there is not a [black-] smith in London but what may easily do the same thing.'[11] As a punishment for his disobedience, and to prevent his escaping his shackles once more, the guards placed him in solitary confinement, handcuffing him as well as stapling him to the floor. For the first time in prison he was practically immobile. His old employer, Mr Kneebone, visited him for a second time soon after this incident; he begged the keepers with tears in his eyes to preserve Jack from 'those dreadful manacles'.[12]

Jack's hopes of escape began to fade; according to one newspaper, he threw himself on the mercy of Jonathan Wild.

Jack Sheppard, the condemned malefactor in Newgate, entertaining no hopes of life, has flung himself upon the charity of Jonathan Wild, who not only furnished him very handsomely with meals of substance in prison, and with proper books of devotion, but has promised him after a decent execution, to take care of his decent interment at his own cost and charge.

There is no other evidence of Jack's turning to Wild in this way and it is possible that *Parker's London News* got its facts slightly wrong, and were talking about Blueskin, instead of Jack. The *Daily Journal* states that it was Blueskin, not Sheppard, who threw himself upon Wild's mercy and this fits in with subsequent events. Neither Sheppard's nor Wild's pride would have allowed one to enter into an association with the other: Jack hated Wild for using Edgworth Bess to find him and for sending Hell-and-Fury Sykes to capture him when he was first arrested; and in turn he had become to Wild a sort of nemesis, humiliating him by slipping through his previously successful clutches. Perhaps Wild deliberately placed the information in the paper as some kind of public relations exercise, hoping that Londoners would look on him with sympathy if he were seen to be helping the man they now regarded as a hero.

PART FIVE

Happy had it been for him if Blake's wound had proved fatal,
for then Jonathan had escaped death by a more dishonourable wound in
the throat, than that of a penknife.

CAPTAIN JOHNSON,
The Lives of the Highwaymen, 1734

Death

On the day that Blueskin Blake was executed, Jack Sheppard was moved for the last time into the condemned hold (illustration 29, page 216). His cell-mate was a Frenchman named Louis Houssare, 'the French barber', who had violently murdered his wife. Both prisoners were stapled to the floor, and two guards were on round-the-clock duty. The week before Jack's execution 'was a week of the greatest noise and idleness among mechanics [manual workers and apprentices] that has been known in London':

His escape and his being so suddenly retaken made such a noise in the town, that it was thought all the common people would have gone mad about him; there being not a porter to be had for love nor money, nor getting into an alehouse, for butchers, shoemakers and barbers, all engaged in controversies, and wagers, about Sheppard Newgate night and day surrounded with the curious from St Giles's and Rag Fair, and Tyburn Road daily lined with women lest he be hanged Incog [incognito; anonymously].[1]

At nine o'clock on the morning of Monday 16 November 1724, Jack Sheppard was taken out of the condemned hold to the chapel to receive his last rites from the Reverend Wagstaff, one of the prison chaplains. Reverend Purney, the Ordinary, or head chaplain of Newgate, was ill and in the country recuperating; normally, he would have presided over the ceremony for a prisoner as notorious as Jack. The keepers made a profit by charging visitors for the privilege of watching the condemned men in chapel the day before they died. 'For a full two months we have been hindered from going to chapel because the keepers . . . make a great show of the

29. *Jack Sheppard in Newgate* (Anon.)

condemned prisoners in the chapel by which they raise great sums of money.'[2] According to custom, Jack sat in front of his own black-shrouded coffin to hear the service.

The Ordinary's attempts to impose religion (and thus, order) on his charges were invariably met with resistance and mockery. His weekly sermons were marked by the prisoners' irreverence and insolence. They talked throughout the services, sometimes loudly threatening to shoot the Ordinary. They ate and drank off the altar, smoked during the sermons, even relieved themselves in the corners of the chapel. They spat on the Ordinary's pulpit and cut off the tassels from the pulpit cushion. But the blasphemous behaviour of their charges did not unduly worry Newgate's chaplains. They were motivated more by the desire for profit than any altruistic wish to save damned souls. Most Ordinaries published accounts of the condemned malefactors who passed under their gaze, which sold like wildfire. Hogarth places the Ordinary on a parallel with a hawker of last dying speeches in the Tyburn scene of the Idle Apprentice series (illustration 30, page 218): they are the only two figures who look directly out towards the viewer, one placed immediately above the other in the centre of the print. So profitable were their accounts that some Ordinaries even threatened to withhold the Holy Sacraments from those prisoners who refused to tell their story to them. Most prisoners, though, were tempted by the prospect of having enough money for a decent suit of clothes in which to hang, and a coffin. John Allen, Ordinary at the start of the eighteenth century, ran a small funeral business as a side-line to his publishing work.

Some malefactors refused to repent. The last man to be hanged in chains shouted from the scaffold, 'There is no God. I do not believe there is any and, if there is, I hold Him in contempt.' Others were penitent, seeking salvation in the last moments of their lives. One man, converted by the Methodist evangelist John Wesley just before he was hanged, said beatifically as he was dying, 'I feel a peace which I could not have believed to be possible. And I know it is the peace of God, which passeth all understanding.' Wesley's crusade to save the souls of the damned led him to Tyburn in the

30. *Industry and Idleness XI: The Idle 'Prentice Executed at Tyburn* (William Hogarth)
The only person weeping for Tom Idle's imminent death is his mother, who stands
in a cart at the far right with her head buried in her apron. All the other figures,
except the ballad-monger and the Ordinary, who look directly out at the viewer, are
concentrating on the atmosphere and spectacle of the 'Hanging Fair'. Below Mrs
Idle's cart, two small boys are picking the pocket of a vendor as he hawks his wares.

1730s. He tried to convert a gang of highwaymen awaiting execution but they refused to listen. Two nights before they were due to
die, two of the robbers escaped but were caught when trying to release their fellow prisoners. They were hanged wearing 'white cockades in their hats in token of their triumph over this world'. White
cockades were a public protestation of innocence; in this case, they
were also a symbol of the dead men's resistance to Wesley's faith.
He was preaching the surrender of the sins of the world; but he was
trying to teach the rewards of renunciation to men whose lives had
been ruled by a desire for material gain and the pleasures of the
flesh.[3]

After visiting the chapel, Jack was taken by his guards to the Press
Yard where Watson, the Under-Sheriff, made the traditional formal
demand for his body. His fetters (or 'Darbies') were knocked off his
feet with a block and hammer. Jack appeared in high spirits, stam-
mering out witticisms to the guards, but when he saw that his

hands were being rebound he demanded furiously that his handcuffs be removed. Traditionally, as he well knew, condemned men travelled to Tyburn in an open cart with their wrists free, but their arms bound by the rope that would be tied into their noose. Watson jokingly replied, 'You're an imp of mischief and it will be impossible to deliver you safely at Tyburn unless you have irons on your wrists.'[4]

Jack pulled violently away from the Knight of the Halter who was securing him in the cart and raised his manacled hands over Watson's head in an effort to strike him. The turnkeys got hold of him before he brought his hands down, and Watson began searching Jack's person. With a scream of pain, he withdrew his hand from Sheppard's waistcoat pocket, revealing a cut and bloody hand. He had caught it on a sharp clasp penknife, fastened into Jack's inside pocket with the blade pointing out. Seeing there was no point in feigning innocence, Jack laughed delightedly and began telling the guards of his ingenious plan to cut off the rope binding his arms by rubbing it surreptitiously against the clasp knife as the cart bore him to Tyburn. Once he was free, he had planned to

throw himself over among the crowd, and run through the narrow passage [at the Little Turnstile, near Lincoln's Inn Fields], where the officers could not follow on horseback, but must be forced to dismount; and in the meantime doubted not, but by the mob's assistance, he should make his escape.

Secured by heavy handcuffs, his last-ditch plans for escape foiled, Jack was driven through the streets of London towards Tyburn (on the site of Marble Arch). There had been a gallows at Tyburn since 1571, but it was only one of many execution sites in eighteenth-century London – known as the 'City of the Gallows' for the multitude of gibbets a visitor to London passed on his way into the city. Criminals might also be hanged at Newgate, Putney Common, Kennington Common, Smithfield, Finchley Common and the aptly named Execution Dock in East Wapping. Women were burned at the stake outside the church of St Bartholomew the Great, near Smithfield.

The procession to Tyburn took about two hours. It passed St Sepulchre's Church where the bells traditionally tolled for the miscreants' 'wickedness and sin'. '. . .And knowing it is for you going to your death, may you be stirred up heartily to pray to God to bestow his grace and mercy upon you whilst you live,' exhorted the Ordinary. Jack rode towards the gallows with his noose around his neck and his coffin at his feet. The cart was attended by mounted, liveried Javelin Men and led by one of the City Marshals, proudly holding his silver mace before him.

The streets were thronged with well-wishers; in some places the crowd was so dense the procession had to stop and wait for the way to be cleared. On some hanging days, spectators were trampled to death in the crush. There was a carnival atmosphere as people from all levels of society flooded the streets to see their hero die a noble death. Samuel Pepys got a cramp in his leg from standing on a cart wheel, the better to see all the action, at an execution in 1663; in the next century James Boswell confessed that he was 'never absent from a public execution'. There were often as many as 30,000 people; one hanging in Moorfields in 1767 attracted 80,000 spectators. At Tyburn, permanent wooden grandstands known as 'Mother Proctor's Pews' had been erected to seat the crowd.

The eight annual hanging days were commonly known as 'Hanging Fairs' – with hawkers selling food and drink, taverns and inns serving customers on the street, ballad-mongers and jugglers entertaining the assembly (illustration 30, page 218; Plate XI of *Industry and Idleness*). You could buy 'invitations' to the 'Hanging Match' and cheap broadsheet copies of the victims' last words. Jack's unofficial last dying speech was being sold for a penny or two:

> Like Doctor Faustus, I my pranks have played,
> (By contract with his Master long since made)
> Like him lived gay, and revelled in delight,
> Drank all the day, and whored the livelong night.
> To raise my name above all rogues in [hi-]story,
> I've made chains, bolts, and bars fly all before me:
> But, Hark, the dismal sound! The clock strikes one:

The charm is broke, and all my strength is gone:
The dragon comes, I hear his hideous roar;
Farewell my friends, for now poor Jack's no more.

Cant expressions for hanging abounded in street slang because of the personal relevance hanging had for London's poor. If many of the city's destitute population were driven to crime at some stage in their lives, then many of them, too, would have seen the gallows as a very real spectre. Making a mockery of the government's ritual humiliation of their number was the only way they could diminish its importance. Hanging days were known as the 'Sheriff's Ball'; hanging itself was called 'Dancing the Paddington Frisk' and 'Dangling in the Sheriff's Picture Frame'. When one was hanged one was tucked up, or turned off. One common expression held that hanging was nothing more than 'a wry neck, and a wet pair of breeches'.

Although the threat of the gallows was a very real one to much of the crowd, it did not deter thieves from practising their craft. Instead hanging days almost seemed to encourage them to ply their trade among the spectators distracted by the main event. The moment when the crowd was absorbed in concentration on the dying man was the perfect time for pickpockets to pounce on their unsuspecting prey.

'Sometimes the girls dress in white, with great silk scarves, and carry baskets full of flowers and oranges, scattering these favours all the way they go.'[5] While men saw Tyburn's victims as popular heroes, women often saw them as heart-throbs. In *The Beggars' Opera*, Mrs Peachum sums up the attitude of her sex towards men like Jack Sheppard: 'The Youth in his cart hath the air of a Lord/ And we cry, there dies an Adonis.' Polly Peachum echoes her mother's sentiments as she laments Macheath's death.

Methinks I see him already in his cart, sweeter and more lovely than the nosegay in his hand! – I hear the crowd extolling his resolution and intrepidity! – What vollies of sighs are sent from the windows of Holborn, that so comely a youth should be brought to disgrace! – I see him at the Tree [Tyburn tree]! The whole circle are in tears! – Even butchers weep! – Jack

Ketch [the slang name for the hangman, taken from the name of a real executioner of the seventeenth century] himself hesitates to perform his duty, and would be glad to lose his fee, by a reprieve . . .

Crying girls handed Jack bunches of flowers as he rode past them and men struggled up to him as he sat in his cart to wish him well and shake his hand. Women often outnumbered men on hanging days, and were noted for their vociferous presence, either baying for blood or weeping tears of sympathy for the victims.

When all the prisoners arrive at their destination they are made to mount on a very wide cart made expressly for the purpose, a cord is passed round their necks and the end fastened to the gibbet, which is not very high. The chaplain who accompanied the condemned men is also on the cart; he makes them pray and sing a few verses of the Psalms. The relatives are permitted to mount the cart and take farewell. When the time is up – that is to say about a quarter of an hour – the chaplain and relations get off the cart, the executioner covers the eyes and faces of the prisoners with their caps, lashes the horses that draw the cart, which slips from under the condemned men's feet. . .[6]

The cart stopped at the City of Oxford tavern on the Oxford Road (today's Oxford Street) by Marylebone Fields, and Jack drank a pint of sack (warm fortified wine) with James Figgs, the boxer who had visited him in Newgate. A youth bounded up on to his cart and whispered a word into his ear before jumping off and disappearing into the crush. Jack threw his head back and laughed with abandon at his comment; possibly he had just been told of plans to resuscitate his corpse after he had been hanged for the allotted time. He said gaily, if inexplicably, to Reverend Wagstaff, who rode with him to offer spiritual solace if it was needed, that, 'I have now as great satisfaction at heart as if I was going to enjoy an estate of £200 a year.'

Unlike some of his peers, Sheppard did not choose to use his hanging as a chance to demonstrate his innocence. When the cart stopped at Tyburn and the hangman began his preparations, Jack held out a pamphlet called *A Narrative of All the Robberies, Escapes,*

&c., of John Sheppard, written by himself and printed by John Applebee of Blackfriars, dated 10 November 1724 in the Middle Stone Room at Newgate. He declared that this (with the writing of which he was probably helped by Defoe) should be published as his official confession. He agreed to publicize Applebee's account of his life in return for an assurance that the publisher would arrange his 'rescue', a common practice that involved waiting to collect the near-dead body once it had hung for the mandatory fifteen minutes, and taking it quickly to a doctor, who would try to revive it with warm blankets and wine. Should he survive his execution, his story would attract even more interest than it already had; and Applebee would have had the scoop of the century.

Until the automatic drop was introduced in 1760, hanging more often resulted in unconsciousness than death. There were several famous cases of people being revived after they had been hanged: John Smith, who hanged for two hours in 1709, recovered and lived for ten more years. He was known for the rest of his life as Half-Hanged Smith. Sir William Petty, a famous surgeon, revived an apparent corpse brought to him for 'anatomization', or dissection, in front of students. She lived another fifteen years. By tradition, if the first hanging was unsuccessful, a condemned man could go free because his survival was a sign of divine favour.

Some were not so lucky. Six months after Jack's death, a man condemned to death by hanging was being tied up at Tyburn ready for the cart to move away. But as the sheriff's officers approached him, he

flipped [his head] out of the halter, leapt out of the cart among the mob, [and began] to tear off his shroud; but his hands were tied, and he [could] do but little at it. Jack Ketch leapt upon his back, and the officers surrounded him, so that he was soon taken, [rehaltered], and hanged.[7]

At the last, Jack was subdued and obedient. Once the noose was fastened around his neck, the cart moved out from beneath his feet and he was left dangling beneath the gibbet. Because he was so slight, it took several minutes for him to lose consciousness – he did not weigh enough to force his body to drop sharply, and thus break his neck. He writhed and twisted on the end of the rope, with people in the crowd pulling at his legs hoping to ease his pain by breaking his neck, until finally he grew limp and still. 'The hangman does not give himself the trouble to put them [the hanging men] out of their pain; but some of their friends or relations do it for them: they pull the dying person by the legs, and beat his breast, to dispatch him as soon as possible.'[8] The friends of a pirate called John Gow were in such a panic to ensure his quick and painless death that they pulled his legs so hard they broke the rope holding him and he had to be strung up again.

Many victims of the gallows stayed sensible of their situation for several minutes, even after the long drop was introduced. Hangmen were notoriously slapdash about their profession. The body would hang suspended, its bound legs and arms jerking convulsively. Dying men often defecated and urinated in the throes of death; some even ejaculated. Their eyes bulged out of their sockets and a 'bloody froth or frothy mucus' bubbled out of their mouths and noses.

After the allotted fifteen minutes were up, the hearse ordered by Defoe and Applebee to take Jack away and try to resuscitate him approached the dangling body. The crowd, fearing that the hearse was about to take him off to be anatomized, pelted the driver with stones and surged forward to protect the body. Anatomization was an overriding terror of men condemned to death, either from a simple fear of being cut up, whether dead or alive, or perhaps from a distant hope that they might be revived if they had not been dissected; Blueskin had hoped that Wild would protect him from the 'Surgeons' Hall' (illustration 31, page 226; *The Reward of Cruelty*). Onlookers fought fiercely to shield the victims' bodies from the doctors' hearses that skirted the edge of the crowd on execution days, seeking to save one of their own from something they themselves feared. Foremost in their minds must have been the awareness that the dead man might just as easily have been them. They were compelled by a sense of solidarity with the victim as well as traditional religious beliefs in the sanctity of the corpse, and the importance of a proper burial because the soul's resurrection on Judgement Day was believed to depend on the corpse's integrity after death.[9] Dick Turpin's body was exhumed a few days after his burial, by a crowd who feared it had been taken away to be dissected; it was carried triumphantly through the city of York, where Turpin had died, on the shoulders of four men.

The desire of the poor to save the bodies of the hangman's victims was compounded by the feeling that the educated classes were exploiting and desecrating their dead heroes by using them as scientific experiments. The lower classes believed that the corpses of condemned men had mythical, almost magical powers which were defiled by dissection. The ancient Romans thought that the blood of criminals was a cure for epilepsy, while the 'death sweat' of a condemned man was held to cure the King's Evil. A withered limb would be made whole again by placing it on the neck of a recently hanged man, and touching the hand of a hanged man could cure a multitude of ailments ranging from cancerous growths to ulcers. The hand of a hanged man could also make a barren woman fertile. Shopkeepers thought their business would improve if they kept the fingers of a felon in their shop; a small bone taken from a criminal's corpse and carried in a purse was supposed to keep it from being empty. The hangman did a roaring trade after execution days by selling the rope used to hang the felons for a shilling an inch; it was meant to bring good luck.

In the crush, Jack's body was torn and dragged about; eventually, relative peace was restored, and what remained of the corpse was taken to the Barley Mow tavern. Later that night, when his friends attempted to take it away to bury it, another riot broke out outside the tavern. Finally, at about midnight, Jack was interred in the churchyard of St Martin-in-the-Fields.

Two weeks later *The Harlequin Sheppard*, a popular 'opera', opened in a Drury Lane theatre, the first in a long line of dramatizations of Jack Sheppard's short life.

31. *The Reward of Cruelty* (William Hogarth)

The corpse of Tom Nero lies on the dissecting table in the Royal College of Surgeons, the noose still around his neck. The doctor who surveys the scene looks down from his throne like Christ in Judgement. The two skeletons hanging on either side of the room belonged to other (real) convicted highwaymen. At the bottom left of the engraving, a cauldron full of bones bubbles like some strange pagan ritual vessel.

So amazing have been the actions of this desperado, that, we hear, they have got *The Escapes of Jack Sheppard, or Harlequin in Newgate*, now in rehearsal at the new playhouse; Mr Lun not doubting but to make as much of him as he has done of Dr Faustus [another popular play]. The person who plays Sheppard, it seems, went to see the original in Newgate; who told him, he should be glad to have it in his power to play his own part.[10]

The most successful and enduring play based on Jack Sheppard's life was undoubtedly John Gay's *The Beggars' Opera*, first staged in 1728. It was performed more than any other piece in the eighteenth century, and there was at least one production every year from 1728 until 1886. Although Macheath, the central character, was a highwayman rather than a house-breaker, he had been based in part on Sheppard, and his enemy, Peachum, was clearly modelled on Sheppard's antagonist Jonathan Wild. Gay had planned to write about Wild ever since meeting him at the races at Windsor in 1719. Wild had 'discoursed with great freedom on his profession, and set it in such a light, that the poet imagined he might work up the incidents of it for the stage'. Gay had discussed his idea for a 'Newgate Pastoral' with his friends Alexander Pope and Jonathan Swift, neither of whom thought his play would succeed. But succeed it did. It was said to have made Gay rich, and Rich (the producer) gay. Gay, who had lost everything when the South Sea Bubble burst in 1721, made between £700 and £2,000 from the musical. Lavinia Fenton, who played Polly Peachum, became the most celebrated woman in London. The Duke of Bolton made her his mistress, with an annual allowance of £400; scandalously, he later married her. William Hogarth painted scenes from the play, song-books were published, prints of the characters engraved, 'Beggars' Opera' playing cards and fans issued.

Daniel Defoe was one of the contemporary writers who took a firm stand against what he saw as the corrupting influence of *The Beggars' Opera*.

We take pain to puff 'em [rogues] up in their villainy, and thieves are set out in so amiable a light in *The Beggars' Opera* that it has taught them to value themselves on their profession, rather than be ashamed of it, by making a highwayman the hero and dismissing him at the last unpunished.

In Jack Sheppard's autobiography, most probably ghost-written by Defoe, Jack says he hopes his story will 'prove a warning to all young men'. From the little we know about Jack, it seems unlikely that this sentiment originated from him. More probably it was inserted by Defoe, trying to add a moral to the story of the outlaw's life. Defoe was very concerned about the negative influence glamorous, escapist crime stories had on their impressionable readers. ' 'Tis something strange,' he wrote in the preface to his life of Jonathan Wild, 'that a man's life should be made a kind of romance before his face, and while he was on the spot to contradict it; or, that the world should be so fond of a formal chimney-corner tale, that they had rather that a story should be made merry than true.'

Defoe was not wrong about the image characters like Sheppard and Macheath projected. A boy of seventeen who was tried at the Old Bailey declared himself 'so delighted with the spirit and heroic character of Macheath, that on quitting the theatre he laid out his last guinea on the purchase of a pair of pistols, and stopped a gentleman on the highway'.[11] And the attraction persisted throughout the nineteenth century. A Manchester boy in the 1840s claimed he saw the play *Jack Sheppard* 'four times in one week', spending 6d. of his weekly 6s. 6d. salary. R. H. Horne, a nineteenth-century writer, commented that although common people had no knowledge of biblical figures they knew intimately 'the character and course of life of Dick Turpin, the highwayman, and more particularly of Jack Sheppard, the robber and prison-breaker'.[12] This state of affairs was traced directly back to the popularity of *The Beggars' Opera*:

Rapine and violence have been gradually increasing ever since its first representation . . . Young men, apprentices, clerks in public offices, and others, disdaining the arts of honest industry and captivated with arts of idleness and criminal pleasures, now betake themselves to the road, affect politeness in the very act of robbery, and in the end become victims to the justice of their country.[13]

William Harrison Ainsworth's novel *Jack Sheppard* was published in 1839. He and Charles Dickens visited Newgate together in 1837, Ainsworth researching *Jack Sheppard*, and Dickens collecting notes for what became *Oliver Twist*. Nine new plays based on Jack's life were released in the year after Ainsworth's novel was published, but after 1840 any play with the name 'Jack Sheppard' in its title was banned by the government following the murder of 72-year-old Lord William Russell by his valet, Courvoisier. At his trial, Courvoisier claimed he had gone to his master's bedroom to kill him after reading *Jack Sheppard*. Dickens described watching the valet hang:

No sorrow, no salutary terror, no abhorrence, no seriousness; nothing but ribaldry, debauchery, levity, drunkenness, and flaunting vice in fifty other shapes . . . I hoped, for an instant, that there was some sense of Death and Eternity in the cry of 'Hats Off!' when the miserable wretch appeared; but I found, next moment, that they only raised it as they would at a play – to see the stage the better, in the final scene.

Jack Sheppard also inspired the painter and engraver William Hogarth. Hogarth's father-in-law, Sir James Thornhill, had painted Sheppard in Newgate. It is not known if Hogarth, Thornhill's apprentice, accompanied him on this assignment, but Hogarth must have seen the portrait (which has since been lost). The features of Tom Idle, the idle apprentice in *Industry and Idleness*, are supposedly derived from Thornhill's portrait of Jack Sheppard, and Tom's life mirrors that of the real Jack. Unlike Defoe, who puts words into Jack's mouth to make his story a better example to other young men, Hogarth allowed his account to stand alone. Jack's end was the only moral he needed: Hogarth let it speak for itself.

William Hogarth (self-portrait, illustration 32, page 230) was almost unique among his contemporaries for his interest in, and sympathy with, the lives of the eighteenth-century underclasses. Most artists of this period concentrated on works commissioned by their wealthy clientele, usually of a religious, heroic or commemorative nature; Hogarth, like the writers Defoe and Fielding, preferred to look at society as a whole. Whereas he painted portraits of members of the

32. Self-portrait (William Hogarth)

aristocracy and merchant classes, he chose to use engravings – their complex narrative schemes often novelistic in their conception – to illustrate a side of life largely ignored by other painters of the time.

Where Hogarth was brought up played a significant part in forming his mentality. He was born in Bartholomew's Close, an area of London like Spitalfields, where Jack Sheppard was born, that was noted for its dissenting, radical population. Newgate Prison was two minutes' walk away; the procession of the condemned men passed through Smithfield on its way to Tyburn. The raucous Smithfield meat market was practically on his doorstep. St Bartholomew's Fair, held annually at Smithfield, was thronged with strolling players like the ones to whom the young Jonathan Wild had been attracted in Wolverhampton. Criminals, who saw fairs as places of business, congregated at St Bartholomew's Fair, plying their various trades (illustration 23, page 145; *Southwark Fair*). Jonathan Wild's thief-taking predecessors used fairs as he did, to display their strength and keep in contact with the men and women who worked for them. These characters, alienated from normal society, whom Hogarth depicts time and again in his engravings, had been known to him from his earliest years, and his empathy with figures such as Moll Hackabout and Tom Idle sprang from his background and upbringing.

William Hogarth was born on 10 November 1697, the son of a Latin scholar who spent much of his son's youth in a debtors' prison. Although Hogarth was middle class, in that he was well ed-ucated and the son of a scholar, the poverty in which he grew up as a result of his father's debts meant that he never felt he belonged to the newly prosperous mercantile class of early eighteenth-century London. He was a child neither of the street, because his education and birth lifted him above it, nor of the emergent middle class, which his family lacked the funds to belong to.

These childhood influences allowed Hogarth to bring a special understanding to his illustrations of the lives of outcasts. Ronald Paulson argues that his sympathetic attitude can be seen most clearly in the series *Industry and Idleness*, where Hogarth, ostensibly lauding the rise to wealth and responsibility of Francis Goodchild, the Industrious 'Prentice, in contrast to the dissolution of Tom Idle, the Idle 'Prentice, is in fact looking up at the progression of events from the perspective of Tom Idle. The hero of the piece is really a villain; and the good-for-nothing Tom no more than a vic-tim of circumstance.

In Plate I (illustration 5, page 35), Francis Goodchild and Tom

Idle sit at their looms, watched over by their stick-wielding master. Goodchild sits in the light, beneath a window, weaving away industriously, a clean copy of the *'Prentices' Guide* at his feet, his coat brushed and neat. Idle sleeps off a hangover in the dim light that reaches his rickety loom, clad in a ragged jacket, a tattered copy of the *'Prentices' Guide* on the floor beside him. Paulson sees Idle's drinking and whoring as symptoms of his condition, rather than the causes of it. Idle had been consigned by his master to a poor quality loom in a dark corner, given a torn-up guide to his duties, his clothes left unmended, his education neglected; Goodchild sits, literally and metaphorically, in the light. Idle's fate has been imposed on him with his name; he would have to work twice as hard as Goodchild to escape the taint of the expectations his name carries with it.

Is [Goodchild] good because his name inclines others to expect good of him and treat him well, or is he named (allegorically) to correspond to his good character? Have others been prejudiced against Idle by his name and so discouraged him that he has taken on the qualities which his name assigned him?[14]

While on the surface, Hogarth holds Goodchild up as an example of the ideal apprentice, an apprentice looking at the series would notice immediately the sinister implications of Goodchild's swift marriage to his master's daughter and the insidious, inexorable takeover of his master's business. Hogarth, who had seen himself as an idle apprentice, indulging in the stereotypical apprentices' pastimes of gambling, drinking and whoring, could hardly have been unaware of the impression his portraits of Goodchild and Idle would create in the minds of their real-life counterparts. Hogarth was saved by his ambition and creativity, which served to free him from the drudgery of his 'long apprenticeship', but Tom Idle had no avenues of escape except those open to Jack Sheppard and others like him: taverns, gin shops, brothels, flash-houses and eventually, inevitably, the gallows.

Decline

Jonathan Wild, who had been so instrumental in the capture and conviction of Jack Sheppard and Blueskin Blake, found that his popularity, far from rising as a result of these successes, was on the wane. For the common people of London, Jack's adventures had been a joyful respite from their dreary, struggling lives. When he died they mourned their loss. And Jonathan was the object of their grief and anger.

Wild had needed to remove Jack. Throughout his career, he had focused his energies on ridding London of any groups of criminals who worked independently of him. He had purged the capital of five major gangs of highwaymen and footpads and by 1724 most of the members of the city's criminal underworld were under his control. All, that is, except Sheppard, whose charisma and charm attracted into his sphere men such as Blueskin, who had once been part of Wild's 'Corporation of Thieves'. Jack's emphasis on loyalty to one's associates and independence from authority – both government authority and its mirror image within the criminal hierarchy – challenged all that Wild had achieved since his years in Wood Street Compter. Jack Sheppard was a maverick, the wild card that threatened to destroy Wild's criminal empire by undermining the principles of selfishness and suspicion on which he based his control over his Corporation.

Wild had been seriously wounded by Blake's attack in the Old Bailey. He was confined to his bed for several weeks – to his chagrin, no doubt missing Jack's execution – while his throat healed. He was lucky to have survived. In the eighteenth century even a small cut could prove fatal since there were no antibiotics. Minor ailments lingered for months, surgery was rare and very dangerous without anaesthetics, and liquor and opium were the only effective pain relievers.

Despite the increasing confidence that disease 'was a foe medical science could vanquish',[1] there were as yet few scientific advances to improve the health of the mass of the population. Physical defects either at birth or as the result of an accident could not be corrected surgically, so the sight of a twisted cripple or mutilated, scarred face would have been common. Indeed these people might even capitalize on their misfortune by displaying themselves to curious crowds at fairs and markets. Quacks abounded, like the 'dentist' in the window of Hogarth's *Night* (illustration 33, page 235), exploiting victims of the dread diseases of the age – smallpox, leprosy, consumption, tetanus – through a mixture of sham medical knowledge, dressed up with a few words of Latin, and the terror and pain of their patients. Their remedies contained ingredients such as live hog-lice and worms, goose shit and ground human bones. Extravagant claims were made in advertisements like this one, which were pasted on the walls of coffee-houses and inserted in newspapers:

Purging sugar plums for children and others of nice palates, nothing differing in taste, colour, etc. from sugar plums at the confectioner's, having been experienced by thousands to sweeten and purify the blood to admiration, kill worms, cure green sickness in maids, pale looks in children, rickets, stomach aches, King's evil [scrofula], scurvies, rheumatisms, dropsia, scabs, itch, tetters [skin eruptions], etc. Good in cases where purging is necessary, doing all that is possible to be done by purging medicine being the cheapest, fastest, pleasantest medicine in the world. Fit for persons of all ranks, ages, and sexes; price is on the box, to be had only at Mr Spooner's at the [sign of the] Golden Half Moon in Lemon Street, Goodman's fields, near Whitechapel, with directions [for use].

Some remedies were hailed as total panaceas, like the 'Pectoral, Healing, Balsamick, Chymical QUINTESSENCE' advertised in one newspaper. Even hypochondria had a cure: 'famous drops for Hypochondriack Melancholly, which effectually cure on the spot'.

Many reputable doctors had a touch of the charlatan: Dr Richard

33. *Night* (William Hogarth)

The overturned stagecoach and the fire in the background conjure up an image of disorder and chaos. The man following the link-boy on the left is a portrait of the magistrate Thomas de Veil, whose strict enforcement of the Gin Act provoked riots in 1738. He is shown drunk, clothed in full Freemason regalia, as a woman empties her chamber pot on to him from an upstairs window.

Mead, medical adviser to Queen Anne, sat daily in Batson's coffee-house writing prescriptions at half a guinea a go for apothecaries whose patients he didn't even see. Despite popular dependence on these men, through necessity rather than choice, they were universally derided:

> But baneful quacks, in physick's art unread,
> To weaving, cobbling or tumbling bred,
> Or else poor scoundrels, who for scraps & thanks,
> Swept stages for their master mountebanks,
> These to the world destructive slops commend
> And do their poys'nous cheats to live extend,
> By vain pretences pick the patients' purse,
> And with sham med'cines make 'em ten times worse.[2]

But medical advances were being made. Lady Mary Wortley Montagu brought back to England in 1718 a technique of inoculation she had seen practised successfully in Turkey, which was soon in common use by the upper classes. It was considered a marvel:

We are certainly informed that Mr Horace Walpole, son to the Right Honourable Robert Walpole Esq [later Prime Minister], who was inoculated for the smallpox three weeks since by Mr Maitland, apothecary in Pall Mall, has had the disease very fair and favourable, and is recovered to the great satisfaction of all his friends.[3]

William Harvey had published his theory of the circulation of blood in 1628; thirty-nine years later, in 1667, the first blood transfusion was performed at London's Royal Society. The widespread use of criminals' corpses for anatomical research and demonstration greatly increased surgeons' knowledge of the human body. Several new hospitals opened in London over the first half of the century, including Westminster General Infirmary in 1719, Guy's Hospital in 1725, St George's Hospital in 1733 and the London Hospital in 1752.

Eighteenth-century men lived, on average, to between forty and fifty years of age. Wild was an old man of forty-one or forty-two when Blueskin stabbed him, and found it difficult to recover his drive. He was not as strong as he had once been, and his successes had softened him. The ruthlessness he had possessed as a younger man was diluted by his mature desire to become an accepted part of London's bourgeois élite. He no longer judged situations as adroitly; his reactions had become blunted.

As soon as he recovered, Wild turned his attention to a crisis which had sprung up concerning one of his men, Roger Johnson, a hardened malefactor. He had been arrested in 1718 for 'Preaching the Parson', a confidence trick by which, disguised as a churchman, he exchanged forged coins for real ones. Tried and condemned to death, he informed on his own mother in order to obtain his freedom. He began working for Wild soon after his release from prison. In the early 1720s Wild bought a ship and placed Johnson in it as captain. Johnson ferried the sloop back and forth between London and Flanders, taking stolen goods which could not be sold in England to a warehouse in Flushing for resale in Europe, and then smuggling foreign goods back into London. He masqueraded as a respectable trader, advertising that he was to be found at the Graecian coffee-house, on the Exchange, to conduct business.

Johnson, suspecting one of his sailors of stealing some valuable Holland cloth which they were bringing to England to sell, stopped the man's wages. The sailor, furious at the accusation, went to see an old enemy of Johnson's called Tom Edwards, who owned the Goat tavern in Long Lane, and told him when Johnson was expected in London. Soon after Johnson's arrival, Edwards procured a warrant for his arrest. This was an easy enough process for a man like Edwards whose underworld associations would have brought him into contact with corrupt constables or JPs who had the right to issue warrants, and would do so for a price. The two men met outside the Black Lyon alehouse in the Strand (not the Black Lion in Drury Lane where Jack Sheppard had been corrupted by Edgworth Bess and her friends) and Edwards took Johnson into custody. Johnson, however, managed to get a messenger to Wild. Pausing only to collect a constable and a warrant, Wild rushed over to the Goat, released Johnson, and had Edwards arrested.

Within a few days Edwards had procured his own release from

Wood Street Compter. Knowing the way to get at Johnson was through Wild, he obtained a warrant to search one of Wild's warehouses and seized the contraband goods Wild and Johnson kept in storage there. Wild, apoplectic with rage but aware that he could not implicate himself in a dispute over what were clearly stolen goods, could do no more than try to claim them in Johnson's name. He had Edwards rearrested, but Edwards's agents, in turn, sent out constables to arrest Johnson. This they did, but once again he was able to send for Wild in the nick of time. Wild, attended by Quilt Arnold, arrived at the alehouse in Middlesex where the constables were having a drink before placing Johnson in custody. A fight broke out, Wild and his men emerged victorious, and Roger Johnson once more escaped the clutches of the law. Meanwhile, Edwards had bailed himself out of Marshalsea Prison and had sworn revenge on Wild and Johnson.

This incident only confirmed to the public what they had suspected since Wild's feverish pursuit of Jack Sheppard: that Jonathan Wild, far from being the public-spirited benefactor he pretended to be, was a self-serving, professional villain. It was obvious that his interests had been threatened by Edwards's assault on Johnson; and that Johnson himself was little more than a smuggler, a pawn in Wild's game. Afraid of the wrath of Tom Edwards, and aware that the law would not back him if he tried to bring the affair into the open, Wild went into hiding for several weeks. He tried to stem the rising tide of antipathy towards him by putting advertisements in newspapers offering a reward of ten guineas to any person who discovered the source of the rumours circulating about him.

When he thought the affair had blown over, Wild came out of hiding to attend to business. On Saturday 6 February he was summoned to Leicester House, the London residence of the Prince and Princess of Wales, to offer his opinion about a gold watch which had been stolen from one of their attendants; Wild advised them that the watch was 'past all hopes of recovery'. This uncharacteristic failure to act, to take advantage of the social and professional cachet of being consulted by Leicester House, shows how distracted he was by the affair with Johnson and Edwards, and how his wound and long illness had sapped his strength.

Just days after this honour, on 15 February 1725, Wild was arrested. Thomas Jones, constable in the parish of Holborn, came to Wild's office in the Old Bailey, seized him and Quilt Arnold and took the two men to Sir John Fryer, a magistrate, 'who, being indisposed, sat up in his bed to examine him [Wild]'. Wild was charged with helping Roger Johnson, described as a 'highwayman', to escape from a constable at a tavern in Bow, Middlesex. He was taken to Newgate and placed in custody.

No proceedings were brought against him at first, but Constable Jones's affidavit stated that there were two people willing to stand evidence against Wild in court. John Follard, a thief, and Thomas Butler, a 'Passing Lay', or card shark, had agreed to charge Wild with a capital crime in return for immunity. Significantly, Thomas Butler's brother owned the Black Lyon alehouse on the Strand outside which Thomas Edwards had first arrested Roger Johnson. A 'Warrant of Detainder' was also issued, charging Wild with 'forming a kind of Corporation of Thieves of which he was the head or director'. In twelve points, it detailed his crimes: organizing of robberies; using returned transported convicts as virtual slave labour; receiving, concealing, altering, smuggling and selling stolen goods; and finally selling 'human blood' by regularly giving up to the gallows in return for the government's cash reward some of the criminals who worked for him. He was accused of carrying a silver staff as a spurious display of the authority he assumed. Another section indignantly pointed out that he often charged well over half the value of the goods he recovered for clients: the implication being, that while it was all very well to be a thief-taker and receiver, Wild had abused his clientele by monopolizing the trade, and thus being free to demand the fees he wanted because people were in thrall to the thieves who overran London at Wild's command.

The newspapers, for so long Wild's greatest tool of promotion, turned against him. He was referred to sarcastically as 'Honest Mr Wild'. In the spring of 1725 the *Original London Half-Penny Weekly*

serialized an unflattering version of his life. There was endless conjecture as to precisely what crimes he would stand trial for.

The particulars of his [Wild's] accusation are as yet uncertain, but we hear
that very great bail has been refused, which occasions various speculations,
some being apprehensive of the loss of his intelligence and protection by
his being obliged to travel [i.e., no longer working], and others entertaining
the more dismal opinion, that he'll leave the world in his own way . . .

But few doubted what his eventual fate would be. 'The general
opinion is, there will be work for a hangman.'[4]

Public opinion swung further and further away from Wild. William Duce, a footpad against whom he had given evidence in court,
accused Wild of being worse than the thieves at his control, para-
sitically sucking them dry for his own advantage. 'There is not a
greater villain upon God's earth than Jonathan Wild. He makes it
his business to swear away honest men's lives for the sake of the
reward, and that is what he gets his livelihood by.'[5] Blueskin's assault on Wild in front of the Old Bailey had opened the floodgates;
from that point on, he was a sitting target. And it was not just
thieves who were emboldened to speak out against him. Defoe
summed up the new attitude to Wild in his *Life of Jonathan Wild*,
stressing the collective guilt of those who, even though suspecting
his active association with criminals, had chosen to turn a blind eye
because the service he offered was so useful.

I think it unpardonable, that a man should knowingly act against the law,
and by so doing powerfully contribute to the increase, as well as safety and
maintenance, of pilferers and robbers, from no other principle, than a criminal selfishness, accompanied with an utter disregard to the public; yet
nothing is more common among us. As soon as anything is missing, suspected to be stolen, the first course we steer is to the office of Mr Jonathan
Wild . . . Here we are so far from hating our enemy, that we proffer him a
recompense for his trouble, if he will condescend to let us have our own
again; and leaving all revenge to God, to show that we are willing to forgive
and forget, we consult, in the most effectual manner, the safety of a person
that deserves hanging for the wrong he has done us.

However, Wild did not seem unduly disturbed by recent events, his conviction that he had served the public too well for them ever to turn against him apparently unshaken by his arrest. His work had taken him to Newgate many times throughout his career, so although he had never stayed there before he soon settled in. He lived in luxury, sleeping on a flock mattress between his own sheets, drinking his favourite wine brandy, and conducting business in his cell as if it were his own office. His agents visited him daily, and he issued orders according to his usual habits.

On 10 March Wild invited a lace-seller, Catherine Steatham, to visit him in his cell at Newgate. She had come to his office at the end of January offering twenty-five guineas for the restoration of some lace which had been stolen from her shop. When they met in Newgate, Wild told Mrs Steatham he had found her lace, and that when it was delivered back to her she should pay the messenger ten guineas. The grateful old lady begged him to let her give him a reward for the trouble he had gone to on her behalf. Magnanimously, Wild refused to accept anything. 'As you are a widow and a Christian I desire nothing more of you but your prayers, and for them I shall be thankful.'[6]

On Thursday 5 May 1725 another trial, unconnected to Wild or Sheppard but which attracted an equal amount of interest, began. It was the trial of Thomas Parker, Earl of Macclesfield, Walpole's Lord Chancellor and close personal friend of King George I, who was also the stepfather of Dr Johnson's friend the journalist Richard Savage, later convicted of murder and then pardoned in an eighteenth-century *cause célèbre*. In a dispute with a stranger in the private gaming room of Robinson's coffee-house in 1727, Savage ran him through the chest with his sword. Macclesfield stood accused of receiving bribes, selling offices and embezzling over £100,000 of Chancery funds. Represented by the same lawyer who had defended the notorious Dr Sacheverell, Macclesfield got off lightly. He was fined £30,000, which he paid easily (having lined his pockets so thickly during his years in office), and earned his freedom from the Tower of London on 21 July. George I was so upset by the harsh treatment accorded his friend that he promised to pay him back out of the Privy Purse, in £1,000 instalments, but died having made only one payment.

Grub Street seized on the parallels between the cases of Wild and Macclesfield with shameless gusto. As early as 1723 John Gay had written scathingly of professional politicians, 'I cannot but wonder that the talents for a great statesman are so scarce in the world, since so many of those who possess them are at every month cut off in the prime of their age at the Old Bailey.' In *Mist's Weekly Journal*, the editor, Nathaniel Mist, called Wild 'that celebrated statesman and politician', comparing the skills he had used to dominate the London underworld with those Walpole deployed to control Parliament. Both used a complicated system of spies and informers, playing on their followers' fears of being betrayed before they were able to turn evidence themselves. Both sacrificed pawns with impunity when they were no longer needed; and the success of both crucially depended on making the public believe that it needed the services they provided.[7] While Walpole created the illusion that without his leadership the government of the country would fall apart, Wild was able to make people believe that he was the last bulwark against the rising tide of crime – at the same time encouraging and stimulating its very growth.

In response to the trials of Macclesfield and Wild, the Tory Duke of Wharton suggested that instead of being hanged, Jonathan Wild should be set the task of recovering the £8,000,000 Exchequer deficit which, Wharton implied, was due to the corruption of Walpole's government:

> From sunset to daybreak, whilst folks are asleep,
> New watch are appointed th'Exchequer to keep
> New bolts and new bars fasten every door,
> And the chests are made three times as strong as before;
> Yet the thieves in the day-time the treasures may seize,
> For the same are entrusted with care of the keys;
> From the night to the morning 'tis true, all is right,
> But who will secure it from morning to night?

Quoth Wild unto Walpole, 'Make me undertaker,
I'll soon find the rogues that robbed th'Exchequer,
I shan't look among those that are used to purloining,
But shall, the first, search in the chapel adjoining.[8]

But it was Wild, the upstart, who was punished for his sins, whereas the rich, titled, well-connected Macclesfield eluded justice.

Wild's name became a metaphor for political corruption almost as soon as he was arrested. *Mist's Weekly Journal* published an article in June 1725, two weeks after Wild died, calling him a 'Great Man', a term commonly used to describe politicians and statesmen.

He [Wild] bore a very great veneration for men of parts, and was often heard to say, that men of wit, who have no other inheritance to maintain them, should ride the world, and bridle and saddle the rest of mankind one way or another . . . It was his opinion, that men of parts (in which clause he sometimes included thieves and idle fellows) should be maintained by the public, and whether it was done by picking their pockets, or boldly taking their money by force, he thought it much the same thing.

This was the first explicit comparison of Wild with the corrupt politicians headed by Walpole against whom Tory writers such as Swift and Pope railed. *The Beggars' Opera* was another anti-Walpole tract. Mr Peachum, the character based on Jonathan Wild, was also a satirical portrait of Robert Walpole. 'In one respect indeed, our employment may be reckoned dishonest, because, like great statesmen, we encourage those who betray their friends,' says Peachum to the turnkey, Lockit. He sings:

The priest calls the lawyer a cheat,
The lawyer be-knaves the divine,
And the statesman, because he's so great,
Thinks his trade is as honest as mine!

Alexander Pope, who helped his friend Gay revise the play, added these lines to Macheath's part as he prepares to die at Tyburn:

Since laws were made for every degree
To curb vice in others as well as in me

I wonder we hadn't better company
Upon Tyburn Tree. . .

Gay's attacks on Walpole's political corruption were underlined by the slights against him as a womanizer. The love triangle between Macheath, Polly Peachum and Lucy Lockit echoes Walpole's relationships with his wife and his mistress, Molly Skerrit. Macheath's wanton seduction of the innocent Polly is intended as an analogy of Walpole's rape of the English nation.

The play's barbs stung their target. In February 1728 Jonathan Swift wrote to Gay to discuss Walpole's reaction to *The Beggars' Opera*. 'Does Walpole think you intended to affront him in your opera? Pray God he may, for he has held the longest hand at hazard [a dice game] that ever fell to any sharper's share, and keeps his run when the dice are charged.' In 1737, as a direct result of the violent political antagonism of *The Beggars' Opera*, Walpole put through Parliament a bill requiring all plays to be licensed by the Lord Chamberlain, the first act censoring the theatre for many years.

The most outspoken attack on Walpole and his administration using Wild as metaphor was Henry Fielding's novel, *Mr Jonathan Wild the Great*, published in 1743. Fielding, later the reforming magistrate of Bow Street, compared Wild's criminal organization directly with Walpole's control of the government. He outlined his intentions in the book's introduction:

Here, they will meet with a system of politics not unknown to Machiavel; they will see deeper stratagems and plots performed by a fellow without learning or education than are to be met with in the conduct of the greatest statesmen who have been at the heads of governments.

And, indeed, when things are rightly compared, it will be found that he had a more difficult game to play; for he was blind to the eyes of the world, to find out what tricks to evade the penalties of the law; and, on the other side, to govern a body of people who were enemies to all government; and to bring those under obedience to him who, at the hazard of their lives, acted in disobedience to the laws of the land.

Both men shared the same selfish ambitions, Fielding argued – to derive the greatest personal gain and power from their manipulation of the public. 'I had rather stand on the summit of a dunghill,' says the fictional Wild, 'than at the bottom of a hill in Paradise.' Fielding based his character's life loosely on Wild's, but was more interested in the similarities in method and aim shared by Walpole and Wild than in any historical accuracy.

The same parts, the same actions, often promote men to the head of superior societies, which raise them to the head of lower; and where is the essential difference, if the one ends on Tower Hill [where nobles were executed], and the other at Tyburn? . . . A cod's head is a cod's head still, whether in a pewter or a silver dish.

The criminal underworld, in which the novel was set, was used as a metaphor for the government; cant emphasized the esoteric nature of this corrupt world. This is clear in the fictional Wild's definition of honour: 'Nor can any man possibly entertain a higher and nobler sense of that word, nor a greater esteem of its inestimable value, than myself. If we have no name to express it by in our cant dictionary, it were well to be wished we had.'

Trial

Jonathan Wild was heard to say, two days before he went to court, that he wished he had been killed by Blueskin Blake and thus avoided the ignominy of having to stand trial for his crimes. His feelings were reflected in a contemporary ballad supposedly sung by him at this period, called 'The Complaint of Jonathan Wild'.

> Ye Britons! Cursed with an unthankful mind,
> Forever to exalted merit blind,
> Is thus your constant benefactor spurned?
> Are thus his faithful services returned?
>
> More generous Blueskin! – O, that thy design
> Had ended this unhappy life of mine!
> O, that success had crowned the stroke you gave!
> Then I had gone with honour to the grave!

But Wild remained convinced that the public service he had provided over the years would stand him in good stead, and as part of his defence, he took with him to the Old Bailey on 15 May 1725 a carefully compiled list of the felons he had brought to justice. It named thirty-five highway robbers, twenty-two house-breakers and ten returned transportees, and continued,

Note, several others have been also convicted for the like crimes, but remembering not the persons' names who have been robbed, I omit the criminals' names.

Please to observe, that several others have also been convicted for shoplifting, picking of pockets, &c. by the female sex [i.e., by whores], which are capital crimes, and which are too tedious to be inserted here, and the prosecutors not willing to be exposed.

In regard therefore of the numbers above convicted, some, that have yet escaped justice, are endeavouring to take away the life of the said

JONATHAN WILD

Jonathan seemed oblivious to the fact that this proud broadcasting of his successes merely darkened his name in the eyes of the public. Once his activities had been exposed, anything he said in his defence only implicated him further in the tortuous maelstrom of crime from which he had for so long feigned dissociation. 'He thought his being useful in the first (serving the public by detecting some criminals) would protect him in being [branded] criminal in the last; but here he was, we say mistaken, and fell into a snare which all his pretended merit could not deliver him from.'[1] Surprisingly, Wild was tried neither for the list of felonies he was accused of on the Warrant of Detainder presented to court, nor for the crimes with which Follard and Butler had agreed to charge him when he was first arrested. Wild 'saved them that trouble [of standing as witnesses] by committing a felony'.[2] He stood accused of stealing fifty yards of lace, worth £40, from Catherine Steatham's shop in Holborn, on 22 January 1722, and of receiving stolen goods (the same lace). Catherine Steatham was the woman who had visited Wild at Newgate in March, for whom he had recovered the lace while he was in prison.

Henry Kelly and Margaret Murphy claimed that Jonathan Wild, finding them having a drink with his 'wife' and Mrs Johnson, Roger's wife, in his house in the Old Bailey, had put them up to robbing Mrs Steatham.

'I'll tell you what . . . there's an old blind bitch, that keeps a shop within twenty yards of Holborn Bridge, and sells fine Flanders lace; and her daughter is as blind as herself. Now if you'll take the trouble of calling upon her, you may speak with [steal] a box of lace. I'll go along with you, and show you the door.'

The trio had walked up to Holborn, Wild pointed out to them Mrs Steatham's shop, and Murphy and Kelly had entered and stolen a box of lace. 'At last the old woman stept upstairs to fetch another piece, and in the meantime I took a tin box of lace, and gave it to Murphy, who put it under her cloak.' They went outside, found Wild, and returned to his office where he examined the contents of the box. Kelly stated,

> He asked us, if we'd have ready money, or stay till an advertisement came out? Stock was pretty low with us at that time, and so we chose ready money, and he gave us three guineas, and four broad pieces.
>
> 'I can't afford to give any more,' says he, 'for she's a hard-mouthed old Bitch, and I shall never get above ten guineas out of her.'

Margaret Murphy corroborated Kelly's evidence, adding that Wild had told them he couldn't afford to give them more money for the lace, 'for, though I have got some influence over her, by helping her to goods two or three times before, yet I know her to be such a stingy old bitch, that I shan't get above ten guineas out of her'.

Then Catherine Steatham took the stand. She testified that on discovering the lace had been stolen, she rushed to Wild's office in the Old Bailey to engage his services. Not finding him there, she had advertised independently, offering fifteen guineas for the return of the missing lace, with no questions asked. Soon after, she went back to Wild's office and told him she would give twenty or twenty-five guineas to have her property back; he told her she would have to wait, according to his usual practice, while he looked into the affair – even though the lace had been in his possession since the day it was stolen. 'Don't be in such a hurry,' says he; 'I don't know but I may be able to help you to it [the lace] for less, and if I can I will. The persons that have it are gone out of town; I shall set them to quarrelling about it, and then I shall get it the cheaper.'

When she visited Wild in gaol, he charged her only ten guineas for the lace on behalf of the thieves (although the money went straight into his pocket), and refused to accept any direct payment for himself – probably hoping that by being seen to do her a good turn, he would secure her loyalty. He told her,

I don't do these things for worldly interest, but only for the good of poor people that have met with misfortunes. As for the piece of lace that is missing [one piece was not returned with the rest], I hope to get it for you ere long, and I don't know but that I may help you not only to your money again but to the thief too; and if I can, much good may it do you. And as you are a good woman and a Christian, I desire nothing of you but your prayers, and for them I shall be thankful. I have a great many enemies, and God knows what may be the consequence of this imprisonment.

The combined testimonies of Steatham, Murphy and Kelly show the unabashed duplicity that characterized Wild's behaviour. On one hand, he was all conniving conspiracy, ruthlessly planting the idea of crime in the minds of his companions; on the other, he was a charming businessman, helping to solve problems with all the modest goodwill in the world.

Appearing 'very much dejected', Wild replied to the charges with a plea for mercy on account of his supposed ceaseless fight against crime, his harsh Staffordshire accent untainted by nearly twenty years in London:

My Lord, I hope even in the sad condition in which I stand, I may pretend to some little merit in respect to the service I have done my country, in delivering it from some of the greatest pests with which it was ever troubled. My Lord, I have brought many bold and daring malefactors to just punishment, even at the hazard of my own life, my body being covered with scars I received in these undertakings. I presume, my Lord, to say I have done merit, because at the time, they were esteemed meritorious by the government; and therefore I hope, my Lord, some compassion may be shown on the score of those services.

It proved impossible to convict him of theft proper, but after only half an hour's deliberation, the jury found Wild guilty of receiving stolen goods, under the so-called Jonathan Wild Act, and sentenced him to death. It was ironic that he should finally have been charged only with a crime that had taken place after he was committed to Newgate, and that he should have been convicted for so relatively petty a theft. But although it was less spectacular than some of the robberies with which Wild had been involved, the

Steatham robbery was typical of the way in which he had made his name and his fortune. It was poetic justice that he should be condemned for a minor misdemeanour, when he would have gloried in standing trial, very publicly, for an audacious, scandalous, miraculous heist worthy of Claude Duvall, or of Jack Sheppard.

Undeterred by the court's response to his pleas for mercy, Wild wrote to the king hoping to obtain a pardon on account of his services to society. He 'could not be made to believe he should suffer at last, for what he had publicly done unpunished so long'.[3] He even tried to use his wife's distress to his advantage. Mary Brown, or Wild, had attempted to commit suicide the day after his sentence was passed, 'but someone coming into the room accidentally, cut her down; by which means she had a reprieve against her will'.[4] He begged,

'Tis nothing but your Majesty's wonted goodness and clemency that could encourage me to sue for your royal favour and pardon. . .

For since your Majesty has many times been graciously pleased to spare the lives even of traitors themselves, I cannot but hope for a reprieve from so good a prince, whom I can esteem no less than an inexhaustible fountain of mercy; wherefore, most dread and august sovereign, humbly prostrating myself at your royal feet, I presume to set forth my wicked and melancholy circumstances and from your bounty to seek that favour which is nowhere else to be found.

I have indeed been a most wicked and notorious offender, but was never guilty or inclined to treasonable practices, or murder, both of which I hold in the utmost detestation and abhorrence which affords me great comfort in the midst of my calamity and affliction.

I have a sickly wife loaded and oppressed with grief, who must inevitably go to the grave with me, if I suffer; or lead a most miserable life, she being already *non compos mentis*.

If I receive your Majesty's royal favour of a reprieve, I do firmly resolve to relinquish my wicked ways and to detect (as far as in me lays) all such who shall persevere therein, as a testimony of which, I have a list ready to show to such whom your Majesty shall appoint to see it, which is all that can be offered by your Majesty's most dutiful, loyal and obedient petitioner.

This list mentioned by Wild in his petition might have been the list he produced in court, but it sounds as if it contained new information on criminals who might be convicted as a result of his complicity and intended reform. It is surprising, then, that no efforts were made to discover with what revelations he had hoped to buy his freedom.

Back in Newgate, waiting for a response to his petition, Wild confronted the prospect of death while Mrs Steatham collected the forty pounds she was owed by the government for bringing him to justice. Although Fielding's Jonathan Wild, when asked if he was afraid to die, boldly answered, 'Damme, it is only a dance without music,' the real Jonathan Wild was plagued by terror at his impending fate. It was driving him insane. He refused to eat after returning from the Old Bailey. His old ailment, gout, had hit him badly. He refused to go to church, because he thought that everyone would stare and 'discompose' him.

He never went to the chapel during the whole time that he continued under sentence of death, saying, he was lame, and unable to support himself on his legs [because of the gout], and much more unable to go up so far. Another reason, he added, was, that certain enemies of his, among the crowd, would not only interrupt his prayers by pointing, whispering, &c. but would, he had reason to believe, insult him, and if they dared, would raise a tumult and riot on his account. Therefore, as he knew that to pray to God without attention or regard to Him, was worse than wholly to omit prayers, and as he knew he could not attend to his duty amidst so vast a crowd as appeared at the chapel, he earnestly desired he might never be carried to it.[5]

On the night before he died, he summoned Reverend Purney, the Ordinary, to his cell, and asked to receive the Sacrament. He was obviously in a state of panicked desperation. He asked the exact meaning of the biblical phrase 'Cursed is every one that hangeth on a tree.' He inquired about the disposition of the soul when it was first separated from the body. He wondered where exactly the next world was situated. He admitted that he knew his remaining hours on earth should be devoted to religious contemplation and spiritual reckoning. Later that night he sent for the Ordinary again. 'How,' he asked, 'did the noble Greeks and Romans, who slew themselves, come to be so glorious in history?' Purney told him that heathens considered suicide cowardly, but that Christians were far more strongly opposed to it. Subdued, Wild replied he knew that suicide was sacrilegious.[6] But the necessity of proving his bravery – and the knowledge that he would not be able, sober and undrugged, to face his maker without fear – forced him to try to take his own life. Even the prospect of being buried at dead of night at a crossroads, to diffuse the evil emanating from a suicide's corpse, did not deter him. In the small hours of the morning he took so large a dose of laudanum (opium dissolved in an alcohol solution) that his system, weakened by four days' fasting, rejected it. Two fellow prisoners tried to rouse him by walking his slack body up and down in the cell. Wild was dripping with sweat, his eyes glazed, his head lolling on his shoulders. Finally he vomited violently, and sank into a coma.

As Fielding caustically remarked describing the fictional Wild's death at the gallows: 'He must be a fool, who is ashamed of being hanged, who is not weak enough to be ashamed of having deserved it.'

Hanging

Still 'stupefied and insensible', Wild was carried to the prison chapel to hear the final service. Although earlier he had requested a closed carriage to take him to Tyburn, he was put into the usual open cart, seated between two chaplains. 'At his coming into the cart at Newgate, they [the mob] set up the loudest shouts and huzzahs that ever was heard, which was continued all the way to the place of execution. A temper very uncommon, and indeed very unbecoming, on so melancholy an occasion,' commented the *Daily Journal*. 'Never was there seen so prodigious a concourse of people before, upon any occasion,' reported *Mist's Weekly Journal*. All along the procession route people lined the roads, shouting out curses and insults, pelting him with stones, handfuls of mud and dung, even rotten fruit, vegetables and eggs, and the carcasses of dead cats and dogs. Traditionally, spectators saved these objects for hanging days when they knew a villain was to die.

Contrary to the general behaviour of the street in such cases, instead of compassionate expressions and a general cast of pity which ordinarily sits on the countenances of the people when they see the miserable objects of justice go to their execution, here nothing was heard but cursings and execrations, abhorring the crimes and the very name of the man, throwing stones and dirt at him all the way, and even at the place of execution.[1]

No white-clad girls held bunches of flowers up to Jonathan's cart as they had for Jack Sheppard; no defiant crowds celebrated his exploits. Hawkers sold 'Invitations' to Wild's hanging, addressed to 'all the thieves, whores, pickpockets, family felons, &c., in Great

Britain and Ireland. . .' (illustration 34, page 255). Jonathan might have congratulated himself morbidly on the fact that 'the famous Jack Sheppard had a tolerable number to attend his execution; but no more to be compared to the present, than a regiment to an army'.[2] But the turnout would have been cold comfort, for every face in the crowd looked on Wild with disgust and hatred. 'In all that innumerable crowd, there was not one pitying eye to be seen, nor one compassionate word to be heard; but on the contrary, wherever he came, there was nothing but hollowing and huzzas, as if it had been upon a triumph.'[3]

The size of the crowds that gathered at Tyburn on hanging days made individuals feel their actions would go unnoticed. Men and women, rendered anonymous by the throngs surrounding them, felt free to heckle the hangman or his victims, to hurl abuse at the dying men or the authorities that had condemned them. Being part of a crowd created the illusion of individual anonymity, like that felt by a rioting mob. This mass hysteria stimulated the release of pent-up feelings of frustration and fury, directed either at the government or its victims.

Wild, who had once gloried in his successes at hanging days – 'I must go and drink with the fellows I condemned last Sessions; they die tomorrow, and old friends should part like friends,' says Wile, the character based on Wild in the 1728 play *The Quaker's Opera* – was humbled and humiliated before the jeering mob.

I shall here take notice, that every execution day, Jonathan being mounted on horseback, he would in great triumph ride a little way before the criminals that were going to die, and at some taverns in the way call for half a pint of wine, telling the people about him, with the greatest exultation, and joy, imaginable, that some of his children were coming, they were just behind: so when he went deservedly to be hanged, several thieves went a little way before the cart, telling people, their father was coming, he's just behind.[4]

Jonathan recovered his senses a little during the interminable journey to Tyburn. Some observers thought he looked remorseful.

34. *An invitation to Jonathan Wild's Hanging* (T. Cox)

A broadsheet sold by hawkers like those in Plate XI of *Industry and Idleness* on the day Wild was hanged.

As he passed by Holborn Bridge, being put in mind of the lace womans house [Mrs Steatham's] upon whose account he was cast, he turned himself that way, and shook his head and hand with an air of sorrow, which motion the old woman returned, as was supposed, by way of forgiveness.[5]

A few moments later, 'he had his head broke [cut] by a stone thrown from a window, so that the blood ran down him; and other insults of a barbarous nature were offered to him'. Still only semiconscious, Wild arrived at the gallows with his three companions. The hangman 'turned off' the two highwaymen, William Sperry and Robert Sanford, while Robert Harpham, a coiner, sang psalms as he waited to be hanged. Wild, dazed, joined mechanically in the singing. Harpham, meek and repentant, was the state's ideal public executionee. Loudly and clearly, he desired the crowd to take his untimely and ignominious death as a warning, and stepped forward calmly to die. The mob, inflamed by the hangman's decision to leave Wild until last, 'threatened to knock him [the hangman] on the head if he did not immediately perform it [Wild's hanging]'.[6] The executioner swiftly cut down Harpham's body, and strung Wild up in his place. Because he was still heavily drugged, he died with no difficulty, wearing his nightshirt and wig.

The first man to hang in a shroud, or nightdress, was the highwayman James Wright, whom Wild had brought to his death after he robbed the Lords Burlington and Bruce. The custom of wearing a shroud to be hanged was meant to indicate humility in the face of one's impending judgement at the gates of Heaven. It underlined the fact that man brought nothing into this world at his birth, and took nothing out of it at his death. For highwaymen, whose lives had been devoted to avaricious gain, this reminder was particularly poignant.

Another traditional costume worn by condemned men was a wedding suit. Hanging and marriage had long been linked in common slang. The terms for both were the same: to be hanged, and to be married, were to be 'noozed', or noosed; hanging days were known as 'Hanging Matches'. These connections extended across the Channel: the guillotine, in French slang, was known as the Maiden. The other type of death in which wedding symbolism played a part in the eighteenth century was that of young, unmarried girls. Their corpses were dressed like brides, just as many criminals went to their deaths dressed as grooms. Both were seen by their friends and families as wasted lives, brought to untimely and unjust ends. Most criminals – over three-quarters of those hanged at Tyburn – were aged between twenty and thirty, cut down at the peak of their strength and fertility. At hanging days the connection with marriage was underlined by the presence of young girls dressed in white, handing bunches of flowers up to the condemned men as they were drawn through the crowds to the gallows. So too at the funerals of virgins did their attendants dress in white and garland themselves with flowers.[7]

He that is to be hanged, or otherwise executed, first takes care to get himself shaved, and handsomely dressed, either in mourning or in the dress of a bridegroom; this done, he set his friends at work to get him leave to be buried, and to carry his coffin with him, which is easily obtained. When his suit of clothes or nightgown, his gloves, hat, periwig, nosegay, coffin, flannel-dress for his corpse, and all those things are bought and prepared, the main point is taken care of, his mind is at peace, and then he thinks of his conscience. . .[8]

While some men went to the gallows in a nightshirt, and some wearing their wedding suits, many others simply dressed in whatever finery they could manage. To die with a flourish, wearing a costume of glorious ostentation, was a final way of displaying defiance. Just as some felons wore white cockades to protest their innocence and their hostility to the authorities that had, in their eyes, unjustly condemned them, so others used the splendour and richness of their clothes to show their bravado and resistance.

Sixteen-String Jack, alias John Rann, a highwayman hanged in 1774, was famous for his gorgeous clothes and the pride he took in his appearance. His nickname came from the eight silk ribbons he wore instead of the usual buckle at each knee, holding up his breeches;

the first time he appeared in court his irons were tied up with blue ribbons. He was arrested seven times, and acquitted the first six times he was tried. At his seventh trial, for which he appeared in court 'dressed in a new suit of pea-green clothes, his hat bound round with silver strings; he wore a ruffled shirt, and his behaviour evidenced the utmost unconcern', he was convicted and condemned to death. The following Sunday, three days before his execution, he was allowed to invite seven women of his acquaintance – all prostitutes – to dine with him in his cell at Newgate; all, including Jack, 'were remarkably cheerful'.[9] His insouciance was as greatly admired as his elegance: one was part of the other.

Nathaniel Hawes was another highwayman to whom dying beautifully dressed was of overriding importance. He had informed on his partner, John James, to Jonathan Wild, and James was hanged on Hawes's evidence. He himself was captured soon after by a man he was trying to rob; turning the tables on Hawes, the victim became the aggressor, and Hawes was taken ignominiously back to Newgate. He refused to plead at his trial because the judge would not give him back the stolen clothes he had been arrested in and which he wanted to wear at his execution. He translated the issue of his clothes into a moral debate:

The court was formerly a place of justice, but now it is become a place of injustice. I doubt not that you (indicating judge and jury with a sweep of his hand) will receive a severer sentence than that you pronounce on me. And for my part I make no question of dying with the same resolution with which I have often beheld death and will leave the world with the same courage with which I have lived in it.

The judge, shocked at this display of open contempt, sentenced Hawes to *peine forte et dure*, a method of torture used to force unrepentant defendants to plead, which was abolished in 1772.

The prisoner shall be sent to the prison from whence he came, and put into a mean room, stopped from any light, and shall there be laid on the bare ground, without any litter, straw, or other covering, and without any garment about him, except for something to hide his privy members. He shall lie on his back, his head shall be covered and his feet be bare. One of his arms shall be drawn with a cord, to one side of the room, and the other to the other side; and his legs shall be served in the like manner. Then there shall be laid upon his body as much iron or stone as he can bear, or more. And the first day after, he shall have three morsels of barley bread, without any drink; and the second day, he shall be allowed to drink as much as he can, at three times, of the water that is next the prison door, except running water, without any bread; and this shall be his diet till he dies.

Although Hawes replied grandly – '. . .as I have lived with the character of the boldest fellow in my profession I am resolved to die with it and leave my memory to be admired by all the gentle men of the road of succeeding ages' – the prospect of *peine forte et dure* was awful. While some men, such as Giles Cory, accused of witchcraft in the Salem Witch Trials of 1698, held firm and refused to break their silence, dying after days of pressure and starvation, most capitulated after a short time. Despite his bluster, Hawes lasted only seven minutes under a relatively light weight of 250 lb. before he consented to plead – without his suit of clothes.

How one reached the place of execution was also important. Wild's request to be driven to Tyburn in a closed carriage was refused. He wanted to be enclosed, away from the prying, gloating eyes of his enemies, just as he had wanted to avoid exposure to the insulting taunts of his fellow prisoners at Newgate's chapel. Jenny Diver, the most famous pickpocket of her generation, was allowed to drive to Tyburn in a private coach, attended by her clergyman. Some criminals, however, revelled in their celebrity as they rode to their deaths. Edward Burnworth and his gang of footpads threw pennies into the crowd, like processing royalty, as they were driven to the gallows at Kingston.

While the crowd's response was vital to the spirit of the condemned men as they were 'turned off', it also played a part in overseeing the procedure of the hanging. The spectators watched carefully for any abuses of authority by the officials performing the rituals. They made sure the dying man did not suffer unduly; that his dying words were listened to, whatever his views; and that his last requests were heard. A man unjustly convicted might have a collection taken up for the support of his family. Certain types of crime, however, attracted a violent response from the crowd: sexual crimes, particularly directed towards children, elicited deep disapproval; informers were always treated harshly. On the whole, though, the collective grief and shame many must have felt watching these spectacles of punishment and death were purged by their demonstrations of contempt for the system that had allowed them to happen. The mob's insistence on the rights of the dying men, and the elaborate superstitions and rituals surrounding the execution and burial of criminals, was a way for the common people to assimilate and accept the constant drain of the finest and boldest of their number.

Wild may not have been considered the finest or the boldest, but his friends were still concerned about the fate of his corpse. He was buried at dead of night, in secret, next to the body of his 'wife', the devout Elizabeth Mann, to whose memory he had remained loyal since her death. A few days later, his grave was opened up and his body stolen. There was no direct evidence of what happened to it, but a report in the *Daily Journal* on 15 June hazarded a guess.

Last Sunday morning there was found upon Whitehall Shore, in St Margaret's Parish, the skin, flesh, and entrails (without any bones) of a human body: the coroner and jury that sat upon it, ordered it to be buried, which was done on Tuesday last, in the Burial Ground for the Poor, and the surgeon who attended, gave it as his opinion, that it could be no other than the remains of the dissected body. It was observed, that the skin of the breast was hairy, from whence people conjecture it to be part of the renowned Jonathan Wild.

If it was, indeed, Jonathan Wild, how horrified he would have been that his final resting-place was the Burial Ground for the Poor.

In 1847, over a century after Wild's death, a skeleton reputed to be that of Jonathan Wild was donated to the Royal College of Surgeons by one Dr Frederick Fowler in the wake of a flurry of public interest in Wild after the enormous popularity of plays and novels about Jack Sheppard since the publication of William Harrison

Ainsworth's *Jack Sheppard* in 1837, and particularly the recent exca-
vations of Wild's headquarters at the Red Lion tavern in West
Street. If, as the *Daily Journal*'s report suggests, Wild's body had
been excavated and anatomized just after he died, his skeleton
might well have been kept by the doctor who had overseen the operation; it is more than likely that the doctor who kept it would also
have kept a record of its identity.

In 1802, the most famous phrenologist of the day, Mr Deville,
carried out an examination of a skull, unaware that it was that of
Jonathan Wild. Thirty-eight years later, on 22 March 1840, his report was published in the *Weekly Dispatch*:

This is the skull of an individual possessing some useful faculties for me-
chanical operation, going about and comprehending things readily; but he
is a singular character, with a large portion of the brain in the region of
propensities. And under disappointment of his own importance, pecuniary
difficulties, or intoxication, he would be very likely to commit crime. He
would be fond of offspring or children, but not a kind parent, as the man-
date must be obeyed. He would be the associate of a female, and probably
a married man, but liable to jealousy, being a doubter of the integrity of
others towards himself; and while in this state of feeling, he would be liable
to do injury to those offending him, and, if opposed, murder might be the
result of such an organization. He would be conceited, self-willed and ob-
stinate; and if opposed in his own views, his passions would run very high.
He would, without much hesitation, appropriate to his own uses the property of others; but, in so doing, show some ingenuity and cunning, it being
difficult of detection. He would, at times, manifest some feeling for religion
and might follow some sect, and at times hold forth upon the subject; but
I doubt much the integrity on it, being more to screen and cover the animal
propensities. He would be a talker in his own society – a knowing and conceited individual. He has had some notions of music, and, having some
command of words, would be likely to become the songster of his society
– such as an organization preferring society where he could become the
hero of a public-house party. From the character of the bones, it appears
to be the skull of an elderly man, whom I consider as having had the power
of becoming useful, but from the preponderance of the animal, I consider
him an aged sinner.

Epilogue

Wild left behind him a vacuum. He had become irreplaceable as a thief-taker. But not to his last 'wife', Mary Brown, despite her attempts barely a month before to kill herself. His most loyal servant, Quilt Arnold, was courting his master's widow.

We hear that the relic of Jonathan Wild is actually contracted to Quilt Arnold, her husband's journeyman, and is resolved to marry him at all hazards; 'tis remarkable, that this wretched woman hath had two husbands and a kinsman executed at Tyburn within these ten years: moreover, her uncle, Mr Spurling, a turnkey at Newgate, was murdered at the Sessions House, for which fact a man and a woman were executed before Newgate; so unfortunate her family hath been. Therefore, what encouragement a person of Mr Arnold's character hath to venture on her, is a secret,

related the *Daily Post* only two days after Wild's death. It remains unknown whether or not Quilt Arnold married Mary, but just before Wild's execution he was 'ordered to remain [in prison] till the ensuing assizes for Essex, when he is to be removed thither to be tried for a capital crime charged upon him in that county'.

Wild's son, born just before he left Wolverhampton to seek his fortune in London, was in the capital at the time of Wild's death. At nineteen years of age, he was only a little younger than Jack Sheppard. The newspaper reports give no indication of whether or not the young Wild had come to London before his father's arrest, hoping, as his uncle Andrew had done, to use his influence to carve a career for himself in London's underworld; or whether he disapproved of his father's successes, and came to the city before his death only for a final reconciliation. The *London Journal* speculated that he was headed for Holland, 'unable to bear the reflections that may be cast on him on account of his unfortunate father; who, 'tis said, had left him £300'. In fact, the young man sold himself as an indentured servant, and travelled to the New World, a voluntary transportee. Perhaps he hoped that in the American colonies the shameful fact of who his father was would pass unnoticed.

Andrew Wild, who had come to London hoping to capitalize on his brother's success, and had kept a 'case', or flash-house, during Jonathan's criminal ascendancy, was put into the Wood Street Compter for debt in 1725; nothing more was heard of him. Perhaps without the protection of his brother he was unable to keep his business going. Jonathan's other brother, John, who had been involved in the royalist demonstrations in Wolverhampton in 1715, remained in his home town, as did his two sisters, who were married to a buckle-maker and a comb-maker.

Edgworth Bess, Jack Sheppard's first love, was committed to Tothill Fields Bridewell, a house of correction, 'for seducing a shopkeeper's son to go a-thieving with her' in April 1725. A year later she was in court again. Six stolen silver spoons had been found among her possessions. At first she claimed they 'were left me by my dear, John Sheppard, and I have just fetched them out of pawn', but when her accomplice – yet another impressionable young man – confessed, she was convicted and sentenced to be transported to the American colonies.

Public reactions to Wild's execution varied. As shown at his hanging, the common people of London celebrated his death. To them he was a villain, playing on people's desperation to bind them to him. A satirical pamphlet published after his death revealed the extent to which public opinion had swung against him when his ruthless recruitment of thieves was revealed.

Let them be men picked and chosen for their resolution, men that will do or swear anything, who, not having drunk of the milk of human kindness, have no feeling for their fellow creatures but would as soon strike a man down the skull with a hanger as the unfeeling butcher does the ox.[1]

The educated classes were more ambivalent. Once Wild's office had closed, there was nowhere to turn to retrieve stolen property. ' 'Tis remarkable that since the dissolution of Jonathan Wild, not one felon has been convicted capitally, which by some is attributed to a reform amongst the rogues and by others to the want of a proper person to detect them,' reported the *Daily Journal* six weeks after Wild's death. Cesar de Saussure was more forthright:

Many persons in England think more harm than good was done by the execution of this famous thief. They say there is no one now to go to who will help you to recover your stolen property – and, while the government has certainly got rid of a robber, he was only one, and by his help several were hanged every year.

Jonathan's death provided rich pickings for London's satirists and verse-makers. *Jonathan Wild's Advice to his Successor*, written by an anonymous Grub Street writer, advised the applicants to Wild's position of what traits were necessary for success.

And I do not in the least doubt that someone or other may think it worth his while to revive my occupation, especially when he is assured of the means to render himself obscure, it being a function of no small profit, requiring little industry, honour, honesty or conscience, though the appearance of these virtues is as necessary as the non-possession of them. The mask is the *summum bonum* of our sanction, a mask that may be put on at any time without incurring the displeasure of the Black Act or any other in the trammels of the law.

Just as Jack Sheppard had used disguise to facilitate his escapes, so too had Jonathan Wild used his ability to feign sympathy and interest when it was needed to cultivate the business of which his death had deprived London.

Popular ballads mocked the men who had brought Jonathan to his death, then regretted their actions when there was no one who could restore their stolen property to them.

But sure, e'er long, the time will come again,
When watches shall be lost in Drury Lane;
Snuffboxes, finely painted, miss their way,
And rings, and pocketbooks shall go astray;
When Phillis at the ball or masquerade
Shall lose a present from some lover made·
Then you – unthinking monsters! – you that now
Exult at my unpitied overthrow,
Then you'll repent too late: you then in vain,
Will wish to have your Jonathan again!

One of the most interesting treatises against thief-taking was Bernard de Mandeville's *An Enquiry into the Causes of the Frequent Executions at Tyburn*, published as a series of letters in the *British Journal* from 27 February 1725 – twelve days before Wild was arrested. De Mandeville's premise was simple:

The mischief that one man may do as a thief, is a very trifle what he may be the occasion of, as an agent or concealer of felons . . . That rogues should be industriously dispersed throughout the city and suburbs; that different hours and stations should be observed among them, and regular books kept of stolen goods; that the superintendent in this hopeful economy should, almost every Sessions, for a reward, betray, prosecute and hang one or more of his acquaintance, and at the same time keep on his correspondence amongst the survivors, whom, one after another, he sends all to their Triangular Home [the gallows]; that magistrates should not only know and see this, but likewise continue to make use of such a person for an evidence, and in a manner own that they are beholden to him in the administration of justice; that, I say, all these things should be facts, is something very extraordinary, in the principal city, and the home management of a kingdom, so formidable abroad, and of such moment in the balance of Europe, as that of Great Britain.

But it was Lord Chesterfield, writing thirteen years after Wild's death, who summed up the 'great man' best.

At one great period of his life, [Jonathan Wild] seemed rather born to a ribband about his shoulders than a rope around his neck . . . He was certainly a man of parts, and had he set out in the world in an honest, instead of a dishonest road, we might have seen him reckoned a patriot, instead of a pickpocket . . . And it must be confessed, that, in his whole conduct, he showed a steadiness, that wanted nothing but better principles to support it – one almost regrets that such a man should be lost in such a cause.

Bibliography

I am particularly indebted to the following modern historians: J. M. Beattie, M. Dorothy George, Douglas Hay, Christopher Hibbert, Christopher Hill, Michael Ignatieff, Peter Linebaugh, Frank McLynn, Roy Porter, J. A. Sharpe and E. P. Thompson. Their books, listed below, have been of enormous use to me in my research and would also provide excellent further reading for anyone interested in general eighteenth-century history as well as its criminal history.

The works of Gerald Howson and Frederick Lyons on Jonathan Wild and of Horace Bleackley on Jack Sheppard are highly recommended. Bleackley's and Lyons's books are particularly useful as they contain reproductions of many of the relevant eighteenth-century documents.

I would also like to mention several authors who deal specifically with eighteenth-century fiction, and who, because of their literary rather than historical approach, shed a slightly different light on the subject. They are: J. Bender, I. Donaldson, P. Earle, Pat Rogers and Ian Watt. P. Wagner's book on the political, cultural and economic impact of erotica in the eighteenth century is fascinating, as is E. J. Burford's amusing look at eighteenth-century Covent Garden life, *Wits, Wenchers and Wantons*.

Practically everything I have written about William Hogarth derives from the many books on him by Ronald Paulson, who is the authority on anything Hogarth-related.

The best eighteenth-century accounts of London's underworld are the contemporary biographies and narratives of notorious London figures including Sally Salisbury, Benjamin Child and Ralph Wilson, as well as the many lives of Jack Sheppard and Jonathan Wild. Also of interest is J. Villette's *Annals of Newgate*, which contains a large number of potted histories of criminals held in Newgate Prison. *Moll Flanders*, by Daniel Defoe, who had an intimate (if disapproving) knowledge of the underside of London life, is the best fictionalized account of criminal London in the early eighteenth century.

Eighteenth-century foreign observers of English life provide further insights into what life was like in the London inhabited by Wild and Sheppard. I have relied heavily on the comments of Cesar de Saussure, Henri Misson and Baron Muralt, all listed below.

John Gay, *Trivia*. Wherever there is an unattributed bit of verse, it is taken from Gay's wonderful ode to early eighteenth-century London.

CONTEMPORARY ACCOUNTS (1700–1800)

Anon., *A New Canting Dictionary*, London, 1735

Anon., *The Foreigner's Guide: Or, a Necessary and Instructive Companion both for the Foreigner and Native in their Tour through the Cities of London and Westminster*, London, 1730

Anon., *Wat Tyler and Jack Strawe: Or, the Mob Reformers*, London, 1730

Anon., *The History of Wat Tyler and Jack Strawe*, London, 1750

Anon. (Gay or Swift), 'Blueskin's Ballad', London, 1724

Anon., *The Life of Jonathan Wilde, Thief-Taker General of Great Britain and Ireland from his Birth to his Death*, London, 1725

Anon., *The History of the Remarkable Lives and Actions of Jonathan Wild, Thief-Taker, Joseph Blake alias Blueskin, Footpad, and John Sheppard, Housebreaker*, London, 1725

Anon., *An Authentic History of the Parentage, Birth, Education, Marriages, Issue and Practices of the Famous Jonathan Wild*, London, 1725

Anon., *News from the Dead: Or, a dialogue between Blueskin, Sheppard and Jonathan Wild*, London, 1725

Anon., *The Whole Life and History of Benjamin Child*, London, 1722

Byrom, J., *Miscellaneous Poems*, London, 1773

Chesterfield, Lord, 'Common Sense', 23 December 1738

Cleland, J., *Fanny Hill*, London, 1749

de Mandeville, B., *An Enquiry into the Causes of the Frequent Executions at Tyburn*, 1725 (reprinted with introduction by M. R. Zirker, Los Angeles, 1964)

de Saussure, C., *A Foreign View of England*, 1725 (trans. Van Muyden, London, 1902)

Dearing, V., and C. E. Beckwith (eds), *Poetry and Prose of John Gay*, Oxford, 1974

Defoe, D., *Robinson Crusoe*, London, 1719

——, *The True and Genuine Account of the Life and Actions of Jonathan Wild*, London, 1726

——, (or 'H. D.'), *The Life of Jonathan Wild from his Birth to his Death*, London, 1725

——, *A Tour through the Whole of Great Britain*, London, 1724–7

——, *The History of the Remarkable Life of John Sheppard*, London, 1725

——, *A Narrative of all the Robberies etc. of Jack Sheppard*, London, 1724

——, *Moll Flanders*, London, 1722

Female Tatler, 1709–1713, London, 1992

Fielding, H., *Amelia*, London, 1751

——, *Mr Jonathan Wild the Great*, London, 1743

——, *The Grub Street Opera* (ed. J. L. Morrissey, Edinburgh, 1973)

——, *An Enquiry into the Causes of the Late Increase in Robbers*, London, 1751

Fielding, J., *A Plan for Preventing Robberies within 20 Miles of London*, London, 1755

Gay, J., *The Beggars' Opera*, 1727 (ed. P. E. Lewis, Edinburgh, 1973)

'G. E.', *Authentic Memoirs of the Life and Surprising Adventures of John Sheppard by Way of Familiar Letters from a Gentleman in Town*, London, 1724

Johnson, Captain C., *Lives of the Highwaymen*, London, 1734

Misson, H., *Memoirs and Observations of his Travels over England*, 1719

Montagu, Lady Mary Wortley, *Selected Letters* (ed. R. Halsband, London, 1970)

Muralt, Baron, *Letters Describing the Characters and Customs of the English and French Nations*, London, 1726

Pepys, S., *Diary* (ed. R. and L. Latham, London, 1987)

Purney, T., *The Behaviour, Last Dying Speeches and Confessions of the Four Male-factors who were Executed at Tyburn on the 24 of May 1725*, London, 1725

Select Trials at the Old Bailey, London, 1734

Smith, Captain A., *Memoirs of the Life and Times of Jonathan Wild*, London, 1726

Swift, J., *Gulliver's Travels*, London, 1726

——, *Collected Poems* (ed. J. Horrell, London, 1958)

Villette, J., *The Annals of Newgate*, London, 1776

Walker, Captain C., *Authentic Memoirs of the Life, Intrigues, and Adventures of the Celebrated Sally Salisbury*, London, 1723

Walker, T., *The Quaker's Opera, or the Escapes of Jack Sheppard*, London, 1728

Ward, E., *The London Spy*, London, 1704

Wesley, J., *The Journal*, London, 1938

The Whole Proceedings of the Trial of Jonathan Wild, London, 1725

Wild, J., *The Humble Petition of Jonathan Wild Humbly Presented to His Majesty*, London, 1725

Wilson, R., *A Full and Impartial Account of all the Robberies Committed by John Hawkins, George Sympson, and their Companions*, London, 1722

LONDON NEWSPAPERS

London Journal

Mist's Weekly Journal

Parker's London News

Weekly Journal, or British Gazetteer

Weekly Journal, or Saturday's Post

PERIODICALS

Spectator

MODERN (POST 1800)

Ainsworth, W. H., *Rookwood*, London, 1837

——, *Jack Sheppard*, London, 1839

Allerton, R., and T. Parker, *The Courage of His Convictions*, London, 1962

Anon., *Jack Sheppard – A Romance of Old London*, London, 1870

Armens, S. M., *John Gay: Social Critic*, New York, 1954

Beattie, J. M., *Crime and the Courts in England*, Oxford, 1986

Ben-Amos, I. K., 'Failure to become Freemen', *Social History*, XVI, 1991

Bender, J., *Imagining the Penitentiary: Fiction and the Architecture of Mind in the Eighteenth Century*, Chicago, 1987

Besant, W., *London in the Eighteenth Century*, London, 1902

Blackett-Ord, M., *Hell-Fire Duke*, Kensal, 1982

Bleackley, H., *Jack Sheppard*, Edinburgh, 1933

Buck, A., *Dress in Eighteenth Century England*, London, 1979

Burford, E. J., *Wits, Wenchers and Wantons*, London, 1986

Bushaway, R. W., *By Rite: Custom, Ceremony and Community in England 1700–1800*, London, 1982

Chancellor, E. B., *The Annals of Covent Garden and its Neighbourhood*, London, 1930

——, *The Eighteenth Century in London*, London, 1920

Chandler, F. W., *The Literature of Roguery*, London, 1907

Cloward, R. A., and L. E. Ohlin, *Delinquency and Opportunity*, London, 1961

Cockburn, J. S. (ed.), *Crime in England*, London, 1977

Cohen, A. K., *Deviance and Control*, Englewood Cliffs, NJ, 1966

Cohen, S. (ed.), *Images of Deviance*, Harmondsworth, 1971

Cohen, S. and A. Scull (eds), *Social Control and the State*, Oxford, 1983

Collins, P., *Dickens and Crime*, London, 1962

Coser, L. A., and B. Rosenburg, *Sociological Theory: A Book of Readings*, New York, 1957

Davis, D., *A History of Shopping*, London, 1966

Davison, L., *et al.* (eds), *Stilling the Grumbling Hive*, Stroud, 1992

Deehiseekayess, J., *Tyburn Tree*, London, 1849

Dickens, C., *Oliver Twist*, London, 1837

Donaldson, I., *The World Upside-Down: Comedy from Jonson to Fielding*, Oxford, 1970

Dunlop, O. J., and R. D. Denman, *English Apprenticeship and Child Labour: A History*, London, 1912

Earle, P., *A City Full of People*, London, 1994

——, *The World of Defoe*, London, 1976

——, *The Making of the English Middle Class*, California, 1989

Foucault, M., *Discipline and Punish*, London, 1977 (trans. A. Sheridan)

Gatrell, V. A. C., *The Hanging Tree: Execution and the English People, 1770–1868*, Oxford, 1994

Gatrell, V. A. C., Lenman, B., and G. Parker, *Crime and the Law*, London, 1980

Genet, J., *The Thief's Journal*, Harmondsworth, 1971

George, M. D., *London Life in the Eighteenth Century*, London, 1925

——, *Hogarth to Cruikshank*, London, 1967

Griffiths, A., *Chronicles of Newgate*, London, 1884

Harris, T. (ed.), *Popular Culture in England, c. 1500–1850*, London, 1995

Hay, D., Linebaugh, P., and E. P. Thompson (eds), *Albion's Fatal Tree*, London, 1975

Hay, D., Linebaugh, P., and E. P. Thompson, *Bulletin for the Society of the Study of Labour History*, 25, 1972

Hibbert, C., *The Road to Tyburn*, London, 1957

——, *Highwaymen*, London, 1967

——, *London: The Biography of a City*, Harlow, 1969

Hibbert, C., *The Roots of Evil*, London, 1963

Hill, C., *Liberty Against the Law*, Harmondsworth, 1996

——, *Reformation to Industrial Revolution*, Harmondsworth, 1969

Hobsbawm, E. J., *Bandits*, Harmondsworth, 1985

Holt, J. G., *Robin Hood*, London, 1982

Howson, G., *Thief-Taker General: The Rise and Fall of Jonathan Wild*, London, 1970

——, *It Takes a Thief*, London, 1987

Ignatieff, M., *A Just Measure of Pain*, London, 1978

Irving, W. H., *John Gay's London*, Cambridge, MA, 1928

Irwin, W. R., *The Making of Jonathan Wild*, New York, 1941

Jackson, P. N., *Dick Turpin, 1706–1739*, Ilfracombe, 1988

Jarrett, D., *England in the Age of Hogarth*, London, 1974

Jesse, J. H., *George Selwyn and his Contemporaries*, London, 1843

Judges, A. V., *The Elizabethan Underworld*, London, 1930

Kidson, F., *The Beggars' Opera*, Cambridge, 1922

Langford, P., *A Polite and Commercial People: England 1727–1783*, Oxford, 1989

Lillywhite, B., *London Coffee Houses*, London, 1963

Lindsay, J., *The Monster City: Defoe's London 1688–1730*, London, 1978

Linebaugh, P., *The London Hanged*, London, 1991

Lyons, F. J., *Jonathan Wild, Prince of Robbers*, London, 1936

McLynn, F., *Crime and Punishment in Eighteenth Century England*, London, 1989

Malcolm, J. P., *Anecdotes of London in the 18th Century*, London, 1808

Malcolmson, R. W., *Popular Recreations in English Society*, Cambridge, 1981

——, *Life and Labour in England, 1700–1800*, London, 1981

Marks, A., *Tyburn Tree*, London, 1908

Marshall, D., *English People in the Eighteenth Century*, London, 1956

Morley, H., *Memoirs of Bartholomew Fair*, London, 1892

Noyes, A., *Collected Poems*, London, 1910

Partridge, E., *Dictionary of the Underworld*, London, 1949

Paston, G., *Side Lights of the Georgian Period*, London, 1902

Paulson, R., *Popular and Polite Art in the Age of Hogarth and Fielding*, South Bend, IN, 1979

——, *Emblem and Expression: Meaning in English Art in the Eighteenth Century*, London, 1975

——, *Hogarth: The Modern Moral Subject 1697–1732*, Cambridge, 1992

——, *Hogarth: High Art and Low 1732–1750*, Cambridge, 1992

Pike, L. O., *A History of Crime in England*, London, 1873–6

Plumb, J. H., *Georgian Delights*, London, 1980

——, 'The New World of Children in Eighteenth Century England', *Past and Present*, 67, 1975

——, *England in the Eighteenth Century*, Harmondsworth, 1950

Porter, R., *English Society in the Eighteenth Century*, London, 1982

——, *London: A Social History*, London, 1994

Pringle, P., *The Thief Takers*, London, 1958

——, *Henry and Sir John Fielding* [no place of publication given], 1968

Quennell, P. C., *Hogarth's Progress*, London, 1955

——, *London's Underworld*, London, 1983

Radzinowicz, L., *A History of English Criminal Law and its Administration from 1750*, London, 1948

Rayner, J. L., and G. T. Crook, *The Complete Newgate Calendar*, London, 1926

Redwood, J., *Reason, Ridicule and Religion: the Age of Enlightenment in England, 1660–1750*, London, 1976

Reed, M., *The Georgian Triumph*, London, 1983

Richardson, A. E., *Georgian England*, London, 1931

Rogers, P., *Hacks and Dunces*, London, 1980

——, *Eighteenth Century Encounters*, Brighton, 1985

Rosenfeld, S., *The Theatre of London Fairs in the Eighteenth Century*, London, 1960

Rude, G., *Hanoverian London*, London, 1971

——, *Paris and London in the Eighteenth Century*, London, 1970

Rudolph, L. I., 'The Mob in Eighteenth Century America and Europe', *American Quarterly*, XI, 4, 1959

Rule, J., *Albion's People: English Society 1714–1815*, London, 1992

Rumbelow, D., *The Triple Tree*, London, 1982

Salgado, G. (ed.), *Cony-Catchers and Bawdy-Baskets*, Harmondsworth, 1972

Schama, S., *Landscape and Memory*, London, 1995

Schultz, W. E., *Gay's Beggars' Opera*, New Haven, CT, 1923

Seccombe, T., *Lives of Twelve Bad Men*, London, 1894

Sennett, R., *The Fall of Public Man*, Cambridge, 1977

Sharpe, J. A., *Crime and the Law in English Satirical Prints 1600–1832*, Cambridge, 1986

———, *Crime in Early Modern England*, London, 1984

———, 'Last Dying Speeches: Religion, Ideology and Public Execution in Seventeenth Century England', *Past and Present*, 107, 1985

Snyder, E., and P. Hay (eds), *Labour, Law, and Crime*, London, 1987

Speck, W., *Stability and Strife, England 1714–1760*, London, 1977

Spierenburg, P., *The Spectacle of Suffering*, Cambridge, 1984

Spufford, M., *Small Books and Pleasant Histories*, London, 1981

Squire, G., *Dress and Society 1560–1970*, London, 1974

Stone, L., *An Open Elite?*, Oxford, 1986

Styles, J., and S. Brewer (eds), *An Ungovernable People*, London, 1980

Survey of London, London, 1957

Thompson, E. P., *Whigs and Hunters*, London, 1975

———, *The Making of the English Working Class*, London, 1964

———, 'Eighteenth Century English Society: Class Struggle without Class?', *Social History*, III, 2, 1978

Tobias, J. J., *Crime and Industrial Society in the Nineteenth Century*, London, 1967

Victoria County History of Staffordshire, London, 1908, 1970 and 1979 editions

Wagner, P., *Eros Revived*, London, 1988

Watt, I., *The Rise of the Novel*, London, 1957

Weitzman, A. J., 'Eighteenth Century London: Urban Paradise or Fallen City?', *Journal of the History of Ideas*, XXXVI, 1975

Wheatley, H. B., *Hogarth's London*, London, 1909

Wilson, C., *England's Apprenticeship 1603–1763*, London, 1971

Notes

PART ONE

London

1. C. de Saussure, *A Foreign View of England*, 1725 (translated by Van Muyden, 1902), p. 38

2. J. Addison in the *Spectator*, 1711. From a collected edition of essays from the *Spectator*, 1712

3. H. Misson, *Memoirs and Observations of his Travels over England*, 1719, p. 302

4. Quoted in R. Porter, *London: A Social History*, 1994, p. 183

5. Quoted in P. Earle, *A City Full of People*, 1994, p. 224

6. I. Watt, *The Rise of the Novel*, 1963, p. 179

7. R. Porter, *London*, p. 162

8. R. W. Malcolmson, *Life and Labour in England, 1700–1800*, 1981, p. 110

9. R. Porter, *English Society in the Eighteenth Century*, 1982, p. 273

10. Mrs Trimmer quoted in C. Hill, *Reformation to Industrial Revolution*, 1969, p. 229

11. Hill, *Reformation to Industrial Revolution*, p. 157

Initiation

1. Captain A. Smith, *Memoirs of the Life and Times of Jonathan Wild*, 1726, p. 2

2. *Victoria County History of Staffordshire*, 1970 edition, Vol. 3, p. 109

3. Anon., *An Authentic History of the Parentage, Birth, Education, Marriages, Issue and Practices of the Famous Jonathan Wild*, 1725, p. 3

4. J. Wild, 'An Answer to a Late Insolent Libel', 1718, Appendix II in F. J. Lyons, *Jonathan Wild, Prince of Robbers*, 1936, p. 249

5. Both quotations taken from Sheehan's essay in J. S. Cockburn (ed.), *Crime in England*, 1977, p. 239

6. J. Bender, *Imagining the Penitentiary: Fiction and the Architecture of Mind in the Eighteenth Century*, 1987, p. 14

7. B. de Mandeville, *An Enquiry into the Causes of the Frequent Executions at Tyburn*, 1725, p. 17

8. Bender, *Imagining the Penitentiary*, p. 45

9. D. Defoe, *The Life of Jonathan Wild from his Birth to his Death*, 1725 (p. xvi in an 1840 edition of Fielding's *Jonathan Wild the Great*)

10. C. Hill, *Liberty Against the Law*, 1996, p. 230

11. W. Speck, *Stability and Strife, England 1714–1760*, 1977, p. 58

12. E. P. Thompson quoted in J. Sharpe, *Crime in Early Modern England*, 1984, p. 117

13. C. Hibbert, *Highwaymen*, 1967, p. 92

14. M. Bakhtin quoted in R. W. Malcolmson, *Life and Labour in England, 1700–1800*, 1981, p. 73

Struggle

1. J. H. Plumb, 'The New World of Children in Eighteenth Century England', *Past and Present*, 67, 1975, p. 65

2. M. D. George, *London Life in the Eighteenth Century*, 1925, p. 228

3. Ibid.

4. Captain C. Walker, *Authentic Memoirs of the Life of Sally Salisbury*, 1723, p. 10

5. J. Villette, *The Annals of Newgate*, 1776, Vol. 1–2, p. 255

PART TWO

Underworld

1. D. Defoe, *The True and Genuine Account of the Life and Actions of Jonathan Wild*, 1726 (reprinted in Penguin Classics, 1986), p. 231

2. R. Porter, *London: A Social History*, 1994, p. 171

3. R. Porter, *English Society in the Eighteenth Century*, 1982, p. 278

4. Captain C. Walker, *Authentic Memoirs of the Life, Intrigues and Adventures of the Celebrated Sally Salisbury*, 1723, p. 12

5. Walker, *Sally Salisbury*, p. 126

6. Ibid., p. xiv

7. R. Paulson, *Emblem and Expression: Meaning in English Art in the Eighteenth Century*, 1975, p. 40

8. *Daily Courant*, 1 May 1731

9. R. Paulson, *Hogarth: The Modern Moral Subject, 1697–1732*, 1992, p. 243

10. H. B. Wheatley, *Hogarth's London*, 1909, p. 274

11. E. Forrest, *A Peregrination*, 1732 (ed. C. Morgan, 1952), p. 7
12. J. M. Beattie, *Crime and the Courts in England*, 1986, pp. 92–3
13. *London News*, 18 February 1719
14. R. Steele essay in the *Spectator*, 1712
15. E. J. Burford, *Wits, Wenchers and Wantons*, 1992, p. 35
16. P. Wagner, *Eros Revived*, 1988, p. 49
17. H. Fielding, *An Enquiry into the Causes of the Late Increase in Robbers*, 1751, p. 1
18. D. Defoe quoted in P. Earle, *The World of Defoe*, 1976, p. 37
19. G. Howson, *Thief-Taker General: The Rise and Fall of Jonathan Wild*, 1970, p. 4
20. Captain C. Johnson, *Lives of the Highwaymen*, 1734, p. 192
21. Howson, *Thief-Taker General*, p. 40

Apprenticeship

1. G. Howson, *Thief-Taker General: The Rise and Fall of Jonathan Wild*, 1970, p. 69; and H. Bleackley, *Jack Sheppard*, 1933, p. 201
2. D. Defoe, *Moll Flanders*, 1722 (Penguin Classics edition, 1989), p. 274
3. G. Salgado (ed.), *Cony Catchers and Bawdy Baskets*, 1972, p. 18
4. Quoted in J. M. Beattie, *Crime and the Courts in England*, 1986, p. 150
5. H. Fielding, *An Enquiry into the Causes of the Late Increase in Robbers*, 1751, p. 76
6. P. Linebaugh, *The London Hanged*, 1992, p. 204; C. Hibbert, *Highwaymen*, 1967, p. 51
7. J. Villette, *The Annals of Newgate*, 1776, Vol. 1–2, p. 42
8. D. Defoe, *The Life of Jonathan Wild from his Birth to his Death*, 1725 (p. xviii in an 1840 edition of Fielding's *Jonathan Wild the Great*)
9. Howson, *Thief-Taker General*, p. 116
10. Villette, *Annals of Newgate*, p. 324
11. Anon., *An Authentic History of the Parentage, Birth, Education, Marriages, Issue and Practices of the Famous Jonathan Wild*, 1725, p. 11
12. Ibid., p. 9
13. *Select Trials at the Old Bailey*, 1734, Vol. 1, p. 269
14. J. Wild, 'An Answer to a Late Insolent Libel', 1718, Appendix II in F. J. Lyons, *Jonathan Wild, Prince of Robbers*, 1936, p. 249 (Hitchin's pamphlet is the first appendix)
15. P. C. Quennell, *Hogarth's Progress*, 1955, p. 134

Dissolution

1. Anon., *The Whole Life and History of Benjamin Child*, 1722, p. 8
2. D. Jarrett, *England in the Age of Hogarth*, 1974, p. 204
3. R. Paulson, *Hogarth: High Art and Low 1732–1750*, 1992, p. 28
4. A. Murphy quoted in H. B. Wheatley, *Hogarth's London*, 1909, p. 287
5. H. B. Wheatley, *Hogarth's London*, 1909, p. 134
6. R. Porter, *English Society in the Eighteenth Century*, 1982, p. 33
7. C. Hibbert, *The Road to Tyburn*, 1957, p. 36
8. D. Defoe, *The History of the Remarkable Life of Jack Sheppard*, 1725, reprinted in H. Bleackley, *Jack Sheppard*, 1933, p. 139
9, Captain C. Johnson, *Lives of the Highwaymen*, 1734, p. 461
10. Defoe, *Jack Sheppard*, reprinted in Bleackley, *Jack Sheppard*, p. 139
11. D. Defoe, *A Narrative of all the Robberies etc. of Jack Sheppard*, 1724, reprinted in H. Bleackley, *Jack Sheppard*, 1933, p. 164
12. Ibid.
13. H. Misson, *Memoirs and Observations of his Travels over England*, 1719, p. 307
14. Baron Muralt, *Letters Describing the Characters and Customs of the English and French Nations*, 1726, p. 38
15. Misson, *Travels over England*, p. 39
16. Defoe, *Narrative of all the Robberies*, reprinted in Bleackley, *Jack Sheppard*, p. 163
17. Defoe, *Jack Sheppard*, reprinted in Bleackley, *Jack Sheppard*, p. 141
18. Ibid., p. 142
19. *Select Trials at the Old Bailey*, 1734, Vol. 2, p. 130
20. P. Linebaugh, *The London Hanged*, 1992, p. 27; and L. I. Rudolph, 'The Mob in Eighteenth Century America and Europe', *American Quarterly* XI, 4, 1959
21. D. Defoe, *The Life of Jonathan Wild from his Birth to his Death*, 1725 (p. xxix in an 1840 edition of Fielding's *Jonathan Wild the Great*)
22. Anon., *The History of the Remarkable Lives and Actions of Jonathan Wild, Thief-Taker, Joseph Blake alias Blueskin, Footpad, and John Sheppard, House-breaker*, 1725, pp. 82–7
23. Johnson, *Highwaymen*, p. 462
24. G. E., *Authentic Memoirs of the Life and Surprising Adventures of John Sheppard by Way of Familiar Letters from a Gentleman in Town*, 1724, reprinted in H. Bleackley, *Jack Sheppard*, 1933, p. 177

25. *London Journal*, 25 July 1724
26. G. E., *Authentic Memoirs*, reprinted in Bleackley, *Jack Sheppard*, p. 178
27. Defoe, *Narrative of all the Robberies*, reprinted in Bleackley, *Jack Sheppard*, p. 162

PART THREE

Business

1. D. Defoe, *The True and Genuine Account of the Life and Actions of Jonathan Wild*, 1725 (reprinted in Penguin Classics, 1986), p. 237
2. B. de Mandeville, *An Enquiry into the Causes of the Frequent Executions at Tyburn*, 1725, p. 3
3. Anon., *The History of the Remarkable Lives and Actions of Jonathan Wild, Thief-Taker, Joseph Blake alias Blueskin, Footpad, and John Sheppard, House-breaker*, 1725, p. i
4. J. Addison in the *Spectator*, 1711. From a collected edition of essays from the *Spectator*, 1712
5. H. Misson, *Memoirs and Observations of his Travels over England*, 1719, p. 39
6. The Abbé Prevost, quoted in R. Porter, *London: A Social History*, 1994, p. 171
7. L. Radzinowicz, *A History of English Criminal Law and its Administration from 1750*, 1948, pp. 299–300
8. F. J. Lyons, *Jonathan Wild, Prince of Robbers*, 1936, p. 140
9. D. Defoe, *The Life of Jonathan Wild from his Birth to his Death*, 1725 (p. xlviii in an 1840 edition of Fielding's *Mr Jonathan Wild the Great*)
10. Anon., *Remarkable Lives*, p. 58
11. *Weekly Journal*, August 1723; quoted in J. Lindsay, *The Monster City: Defoe's London 1688–1730*, 1978, p. 83
12. Both quotations in Duvall's mini-biography in Captain C. Johnson, *Lives of the Highwaymen*, 1734, pp. 91–3
13. 'The High-Pad's Boast', from *The New Canting Dictionary* (Anon.), 1735
14. P. Linebaugh, *The London Hanged*, 1992, p. 187
15. Ibid., p. 203
16. 'H. D.', *The Life of Jonathan Wild*, 1725, p. 29
17. *Weekly Journal*, 20 June 1719
18. F. McLynn, *Crime and Punishment in Eighteenth Century England*, 1989, p. 61. Also, the anonymous *The Whole Life and History of Benjamin Child*, 1722

19. Defoe, *Life of Jonathan Wild* (p. xix in an 1840 edition of Fielding's *Mr Jonathan Wild the Great*)
20. *Daily Journal*, 19 May 1724
21. P. Rogers, *Hacks and Dunces*, 1980, p. 185
22. Quoted in L. Stone, *An Open Elite?*, 1986, p. 409
23. Defoe, *Life of Jonathan Wild* (p. xlvii in an 1843 edition of Fielding's *Mr Jonathan Wild the Great*)
24. C. Caraccioli quoted in R. W. Malcolmson, *Popular Recreations in English Society*, 1973, p. 20
25. C. Hibbert, *London: The Biography of a City*, 1969, p. 103
26. Warrant of Detainder issued at Wild's arrest, February 1725; *Select Trials at the Old Bailey*, 1735, Vol. 2, pp. 204–5
27. M. Ignatieff, *A Just Measure of Pain*, 1978, p. 172

Aspiration

1. D. Defoe, *The Life of Jonathan Wild from his Birth to his Death*, 1725 (p. xliv in an 1843 edition of Fielding's *Mr Jonathan Wild the Great*)
2. E. J. Burford, *Wits, Wenchers and Wantons*, 1992, p. 82
3. P. Earle, *The Making of the English Middle Class*, 1989, p. 12
4. J. Osborn, *The Lives of the Most Remarkable Criminals*, 1735 (ed. A. L. Hayward), 1927, p. 257
5. *London Journal*, 2 May 1725
6. Defoe, *Life of Jonathan Wild* (p. xxxiv in an 1840 edition of Fielding's *Mr Jonathan Wild the Great*)
7. Ibid. (p. xxxvi in Fielding's *Mr Jonathan Wild the Great*)
8. D. Defoe, *The True and Genuine Account of the Life and Actions of Jonathan Wild*, 1726 (reprinted in Penguin Classics, 1986), p. 241
9. Anon., *The History of the Remarkable Lives and Actions of Jonathan Wild, Thief-Taker, Joseph Blake alias Blueskin, Footpad, and John Sheppard, House-breaker*, 1725, p. 45
10. Defoe, *True and Genuine Account*, p. 245

Fame

1. J. Villette, *The Annals of Newgate*, 1776, Vol. 1–2, p. 278
2. *Parker's London News*, 16 October 1724
3. G. E., *Authentic Memoirs of the Life and Surprising Adventures of John Sheppard by Way of Familiar Letters from a Gentleman in Town*, 1724, reprinted in H. Bleackley, *Jack Sheppard*, 1933, p. 185

4. *London Journal*, 7 November 1724

5. D. Defoe, *A Narrative of all the Robberies etc. of Jack Sheppard*, 1724, re-printed in H. Bleackley, *Jack Sheppard*, 1933, pp. 167–8

6. *Parker's London News*, 30 October 1724

7. G. E., *Authentic Memoirs*, pp. 188–9

8. D. Defoe, *The History of the Remarkable Life of Jack Sheppard*, 1725, re-printed in H. Bleackley, *Jack Sheppard*, 1933, p. 149

9. Anon., *The History of the Remarkable Lives and Actions of Jonathan Wild, Thief-Taker, Joseph Blake alias Blueskin, Footpad, and John Sheppard, House-breaker*, 1725, p. iii

10. Ibid.

11. Defoe, *Jack Sheppard*, reprinted in Bleackley, *Jack Sheppard*, p. 149

12. Ibid., p. 150

13. *Daily Journal*, 12 November 1724

14. C. Hill, *Liberty Against the Law*, 1995, p. 124

15. Captain C. Johnson, *Lives of the Highwaymen*, 1734, p. 461

16. Anon., *The History of the Remarkable Lives*, p. iv

PART FOUR

Law

1. Lord Cowper quoted in J. M. Beattie, *Crime and the Courts in England*, 1986, p. 59

2. D. Hay essay in D. Hay, P. Linebaugh and E. P. Thompson (eds.), *Albion's Fatal Tree*, 1975, p. 55

3. H. Fielding, *Amelia*, 1751 (Penguin Classics edition, 1987), pp. 15–16

4. *Daily Journal*, 2 July 1724

5. E. J. Burford, *Wits, Wenchers and Wantons*, 1992, p. 137

6. *Fog's Weekly Journal*, 18 January 1729

7. C. J. Fox quoted in R. Porter, *English Society in the Eighteenth Century*, 1982, p. 22

8. E. P. Thompson, *Whigs and Hunters*, 1975. A detailed account of the events leading up to the Black Act.

9. P. Rogers, *Hacks and Dunces*, 1975, p. 4

10. D. Jarrett, *England in the Age of Hogarth*, 1974, p. 19

11. P. Earle, *The World of Defoe*, 1976, p. 89

12. Ibid., p. 87

13. J. A. Sharpe, *Crime and the Law in English Satirical Prints 1600–1832*, 1986, p. 16
14. Ibid.
15. Ibid., p. 25
16. Anon., *The History of the Remarkable Lives and Actions of Jonathan Wild, Thief-Taker, Joseph Blake alias Blueskin, Footpad, and John Sheppard, House-breaker*, 1725, p. ii
17. O. Goldsmith quoted in C. Hill, *Reformation to Industrial Revolution*, 1969, p. 182
18. Hay, Linebaugh and Thompson, *Albion's Fatal Tree*, p. 49

Punishment

1. J. M. Beattie, *Crime and the Courts in England*, 1986, p. 451
2. Ibid., p. 465
3. M. Foucault, *Discipline and Punish* (trans. A. Sheridan, 1977), p. 48
4. Baron Muralt, *Letters Describing the Characters and Customs of the English and French Nations*, 1726, p. 42
5. C. Hibbert, *Highwaymen*, 1967, p. 95
6. P. Linebaugh, *The London Hanged*, 1992, p. 87
7. Muralt, *Characters and Customs*, p. 42
8. B. de Mandeville, *An Enquiry into the Causes of the Frequent Executions at Tyburn*, 1725, p. 34
9. M. Ignatieff, *A Just Measure of Pain*, 1978, p. 21
10. De Mandeville, *Frequent Executions at Tyburn*, p. 40
11. B. de Mably quoted in M. Foucault, *Discipline and Punish*, p. 16
12. Foucault, *Discipline and Punish*, p. 9
13. S. Emlyn, 1730, quoted in L. Radzinowicz, *A History of English Criminal Law and its Administration from 1750*, 1948, p. 266

Gaol

1. D. Rumbelow, *The Triple Tree*, 1982, p. 82
2. J. Hall quoted by D. Rumbelow, *The Triple Tree*, p. 82
3. A. Griffiths, *Chronicles of Newgate*, 1884, Vol. 1, p. 438
4. Rumbelow, *Triple Tree*, p. 30
5. B. de Mandeville, *An Enquiry into the Causes of the Frequent Executions at Tyburn*, 1725, p. 19
6. G. E., *Authentic Memoirs of the Life and Surprising Adventures of John Sheppard by Way of Familiar Letters from a Gentleman in Town*, 1724, reprinted in H. Bleackley, *Jack Sheppard*, 1933, p. 178

7. *Parker's London News*, 4 September 1724
8. G. E., *Authentic Memoirs*, reprinted in Bleackley, *Jack Sheppard*, p. 180
9. *Parker's London News*, 14 September 1724
10. P. Linebaugh, *The London Hanged*, 1992, p. 33
11. D. Defoe, *A Narrative of all the Robberies etc. of Jack Sheppard*, 1724, reprinted in H. Bleackley, *Jack Sheppard*, 1933, p. 164
12. Ibid., p. 165

PART FIVE

Death

1. D. Defoe, *The History of the Remarkable Life of Jack Sheppard*, 1725, reprinted in H. Bleackley, *Jack Sheppard*, 1933, p. 148
2. W. J. Sheehan essay in J. S. Cockburn (ed.), *Crime in England*, 1977, p. 236
3. J. Wesley, *The Journal*, 8 November 1838, reprinted 1938
4. F. J. Lyons, *Jonathan Wild, Prince of Robbers*, 1936, p. 185. All subsequent uncredited accounts of Sheppard's execution come from here too.
5. H. Misson, *Memoirs and Observations of his Travels over England*, 1719, p. 124
6. C. de Saussure, *A Foreign View of England*, 1725 (translated by Van Muyden, 1902), pp. 124–5
7. *Mist's Weekly Journal*, 1 May 1725
8. Misson, *Travels over England*, p. 123
9. E. P. Thompson, 'Eighteenth Century English Society: Class Struggle without Class?', in *Social History*, III, 2, 1978, p. 157
10. *London Journal*, 21 November 1724
11. C. Hibbert, *Highwaymen*, 1967, p. 104
12. P. Linebaugh, *The London Hanged*, 1992, p. 7
13. P. E. Lewis (ed.), *The Beggars' Opera*, 1973, p. 95
14. R. Paulson, *Popular and Polite Art in the Age of Hogarth and Fielding*, 1979, p. 17

Decline

1. R. Porter, *English Society in the Eighteenth Century*, 1982, p. 283
2. N. Ward, 'The Quack's Club', 1709
3. *Daily Post*, 23 October 1725
4. *Parker's London News*, 8 March 1725
5. J. Villette, *Annals of Newgate*, 1776, Vol. 1–2, p. 178

6. *Select Trials at the Old Bailey*, 1734, Vol. 2, pp. 211–19. Subsequent quotations from the trial also come from here.
7. E. P. Thompson, *Whigs and Hunters*, 1975, p. 216
8. M. Blackett-Ord, *Hell-Fire Duke*, 1982, p. 98

Trial

1. D. Defoe, *The True and Genuine Account of the Life and Actions of Jonathan Wild*, 1725 (reprinted in Penguin Classics, 1986), p. 206
2. *Select Trials at the Old Bailey*, 1734, Vol. 2, p. 275
3. J. Villette, *Annals of Newgate*, 1776, Vol. 1–2, p. 342
4. *Parker's Penny Post*, 26 May 1725
5. *Weekly Journal*, 29 May 1725
6. *Select Trials at the Old Bailey*, 1734, Vol. 2, p. 275

Hanging

1. D. Defoe, *The True and Genuine Account of the Life and Actions of Jonathan Wild*, 1725 (reprinted in Penguin Classics, 1986), p. 257
2. *Mist's Weekly Journal*, 29 May 1725
3. Ibid.
4. Captain A. Smith, *Memoirs of the Life and Times of Jonathan Wild*, 1726, p. 24
5. *Weekly Journal*, 29 May 1725
6. J. Villette, *Annals of Newgate*, 1776, Vol. 1–2, p. 276
7. P. Linebaugh essay in D. Hay, P. Linebaugh and E. P. Thompson (eds), *Albion's Fatal Tree*, 1975, p. 112
8. H. Misson, *Memoirs and Observations of his Travels over England*, 1719, p. 124
9. A. Griffiths, *Chronicles of Newgate*, 1884, Vol. 1, p. 270

Epilogue

1. 'Jonathan Wild's Advice to His Successor', Appendix III, F. J. Lyons, *Jonathan Wild, Prince of Robbers*, 1936, p. 289

Index

Figures in italics refer to illustrations